and inspiring. He possesses the magical ability to transform a two-dimensional environment into a three-dimensional, highly interactive space. We all breathe a little deeper as we take in the evidence-based techniques that bring relief to children who have been holding their breaths, steeling themselves against pain and anxiety."

Deborah Vilas, *MS, CCLS, LMSW, Program Director of Child Life Programs, Bank Street College of Education*

"Somatic psychotherapy has increasingly moved into the mainstream over the past two decades. Neal Brodsky's *Embodied Play Therapy: Healing and Building Identity with Children* is both a logical and bold endeavor. Logical in that children are receptive to embodied expression in a way that most adults have lost, bold in that Mr. Brodsky has opened up a new frontier in child therapy. His synthesis of a wide range of established clinical practices and cutting-edge embodied interventions makes for fascinating and instructive reading. If you work with kids, you won't be disappointed."

Brian Gleason, *MSW, Executive Director of The Center for Embodied Relationships*

"*Embodied Play Therapy: Healing and Building Identity with Children* by Neal Brodsky is a true gift in the realm of child therapy. The author's expertise in sandplay, building rapport with children, and, most importantly, creating body awareness and sensitivity shines through. Due to the many case examples, therapists and parents alike will be able to quickly gain knowledge and understanding of interventions that work to help children achieve more fulfillment, build self-esteem, attain self-control, express themselves authentically, experience joy, and respond appropriately in stressful situations."

Karyne B. Wilner, *PsyD, Director of the Core Energetics Academy and former Assistant Director of the International Institute for Core Energetics, Senior Director of the Brazilian Institute, and Associate Director in Australia. Author of* Releasing Toxic Anger for Women

"What a delightful and informative book about a novel approach to treating children with energy, play, and the compassionate involvement of parents. Neal Brodsky uses his background in film and television to bring a sense of embodied creativity to therapy. The book offers the necessary theoretical grounding and then shines in detailed clinical illustrations of a truly enlivened approach to therapy for children and their families. More than with any other therapy book I have read, I found myself smiling, nodding, and wishing I were in the room when Neal brings us inside the flow of his sessions with children. There is lots here for any therapist who works with children."

William J. Doherty, *PhD, Professor Emeritus at the University of Minnesota and co-author of* Helping Couples on the Brink of Divorce: Discernment Counseling for Troubled Relationships

"Speaking as a director of a body psychotherapy training institute in Central Europe, I am thrilled that my colleague, Neal Brodsky, LMFT, has written such a comprehensive, inspiring book to add to the ever-growing interest in somatic therapy. His clear understanding of what children need to be engaged and fully participate in therapy is an inspiration for all students and therapists who work with children and parents looking for direction for their children. The toolbox he offers with clear instructions is creative, energetic, innovative, and broadens the ideas of play therapy, enabling a clinician to more easily reach a young person. His case presentations offer a view of how enthusiastically children react to Embodied Play Therapy. May his ideas bring forth the ability to use imagination and expression as a beacon of hope for healing our younger generation."

Elizabeth S. Carl, *LCSW, Academic Director, Polish Institute of Core Energetics*

"*Embodied Play Therapy: Healing and Building Identity with Children* employs vivid case studies that bring Neal Brodsky's therapeutic approach to life. Engaging narratives invite the reader along on the healing journey of children in his care, spotlighting the benefits of a holistic approach that engages the clients' imaginations, emotions, senses, and bodies.

In the style of Carl Jung, who shared his childhood play memories in *Memories, Dreams, and Reflections*, Neal Brodsky invites the reader into his personal recollections of key childhood moments where the seeds of his future therapeutic style were sown.

For readers seeking to expand or deepen their play therapy skills, Brodsky's chapter on teletherapy is particularly illuminating

Embodied Play Therapy

This book offers innovative strategies for healing children through movement and play with multicultural, multiracial, and genderfluid considerations.

Dynamic movement and body-centered play therapy techniques and tools provide children with a language and outlet to speak their deep truths in the interest of healing from symptoms, including anxiety, depression, and the inability to sustain attention. Focusing on social, emotional, and relational growth, the author chronicles young people's heroic journeys, searching for identity and safety amid fast-moving currents of societal and familial change. Linking the search for generative power to expressive freedom, chapters explore issues ranging from impulsive/explosive behavior, perfectionism, OCD, childhood fears, family-rooted anxiety, and child-parent connection through a range of in-person and live online video tele-sessions.

Practitioners who work with children, such as psychotherapists, marriage and family therapists, somatic therapists, and play therapists, plus teachers and parents, will embrace this warmly voiced combination of immersive case studies and cutting-edge practical applications.

Neal H. Brodsky, MA, MPA, LMFT, ACCEP, is a licensed marital and family therapist, Core Energetics body counselor, writer, and presenter specializing in holistic therapy for adults, couples, and children.

Embodied Play Therapy

Healing and Building Identity with Children

Neal H. Brodsky

Routledge
Taylor & Francis Group
NEW YORK AND LONDON

Designed cover image: Cover illustrated by Evan P. Neidich

First published 2027
by Routledge
605 Third Avenue, New York, NY 10158

and by Routledge
4 Park Square, Milton Park, Abingdon, Oxon, OX14 4RN

Routledge is an imprint of the Taylor & Francis Group, an informa business

ISBN: 9781032357201 (hbk)
ISBN: 9781032357195 (pbk)
ISBN: 9781003328186 (ebk)

DOI: 10.4324/9781003328186

Typeset in Palatino
by KnowledgeWorks Global Ltd.

For my parents, who kindled and cajoled.

For Judy, who lit the way.

For Emma Jay

and

All the little ones yet to be.

The cases presented in this book are composites of many children. While family configuration and details have been altered, the flow of play and narratives that emerge here came from the voices, minds, and imaginations of children and parents I have known and been honored to play alongside.

Contents

Child's Play

My two hands balance
on the sandbox wall.
Climbing up and over.
Pressing my ear down a moment
Into cool sand.
Listening for what may emerge.

Rising
Grinning
Sandy mask on
my cheek.
Eyes aglitter.

Jumping up
Jumping down.
Trampoline mesh meets
my feet.
Life pumping
through every fiber
of my being.

Chalk
Big as my hand
traces on gray slate ground
An inner monster.
Red and brown
Purple and blue
Beckoning secrets
From darkness into Light.

Sunlight sparkling
syllables
of my story.
Hushed wavelets,
trailing over spring leaves.

—Neal Brodsky

Foreword by Dennis McCarthy

To help children feel comfortable in their bodies, their "own skin," is one of the goals Neal Brodsky aims for in his play therapy work, described in this beautifully written book. Neal is very present in these pages, following D. W. Winnicott's insistence that psychotherapy with the child happens in the overlap of the child playing and the therapist playing (1971/1996, p. 54). His own creative process encourages and accompanies the child's creative process on their journey toward health. Embodied creativity is what affirms our humanity, from the 30,000-year-old cave paintings in France, with animals depicted in motion so beautifully that we can almost hear them breathe; to the play space that Neal sits in with the child, where they too are learning how to move more naturally, more gracefully. Using his "four pillars" approach in which playing, breathing, moving, and feeling are the underpinnings of the work, he guides the child to a deeper place in themself. To help the child discharge negative aggression and replace it with positive aggression via the play process is wonderful to witness. We too breathe deeper, relaxing even as the child he describes does. I particularly enjoyed Neal's reflections after each session in which he attempts to understand what has happened in the child's play and their interactions with him during the session.

The word "psyche," the root word of psychology, means soul or life force. Thus, psychology is the study of life force, and in Neal's embodied play therapy process, he embraces psychology in this, its true meaning. To observe how a child moves and how they don't move gives us much information about what is wrong and how to rectify this and may teach us how to help the child. As they jump or roll or crawl or bounce in Neal's presence, we, the readers, feel enlivened along with the child.

The theories Neal shares near the book's onset are concisely put and form a portal (a favorite word for many children) through which we may view what has informed much of Neal's work. They don't take up too much space; rather, it is the playing child that is the book's focus. Neal urges parents to be a collaborative part of the process by engaging in their own treatment. Ideally, as the child changes in his or her behavior, the parent makes room for these changes by doing their own work, although it is a much easier process to help balance the child's psyche or life force than it is for the adults.

Most theories in psychology ignored the body until recently. The energetic processes from which movement, emotion, and thinking arise were not considered. There were of course exceptions, but these were rarely applied to work with children. Neal's book and the approach he describes are groundbreaking in that they see the centrality of these energetic processes in working with children. Perhaps what is most unique about working with children in a play therapy model, such as Neal's, is that the child fully enjoys the process. As they work through emotional and physical blocks, they have fun.

Dennis McCarthy LMHC/DMT – Psychotherapist/
International Workshop/Seminar Leader

Author: *A Manual of Dynamic Play Therapy* and
If You Turned into a Monster
Editor: *Deep Play: Exploring the Use of Depth in Psychotherapy with Children* and *Speaking about the Unspeakable: Non-verbal Methods and Experiences in Therapy with Children*
Founder: Association for the Healing Power of the Imagination https://www.metamorfosinstitute.com/

Foreword by Sue Erikson Bloland

I can only imagine how gratified my father, Erik Erikson, would be to learn that the description of the stages of child development he presented in *Childhood and Society* (1950/1993) and his own work in play therapy with children in *Toys and Reasons* (1978) have contributed, so many years later, to the extraordinary work with children that Neal Brodsky describes in this book.

Addressing the issue with which he is so often confronted in his work with children between the ages of six and puberty, Neal describes the way he uses Embodied Play Therapy to help children experience a part of themselves that parents may not be so good at encouraging – and may actually be afraid to encourage – a sense of embodied aliveness that almost magically supports the hoped-for outcome of this critical stage of development: a feeling of *competence*. Many adults reading the description of the work Neal does with children during this latency period may wish they had had the benefit of working with him themselves! And anyone who works with children (including parents) will find they are better equipped for the job when they have absorbed the profound message offered in Neal's book: that at this stage of development, it is *themselves* that children need to learn to trust. And the various forms of embodied play therapy that he describes here (and which are part of his uniquely empathic work with children) are especially designed to foster this trust.

Sue Erikson Bloland, LCSW

Author, *In the Shadow of Fame: A Memoir by the Daughter of Erik H. Erikson (2nd Edition 2026)*

Psychotherapist and Psychoanalyst
Supervisor and Faculty Member, Manhattan Institute for Psychoanalysis

Introduction

Embodied Play Therapy offers individual children active movement-based sessions with an adult practitioner to build awareness of breathing and feeling using equipment designed to enhance full self-expression. Through play using pillows, a large foam cube, lightweight bats, and protective punching gloves, along with clay, drawing, and a deep sandbox with an assortment of play figures to place in its depths, a child gets in touch with what's inside them. Along the way, they tap into their innate creative abilities to construct self-affirming stories reflecting positive visions for themselves and their world, while building connection and having fun. This book focuses on the structure, variety, and trajectory of Embodied Play Therapy with children ages 6–13. I hope my stories of children and the solutions they crafted in therapy will suggest productive paths for therapists, parents, teachers, and healers who seek to foster greater aliveness and generative power in young people.

Embodied Play Therapy practice with preadolescent children stimulates the senses. It builds reservoirs of energy that a child may call on later amid the rough and tumble of adolescent and young adult life. When a child is allowed to get out of a chair and move in therapy, oxygen adds fuel and whips up storytelling abilities. Possibilities enter mercurial worlds where roles are more pliant. Creations in clay, sand, or scrawled on paper can bend young consciousness into new and unexpected shapes, hinting at new ways for a child to be with others and with themselves.

Parents want safety for their children. They fear and fixate on what they see as wrong, whether it's wasting time with the wrong devices, the wrong friends, or what some view as childhood laziness contributing to troubles at school. One key part of my job is guiding these parents. Helping some relax. Helping others take action with schools to better match an educational environment to what their child requires. Sometimes I need to cajole and convince a parent to provide more of their precious presence.

DOI: 10.4324/9781003328186-1

A parent with their attention divided between a cell phone and a child robs that kid of a fully shared moment that will never come again. Speaking as an empty nest parent with my kids grown and gone, I remind parents that the release of young people to futures of their own making happens sooner than we think. The time for building a relationship may be "now or never."

What first prepared me to begin dialogues of invention and play with young people?

Snapshots from My Own Story...

Three-year-old Neal. *Playing in the sandbox at nursery school with my blind friend Sandy, who's upset with me and, to my shock, rakes his nails across my face. The vision of sand mixed with my tears pierces my heart.*

Six-year-old Neal. *My yet-to-be-born brother growing daily in my mother's uterus; I've built a skyscraper of blocks nearly to the ceiling of my small bedroom. As I sleep in the darkness, it crashes down, echoing against the hard linoleum floor. My mother bursts through the door, "screaming" in whispers between tightly pinched lips that I've woken our downstairs neighbor. My body goes rigid with shock, my breath catching in my throat. The danger in reaching beyond a certain limit evoked by the image of my mother's torment will constrain how high I will permit myself to go in life for a long time to come.*

Refusing to sleep, I begin standing at the locked door of my parents' bedroom, held captive by my terror of the "green leprechaun" I imagine may jump out at me from under my bed. I want to scream for them in the cold night. Instead, I knock softly. When there is no response, I grit my teeth in silence, curling up on the floor outside the door. My parents take me to a clinical psychologist, where I partake in a bounty of foil-wrapped chocolate candy "Kisses" piled high in a translucent glass bowl on a side table next to his waiting room couch. The doctor prescribes "sleep suppositories," which my parents dutifully slip up my rectum nightly. Undaunted by this drugging, I continue to drag myself to my parents' door until depleted by weeks of what they smilingly call my "persistence"; my Mom and Dad exit to get a few nights away, leaving me in the care of a babysitter who will sleep on our living room couch. I watch the babysitter sleep. She has a method to staunch fears I never thought of before, covering her head with a blanket, leaving only the tiniest opening to breathe. I will use this method well into adulthood to feel safe when I wake in fear.

Seven-year-old Neal. *In the role my parents have cast me, I will be photographed and frozen into the "good big brother" in his ironed white dress shirt, holding and feeding my parents' newborn second son. But inside, I'm also repressing anxiety and anger, which leaks out in bursts. Like the time I punched my friend Joey in the nose right in the middle of a highly detailed miniature city that my class has built on the green linoleum floor with figures we crafted from cardboard, watercolor, and wood. Tiny people live and work in this static tableau that holds everything one might need. Stores to buy food and furniture. A post office. A garage. A fire station. I am shocked to see Joey's tears and the blood he wipes away with his hand. As the call comes to have me removed and escorted down to the Principal's office, I feel shame.*

Eight-year-old Neal. *My parents give me a book called Tony and the Wonderful Door by historical novelist Howard Fast (1968). Like me, Tony lives in New York, a city built on the ruins of Native American villages and hunting grounds. In the backyard of a dilapidated tenement where Tony and his parents reside, a door in the fence between buildings beckons, opening a time travel portal to a deeply forested Manhattan Island hundreds of years ago. Dark-skinned indigenous Americans glide upriver in canoes. Tony's new friend, a native boy, teaches him to play ball with sticks crafted from native hickory.*

For me, restricted to "punch ball" in an asphalt slab playground where rules forbid using bats lest we break a window in the surrounding buildings, *Tony and the Wonderful Door* (Fast, 1968), fuels tantalizing fantasies of childhood freedom. I feel pleasure in Tony's liberation from the confines of his small apartment and construct my own fantasy, imagining how I would move from my room now shared with my brother by carving out space for a bed in our entry hall closet, below the clutter of coats stuffed inside.

Like Tony McTavish Levy, the boy from an immigrant family who opened his wonderful door, I had inherited a healthy dose of confusion as to where I fit in. I hungered to escape the worries of my parents, only one generation from the tattered trauma of family life and legacy disrupted by immigration from Poland, Russia, Austria, and Romania to America. Looking back to Tony's use of imagination as a transport mechanism to move his body far away in time and space, I see the power of what I was learning early, feeling Tony's anticipation of adventure and quickening of heart as a door swung open to new vistas. Tony's story, foretelling my future where, after many twists and turns in life, I would become someone helping children open doors into themselves and their lives.

> **Sixteen-year-old Neal.** *The afternoon sun makes you squint in July at Camp Thoreau, where I work with summering children from NYC as their "film counselor." We have written a script outline for a ten-minute movie about a giant eggplant from outer space landing one night at camp. Building massive papier mache models of the eggplant and his spaceship, we freeze-frame animate these for our chase scene, where scores of campers flee across the open fields from the determined eggplant invader. "You better watch out for the eggplant that ate Chicago; if he's still hungry, the whole country is doomed..." (Greenbaum, 1967) This is my first experience working with kids. Little more than a kid myself, my visceral younger memories spark this urge to combine exuberant energy with fantasy, substance, and movement.*

Other pieces of the puzzle of my journey into Embodied Play Therapy fell into place. As a student at the University of Michigan, it was volunteering at a boys training school to play games with imprisoned "juvenile delinquents" who yearned for freedom. In film school at the New School for Social Research and later New York University, it was my fascination with Francois Truffaut's film *400 Blows* (1959) about a rebellious boy struggling with his parents and teachers that inspired me to write my first script about a boy who runs away from home after being punished by his parents.

During my "first career" in the television industry, it was learning about animation created for children, helping to craft a show on home safety, building funding and educational partnerships for environmental programming focused on conserving our planet for the next generation that touched me most.

My "second career" focused on public service began as a part-time Writing Specialist at a small city public housing authority's after-school center aimed at helping to break the cycle of poverty for children from low-income families. As I transcribed the poetic words coming from these kids, many of whose forebears, like mine, came to these shores from other lands, it fueled my growing dedication to press on and learn more about how I could support their learning. So when the offer came to take a bigger job writing grants to support the centers serving these at-risk children and maintain the Housing Authority's staff serving hundreds of multi-cultural families, I jumped on board full-time. Between my first and second careers spanning two decades there was always a throughline – supporting young people and their parents to challenge their existing conditions and grow.

While I spent my days at the Housing Authority office, I embarked on what became a part-time, five-and-a-half-year course of study in family systems, which, after many nights and weekends, led to a master's degree in Marital and Family Therapy. I would become a therapist, ally, and activist working in the service of young people and families. If that meant learning to help the couples who had those kids or were considering it, I would. If that meant learning how to help kids contain rather than act out rebellious emotions held in mind and body, I would. If that meant writing about kids in pain whose symptoms get them noticed enough to be sent to a professional, I would. My intention was to help young people and the yet-to-be-healed young parts of adults discover energy that could prepare new inner groundwork for a more authentic, fully expressed life.

The focus at Fairfield University's graduate program was "structural family therapy," pioneered by theorists like Salvador Minuchin, who put his ideas into practice, treating entire families at the Philadelphia Child Guidance clinic. Jay Haley and Cloe Madanes had pioneered a "strategic family therapy" emphasizing the function of symptoms in perpetuating feedback loops and rules of family interaction (Nicholas & Schwartz, 2001, p. 352). Michael White and David Epston (pp. 188–189) viewed families as the experts in their own stories and helped families re-author new possibilities through "Narrative Therapy." The professor in my introductory class in marriage and family therapy brought out a mobile, tapping one of its hanging components. Everything moved! I was impressed. The premise: when you work with one part of a family system, you affect the whole. Improvements in a family's youngest representative, a child, could aid its adult members and possibly other siblings, even if they were not participating directly in therapy.

What also drew me into becoming a somatic therapist focused on families was my own pain and fear, rooted in childhood and felt in my body as anxiety. While I'd been a therapy client for much of my adult life beginning in my late twenties, it was the somatic work with practitioners trained at the Institute of Core Energetics based in New York that was especially powerful. That work addressed childhood wounds and developmental trauma while putting me in deeper touch with experiences where I felt abandoned and betrayed as a child that were affecting my adult perception and function.

Growing up in Manhattan, I was afraid. Every time I opened my apartment door, less than two decades after the nuclear bombing of Hiroshima, I faced a yellow and black "Fallout Shelter" sign in the hallway. Even though the school I went to did not have us crawling under our desks as if that would save our skins during the tense days of the Cuban Missile Crisis, I didn't know how long I'd have to live. When my teacher announced to our class that President

Kennedy had been shot, I fixated on the flickering images repeated for days on my family's black and white TV. Just as parents of the children I work with today remember watching the Twin Towers collapse into the Manhattan streets. Again. And again. Trauma cascading in waves from generation to generation on high-definition screens bigger than our children and shimmering in full, bloody color from the devices we clutch in our hands.

Words about the Foundation of This Body-Centered Work

Wilhelm Reich, father of body psychotherapy, was a staunch activist in the arena of childhood education and a regular correspondent with A.S. Neill, schoolmaster, child psychologist, and founder of the progressive boarding school Summerhill in England. Regarding children and their life energy, "Reich held that parents force their children to repress their natural sexuality… These repressions create anxiety, which is held at bay by a stiffening, primarily of the stomach muscles. These in turn remain stiff until the repressions and concomitant anxiety are removed" (Placzek, 1982, p. 11). Also attributed to Reich is the notion "that it is by holding their breath that children are in the habit of fighting against continual and tormenting conditions of anxiety which they sense in the upper abdomen" (p. 11).

From Summerhill, Neill wrote to Reich,

> Your stomach theory is completely proved by the stomachs of the children here. The repressed ones have stomachs like wooden boards, but children begin to loosen up very quickly, and at once begin to be hateful and savage. They kill off their enemies (family ones) eagerly in the forms of cushions and dolls. (Placzek, 1982, p. 22)

Reich's focus on repressed sexual energy made sense coming out of the Victorian-influenced Freudian era. I view sexual energy as a key component of life energy, and from my standpoint as a body-centered play and family therapist, I am focused more broadly on the family role in repressing what appears threatening and the issues that result when families promote limited views of self and self-expression.

Take my own family, for example. There's a photo of me at about 18 months old on my desk, eyes glistening, laughing my head off at the sight of a dancing mobile my parents had attached to the glossy table where they fed me. Full of joy. Yet by age eight, I became a more serious and burdened kid, especially after my teacher told my parents I might become the first Jewish President of the United States. Looking at photos from my later childhood as I approached adolescence, I notice the vigilant squint in my eyes. The droop in my shoulders. I feel the tightness in my belly that began then and whose vestiges remain today, even after so much of my own therapeutic work.

Dr. John Pierrakos (1990), a psychiatrist and mentee of Wilhelm Reich, developed Core Energetics after working with another of Reich's students, physician and psychotherapist Dr. Alexander Lowen on the development of the Bioenergetic approach, a body-centered modality focused on the continuity between body and mind (Lowen, 1975/1994). As a Core Energetics practitioner, I was taught to view the body as "frozen history." In adults, "Blocks are stagnated pools of vital substance that accumulate in the defensive perimeter [of the body] and armor it in dysfunctional patterns that Reich named character structures" (Pierrakos, 1990, p. 24). Beginning in childhood, these blocks congeal patterns of human response into structural defenses and narrow access to one's own inner resources of body, emotion, mind, will, and spirit.

Reich (1983), in his book *Children of the Future*, says, "If the rigid armoring of the human animal is the basic common principle of all his emotional misery; if it is this armoring which puts him, alone among biological species, beyond the pale of natural functioning, then it follows logically that *prevention of rigid armoring is the main and central goal of preventive mental hygiene*" (p. 16).

During the final years of my Core Energetics training, as I began bringing insights from body-centered work to adults and young people, my own life plan began to emerge with greater clarity. John Pierrakos (1990) speaks of the possibility that we may uncover a "Life Plan" through which we seek to shape our efforts and life force to make a positive contribution as a unique though "tiny particle in the sweep of all being through space and time" (p. 225). The exploration process [of uncovering a life plan] "centers on who the person is in the present and where he or she can move in the future" (p. 225).

In my view, preventing inner emotional and body-based blocks to fuller expression of energy and consciousness helps children thrive today, building a fertile embodied self to hatch positive life plans in the future. Piloting "Core for Kids," I tailored methods from Core Energetics for adults to meet the needs of children. As a family therapist, I also sought to aid parents in seeing their part in the difficulties that had landed the family in therapy. This included challenging entrenched defenses and dysfunctional parenting strategies linked to their own childhood experiences. All of this was in service of a child moving more fully into their own unique life expression. You will find examples of my initial experiments cobbling Embodied Play Therapy together in the Addendum: "Core for Kids Playshop: A Group Experience."

Noticing how entrenched problematic behaviors could become in adolescence and young adulthood, I felt an urgency to spend at least part of my career with preadolescent kids whose symptoms ranged from night terrors and phobias to issues of rigidity in high-functioning autism to attention disorders, which I like to reframe as "attention possibility," to explosive or compulsive behaviors. As the years went on, I saw what I suspected early on was true. That many children's lives could improve, along with their familial and other relationships, when they participated in active body-centered play linked with the verbal give and take of talk therapy.

Six-year-old Ricky finds himself in the clatter and fluorescence of a New York City subway car, watching a homeless man who is screaming. His mother, holding Ricky's hand tightly, feels the mingling of her sweat with that of her child. Mom crafts sandwiches for such people each week as part of a group that serves the homeless. Ricky knows this, but the man on the subway is a stranger, and the boy's eyes narrow into tense slits.

In my office, mother and son build a square corral made of wooden blocks around each of their bodies. I imagine they draw comfort from the soft touch of blonde wood rectangles that, together, create a frame emblematic of their common need for safety.

In front of our eyes, the boy's anxiety calms.

Ricky has difficulty holding a pen securely in his hand to write or draw. In the depths of my sandbox, he's been placing the most outrageous fire-breathing dragons, some with two heads, some with three. We practice safe ways to let out the frustration he feels with himself, giving him red boxing gloves and his mother a padded shield for Ricky to wail away at. A few weeks later, Ricky comes up with an idea that will effectively transmute self-directed aggression into getting noticed for positive assertion, a project where he will snap photos of his classmates, giving each one the body of a different dragon that he will design. "Ambitious," mom tells me, a glint of admiration for her son in her eyes.

You will find Ricky's continuing story in several of this book's chapters, including other details of this session above with Mom and another with Dad in Chapter 4: Parents in the Mix, as this boy digs deep to uncover solutions for the issues he's grappling with in his own time and unique way.

I hope you will see, as this book unfolds, how the often surprising and touching connections with children opened new vistas and possibilities not only with these youngsters but also with the parents of children brought to me for treatment. Jumping into embodied play helps children and teaches families some valuable lessons as children, through their play, provide clues for the "inner child" parts of parents that are themselves often hungry for healing.

Just as Tony found his "wonderful door" (Fast, 1968), I would search for mine and finding it, I would share it. Embodied Play Therapy opened so many doors. To therapists from the past who had lived through such difficult times in history, they feared for the world's survival, yet persevered. To kids and parents who taught me about their lives and dreams. To colleagues who joined me in collaborating on healing for clients, for communities, and, along the way, for ourselves.

Reflecting on the reasons why I do this embodied work with children, among my deepest motivations is assisting them in loosening inner constrictions and patterns of behavior that could limit available avenues of expression. Helping children open faculties of curiosity and wonder as they release from repression and fear to explore their potential.

Although many years have passed since my own childhood, I can still feel the splash of water lapping at the hull of Tony's canoe, imagine the joy of movement through the waves, the sharp slap of a wooden bat sending a ball flying across the sky. A deeply embodied experience for Tony, for a younger me who first opened the book, and for the man I became who kept that same threadbare, bound hardcover book until now.

A Note for Readers

My "reflections" in this book on the fruits of Embodied Play, where sand is shaped, worlds of figures vie, or clay monsters battle, are meant solely for you as readers. An example – I never interpret a sandbox in front of a child, rarely for parents. What I do is focus on my own body sensations as clues to what a child may be expressing in the process of play. A reverent silence descending over a child's drawing, the flash of physical power much larger than the small human pushing against the padded shield I hold against her attack, the thrill shooting up my spine as I witness an bat-wielding kid persevere to beat their own hitting contest and the sharp sound of clay flattening into a pancake under repeated impact from the swing of child's rubber-headed mallet. In attuning to a child, I become willing to lower my expectations. To jettison my therapeutic agenda and my judgments. In this way, the leadership of a child is honored and followed. Throughout, my goal is to preserve in me a constancy of curiosity that supports awe in this moment and excitement for what may come next. There is so much magic and mystery in a child's creation beyond what I might know. And a child needs to be free to use the imaginings sparked by their work and play long after this adult has left their life.

References

Fast, H. (1968). *Tony and the Wonderful Door*. Alfred A. Knopf.

Greenbaum, N. (1967). *The Eggplant That Ate Chicago*. Go Go Records.

Lowen, A. (1994). *Bioenergetics: The Revolutionary Therapy That Uses the Language of the Body to Heal the Problems of the Mind*. Arkana.

Nicholas, M. P., & Schwartz, R. C. (2001). *Family Therapy Concepts and Methods* (5th ed.). Allyn and Bacon.

Pierrakos, J. C. (1990). *Core Energetics: Developing the Capacity to Love and Heal*. LifeRythmn.

Placzek, B. R. (Ed.). (1982). *Record of a Friendship: The Correspondence of Wilhelm Reich and A.S. Neill*. Farrar, Strauss, Giroux.

Reich, W. M. (1983). *Children of the Future*. Farrar, Strauss, Giroux. (Original work published 1950)

Truffaut, F. (Director) (1959) *400 Blows*. Les Films du Carrosse.

Part I
The Practice

1

Children in an Anxious Age

Embodied Play Therapy in Context

Not since developmental psychologist Erik H. Erikson (1950/1993) published *Childhood and Society* five years after the liberation of the Death Camps in World War II Europe have humans faced the level of worldwide trauma we are feeling now. War, racial and ethnic conflict, antisemitism, islamophobia, political polarization stoked by personal and group-think biases, cancel culture, hate crime, gun violence, an epidemic of drug use and death by overdose, economic insecurity, and a sense of helplessness amid warp-speed environmental, economic, and societal change.

Children's brains and bodies develop today bombarded by the flashing, image-flooded push and pull of their screens, increasingly subject to anxiety and panic.

We adults are often screen-addicted "technoholics" ourselves. Trying as best we can to be of help to these children, our consciousness, like that of our children, is also fragmented by technology. We become whipsawed by worry and fear, desperate to recover from the bane of our times, a disquietingly felt sense of absence and lack, moving into manic action or freezing in overwhelm.

We live in an epidemic of emptiness. As young and old, we squander precious time, leaving the riches of this very moment,

DOI: 10.4324/9781003328186-3

the present, for the lure of "what comes next." We suffer with stories we've created that our efforts, our relationships, and what we possess are just "not enough."

Nancy Colier (2016), therapist and author of *The Power of Off*, says:

> We need to ask ourselves if we (personally) are raising orphan children, choosing to allow technology to take over as surrogates for our own attention. [She asks us] to become aware of the messages we're sending our children when we consistently stare into our own screens and not their eyes. (p. 82)

Colier (2016) further advises that:

> One of the real consequences of too much time with technology is that it disconnects us from our bodies and leaves us perpetually in our minds. Overfed with information and entertainment we become disembodied heads, cut off from our senses in our physical reality, which then causes us to feel fragmented and uprooted. Our physical senses are what makes us feel grounded and connected in the present moment. The senses are our portal into presence. (p. 220)

In the United States, the prevalence of anxiety in children was estimated at 9.2% for 6–11-year-olds for the years 2022–23 (Child and Adolescent Health Measurement Initiative, 2022–2023). Insecurity in parent-child relationships and the surrounding day-to-day and media-saturated environments of children are other factors to consider as we look at what's contributing to increased anxiety in children.

According to the American Academy of Child & Adolescent Psychiatry (2025a):

> American children spend an average of seven to eight hours per day viewing screen entertainment. Videos

> and programs can be a powerful influence in developing value systems and shaping behavior. Unfortunately, much of contemporary television programming features violence. Hundreds of studies of the effects of screen violence on children and teenagers have found that children may:
>
> - Become "immune" or numb to the horror of violence
> - Begin to accept violence as a way to solve problems
> - Imitate the violence they observe on screens

As this relates to possible childhood responses, the American Academy of Child & Adolescent Psychiatry (AACAP) took this position: "Chronic and persistent exposure to media violence can lead to fear, desensitization (numbing), and in some children an increase in aggressive and violent behaviors" (AACAP, 2025b). Further, AACAP noted that "Violent behavior in children and adolescents can include a wide range of behaviors: explosive temper tantrums, physical aggression, fighting, threats or attempts to hurt others" (AACAP, 2017).

> Parents should limit the amount of time children and adolescents are exposed to screens each day as part of a family plan, to ensure screen time does not interfere with homework, physical activity, reading, connecting with family and friends, and sleep. (AACAP, 2025c)

Anxiety manifests in many ways. Seen especially among younger children I treat are symptoms of separation anxiety, which, as delineated by AACAP (2023), include:

- Refusing to go to school or separate from their parents/caregivers...
- Panic or tantrums at times of separation from parents
- Trouble sleeping or nightmares...

Untreated, these fears can grow into phobias whose symptoms include:

- Extreme fear about a specific thing or situation (e.g., dogs, insects, or needles)
- Fears causing significant distress and interfering with usual activities

Other Factors Now Causing Anxiety to Mount among Children

Pediatric researchers at Texas Tech University (2016) looked at the "Mental and Emotional Health of Children Exposed to News Media of Threats and Acts of Terrorism: The Cumulative and Pervasive Effects." They said:

> Children today have virtually unrestricted access to worldwide media coverage of terrorism acts, which threatens their mental and physical health due to their crude nature....Exposure to terrorism violence through the media, videogames, movies, or news about disasters and/or individual incidents has different implications for the pediatric population, and multiple studies have shown a link to adverse mental health effects in children. These findings highlight the need and importance for primary care providers to receive training to effectively assess and refer children who need therapy to confront and deal with these emotional effects. The effects of exposure to terrorism violence on children might not be apparent for several days, months, or even years. The effects are dosed and triggered by existing psychological problems, adversity, and/or previous victimization. (Leiner et al. 2016)

"Addressing the effects of terrorism violence acts involves much more than just taking care of the direct victim's needs, it requires considering that the bystanders watching these acts in the media are highly vulnerable as well" (Leiner et al., 2016).

My home office is located 20 miles from Newtown, Connecticut, where the 2012 Sandy Hook Elementary School mass murders occurred. One of the current issues facing children here is the effect of "school lockdown" practice drills related to the ever-increasing proliferation of school shootings. Children are afraid, and many parents are frightened when sending their children to school. Currently in the United States, while some states have implemented their own gun laws, others have opted to go the other way, allowing "open carry" of weapons and encouraging school personnel to carry them. This leaves therapists, parents, teachers, and school systems the difficult task of working through everyone's fears and crafting solutions. What I witness today is children holding on in whatever ways they can for dear life.

Since 2015, school shooting incidents in the United States have skyrocketed compared to previous decades. There were 332 shooting incidents at K-12 schools in 2024, resulting in 267 injuries and fatalities (Riedman, 2025). As Koo (2021) states:

> As news involving violence can frighten children, people worry that news portrayals of gun violence are often appalling. Based on cultivation theory and the theory of cognitive development, [our study] examined parents' perceptions of the children's exposure and reactions to news coverage of school shootings. A survey of U.S. parents ($N = 266$) demonstrated that children's exposure to news coverage of school shootings is positively related to children's frightened responses, according to the parents' perspective. Parents reported that children more exposed to the news are more likely to perceive the world as dangerous.

And then there is the portable and addictive access to violent imagery and interaction that many children hold in their phones, pads, and laptops – namely, violent video games. In fact, a 2010 review by psychologist Craig Anderson and others concluded that "the evidence strongly suggests that exposure to violent video games is a causal risk factor for increased aggressive behavior, aggressive cognition, and aggressive affect and for decreased empathy and prosocial behavior" (Anderson, et.al., p. 151).

Anderson's earlier research (Anderson & Dill, 2000) showed that playing violent video games can increase a person's aggressive thoughts, feelings, and behavior both in laboratory settings and in daily life. (American Psychological Association, 2013, p. 772). Also, a consensus of media researchers believes that violent media increases aggression in children, and according to one study, "66.0% of researchers either strongly agree or agree that violent games increase aggression in children" (Bushman et al., 2015).

Weighing in as a family therapist who also works with couples and individual adults (many of whom are parents), the stresses on today's parents contribute mightily to the anxiety of the children I see, as you will see portrayed in many of this book's descriptions of children and their parents in therapy. In many instances, the children who act out represent the tip of a family and societal iceberg, which, if not melting fast, is floating, unmoored from a stable connection. I'd estimate that about 65–70% of the children who've been in my care have come from families where parents were in conflict, separated, or divorced.

When you add to this the strains of unpredictable work schedules, job insecurity, and difficulties for parents in maintaining work-life balance (Luhr et al., 2022), the recipe for childhood anxiety being cooked up is staring us right in the face. Conversations I've had with parents over the past decade have focused my attention on the reality of life today, where parents face questions ranging from day-to-day stressors to life-disrupters. Will artificial intelligence replace my job tomorrow? Why does my child fight me about going to school? Will political instability or climate change force my family to move? Why am I so afraid I can't protect my child?

Embodied Play Therapy gives children an opportunity to get more connected to the primary home they will reside in for the whole of their earthly existence – their own living, breathing, and feeling body. But what happens when that body is of a color, religion, gender expression, or sexual preference perceived as different or of lesser value than others? In the book *Multicultural Play Therapy: Making the Most of Cultural Opportunities with Children* (Ray et al., 2022), the editors, all therapists and professors, highlight unmanageable obstacles experienced by those who are not of the dominant culture. These include microaggressions, messages that their looks or culture do not measure up, and daily reminders they witness in the media of children who look like them being detained in poor conditions (p. 17), some pulled from their homes or separated from parents at the U.S. border.

In his book *Toys and Reasons* (1978), developmental psychologist Erik H. Erikson tells the powerful story of a five-year-old Black boy named Robert who builds a "high, symmetrical and well-balanced block structure" (p. 31), placing the Black figure of a boy on the top. Other human dolls stand up in the scene:

> their *arms lifted,* as if in some excitement (p. 32). [Robert's teacher had noted that he sometimes] "danced around the classroom with his arms stretched sideways... [and she] congratulated the boy on his athletic ability and on the gracefulness of his dancing motions; but he had responded with a despairing gesture and had said 'Yes, but my brain is no good.'" (p. 33)

Erikson, speaking in an era less than a decade from the passage of Civil Rights legislation in the United States and approximately two decades from the Supreme Court decision that mandated desegregation of schools (Koughan & Robertson, 2014, July 15), notes that Robert's "black boy on the very *top* of the construction lies supine...most exposed...in the greatest danger of falling down" (Erikson, 1978, p. 35).

Compare Erikson's story with anecdotes from my work with children almost 50 years later. Part Mexican-American at eight years old, one of my clients sits anxiously in the backseat of her parents' car, stuck behind a caravan of flag-waving Trump supporters before the 2020 U.S. election, and wants to open the door to run. In 2025, and approaching her 13th birthday, a girl asks her mom, "Will there be a civil war?"

A ten-year-old white girl, taught in school that the USA is a nation of immigrants, builds a wall of soft furnishings and smashes through it, even as her father confides what may be influencing the conflicts his daughter may be trying to break through and resolve. "We voted for Trump," he says.

And there are other children. The Jewish boy, hearing the words "You are not like us" from his classmates, hides his Star of David inside his shirt. The girl with autism, shamed by her friends for the way she waves her arms to comfort herself, doesn't want to go to school anymore. The children experiencing discrimination because they are gay and whose minds descend into suicidal ideation (see statistics on LGBTQ youth in Chapter 5: Touchy Subjects). A child who dreams that the world is going up in flames.

And I remember my own childhood like it was yesterday…

> **Four-year-old Neal:** *Watching my mom head toward the steel door of our small Manhattan apartment, the doorbell rings insistently. My parents are progressives in McCarthy-era America, and the two trench-coated men my mother sees through the "peephole" in the door say they are FBI. "Get away from this door," she yells, rising on her tiptoes to her full, four foot ten and three-quarter inch height. They leave, never to return. Mistaken identity. But fear gains a foothold in my heart.*

Different children may be anxious about different things. For one, it may be their performance in school; for another, it's conflict or illness, or substance abuse in the family. For others, it's the approaching transition to adolescence that has them anxious. For still others, it's the reality they face in a fast-changing world. Anxious children in an anxious age, where the adults running their world are having troubles trying to keep it all together.

References

American Academy of Child & Adolescent Psychiatry. (2017, December). *Violent Behavior in Children and Adolescence.* Facts for Families No.55.https://www.aacap.org/AACAP/Families_and_Youth/Facts_for_Families/FFF-Guide/Understanding-Violent-Behavior-In-Children-and-Adolescents-055.aspx

American Academy of Child & Adolescent Psychiatry. (2023, October). *Anxiety and Children*. Facts for Families No. 47. https://www.aacap.org/AACAP/Families_and_Youth/Facts_for_Families/FFF-Guide/The-Anxious-Child-047.aspx

American Academy of Child & Adolescent Psychiatry. (2025a, June). *Screen Violence and Children.* Facts for Families, No. 13. https://www.aacap.org/AACAP/Families_and_Youth/Facts_for_Families/FFF-Guide/Screen_Violence_Children-013.aspx

American Academy of Child & Adolescent Psychiatry (2025b June). *News and Children.* Facts for Families, No. 67. https://www.aacap.org/AACAP/Families_and_Youth/Facts_for_Families/FFF-Guide/Children-And-The-News-067.aspx

American Academy of Child & Adolescent Psychiatry. (2025c, June). *Movies, Media and Children*. Facts for Families No. 90. https://www.aacap.org/AACAP/Families_and_Youth/Facts_for_Families/FFF-Guide/Children-And-Movies-090.aspx

American Psychological Association. (2013, November 1). *Violence in the Media: Psychologists Study Potential Harmful Effects.* https://www.apa.org/topics/video-games/violence-harmful-effects

Anderson, C. A., & Dill, K. E. (2000). Video Games and Aggressive Thoughts, Feelings, and Behavior in the Laboratory and in Life. *Journal of Personality and Social Psychology, 78* (4), 772–790.

Anderson, C. A., Ihori, N., Bushman, B. J., Rothstein, H. R., Shibuya, A., Swing, E. L., Sakamoto, A., & Saleem, M. (2010). Violent Video Game Effects on Aggression, Empathy, and Prosocial Behavior in Eastern and Western Countries: A Meta-Analytic Review. *Psychological Bulletin, 126* (20) 151–173.

Bushman, B. J., Gollwitzer, M., & Cruz, C. (2015). There Is Broad Consensus: Media Researchers Agree That Violent Media Increase Aggression in Children, and Pediatricians and Parents Concur. *Psychology of Popular Media Culture, 4*(3), 200–214. https://doi.org/10.1037/ppm0000046

Child and Adolescent Health Measurement Initiative. (2022–2023). *National Survey of Children's Health. Data Resource Center for Child and Adolescent Health Supported by the U.S. Department of Health and Human Services, Health Resources and Services Administration (HRSA), Maternal and Child Health Bureau (MCHB).* https://nschdata.org/browse/survey?s=2&y=51&r=1&#home

Colier, N. (2016). *The Power of Off: The Mindful Way to Stay Sane in a Virtual World.* Sounds True.

Erikson, E. H. (1978). *Toys and Reasons: Stages in the Ritualization of Experience.* Marion Boyers Publishers.

Erikson, E. H. (1993). *Childhood and Society.* W. W. Norton. (Original work published 1950)

Koo, G. H. (2021). Are You Frightened? Children's Cognitive and Affective Reactions to News Coverage of School Shootings. *Mass Communication and Society, 26*(1), 1–22. https://doi.org/10.1080/15205436.2021.1996609

Koughan, F., & Robertson, M. (2014, July 15). *Separate and Unequal.* PBS Frontline. https://www.youtube.com/watch?v=VS6xOVGKOSg

Leiner, M., Peinado, J., Villanos, M. T. M., Lopez, I., Uribe, R., & Pathek, I. (2016, March 23). Mental and Emotional Health of Children Exposed to News Media of Threats and Acts of Terrorism: The Cumulative and Pervasive Effects. *Frontiers in Pediatrics, 4*(26). https://doi.org/10.3389/fped.2016.00026

Luhr, S., Schneider, D., & Harknett, K. (2022, August). Parenting without Predictability: Precarious Schedules, Parental Strain, and Work-Life Conflict. *The Russell Sage Foundation Journal of the Social Sciences, 8*(5), 24–44. https://doi.org/10.7758/RSF.2022.8.5.02

Ray, C. D., Ogawa, Y., & Cheng, Y. (2022). Cultural Humility and the Play Therapist. In C.D. Ray, Y. Ogawa, & Y. Cheng (Eds.), *Multicultural Play Therapy: Making the Most of Cultural Opportunities with Children* (pp. 13–28). Routledge.

Riedman, D. (2025). *How Many School Shootings? All Incidents from 1966–Present. K-12 School Shooting Database.* https://k12ssdb.org/all-shootings

2

The Four Pillars of Embodied Play Therapy with Children

Movement, Breathing, Feeling, Play

When children are trained to mold their behavior in ways acceptable to those with more power, parts of themselves may move underground, leading to imbalances in their emotional energy. Among the resulting symptoms that we adults have named are:

- Anxiety
- Depression
- Oppositional-Defiance
- Sadness, Loneliness, and Grief

I offer Embodied Play Therapy to support and center a child more firmly in the parts of themselves where strength resides. Introducing that child to inner resources of body, mind, and spirit to help them build greater self-confidence in themselves, within their family, with friends, and in school. The focus here is on the evolutionary process of a child in moments of self-discovery, where the fullness of a child can be celebrated. While this process can contribute to positively adjusting what may be askew in

DOI: 10.4324/9781003328186-4

a child and their family system, it goes beyond just fixing things. Because I function outside the orbit of a family system, I often see ways to renew a child's energies that a family likely has not yet tried.

Parents who choose an Embodied Play Therapist go beyond furnishing just "someone to talk to." They invite a broader inclusion of what's available to a child in therapy. The intake form parents fill out for their children says: *"I specialize in helping clients explore and find balance on a deep, body-centered level. For young people, this often involves dynamic movement and other play that connects them to the healing power of the imagination. Reactions may come up during and after sessions, and I ask you to inform me in parent sessions of what you may notice in your child."*

What's important for parents to realize is that although problems appear to rattle around in their children's heads, children are more centered in the immediacy of growing bodies. Because these children are changing fast, and their worlds are as well, one problem may fade, and another may surface. Within a family unit, the child brought into therapy who stabilizes in an unstable family system may be replaced by another sibling who becomes symptomatic to fulfill a role that keeps attention away from adult problems reflected in one and then another of that family's children.

It may be hard to pinpoint when problems are resolved. That's why I ask parents to notice the "little wins." Has a child who fought you around food choices, what they wear to school, and when they'll head out the door in the morning lightened up in their demands? Are they asking for a hug when they're scared or overwhelmed? Have parents learned to take a breath before flying off the handle? Yes, it's good when we adults take ourselves down a notch and realize we might be more of the problem than we'd like to admit and do something to watch and change our own behavior. It's also a good thing to accept that a certain level of the unknown will remain in children sent for therapy. Within the complex field of family, school, and societal influences, problems may re-surface later in childhood, or resolution may be discovered later, well after a course of Embodied Play Therapy is over. And parents who focus mainly on "what's wrong" may miss certain cues that things are headed in a very right direction.

Because no one size will fit all, in-session activities are adapted to an individual kid's needs. A child will peruse and choose from what they see is available. While some are initially reticent, most seem energized and excited. There's an opportunity to do more than just sit still.

The chief concerns for which children are brought in to see me include:

- Fears and phobias leading to a wide range of issues, including sleep problems and night terrors
- Excessive reliance or overuse of screens (phones, tablets, video games, or TV)
- Hyperactivity resulting in problems with school performance
- Refusal to cooperate with teachers and other authorities
- Reluctance to self-advocate with parents, peers, and at school
- Limitation on which foods a child will eat, often paired with heavy reliance on sugar-rich or ultra-processed foods
- Obsessions and compulsive behaviors, which manifest in symptoms like repetitive handwashing, frequent clothing change, and demands on peers, parents, or siblings that they conform to rules set by the child
- Pushback by children on parental needs for cooperation around family mealtime, getting to school, participation in events involving siblings, or in instances where a child feels uneasy or unsafe, especially at times of transition where a change of location is necessary

The reality is that any of the above is exhausting for kids and parents as families struggle to accommodate. Embodied Play Therapy offers a variety of in-session experiences for children that sometimes involve play together with a parent. In either case, the goal is the same, providing some relief where it may have been lacking before. To build emotional and relational capacity in children and to bring families closer.

Embodied Play Therapy: How We Got Here

The lineage of Embodied Play Therapy includes the founder of body psychotherapy, Wilhelm Reich, the developmental work of Erik H. Erikson, the play excursions of psychoanalyst, theoretician, and former pediatrician D.W. Winnicott, and the work of psychotherapist Dennis McCarthy, whose background combined Dance Therapy, Bioenergetics, and sandplay, rooted in the teachings on imagination of Carl Jung. This led McCarthy (2012) to build a Dynamic Play Therapy palette combining sandplay, work with clay, drawing, and play-informed battles between the young client and therapist. Also part of the lineage are pioneers of play and dramatherapy, Sue Jennings and Clive Holmwood, who synthesized several child development approaches into a Neuro-Dramatic Play process, encouraging messy play, playing with objects, and making stories (Holmwood, 2021, p. 168).

Wilhelm Reich speaks of "armoring" or "rigidities of the character and the chronic spasms of the musculature…as a defense against the breakthrough of emotions" (1950/1983, p. 11). This powerful inner armoring begins as the child confronts opposition within the family to the potentially disruptive energy of their life force, which challenges the structural need of parents to control.

Both Austrian-born Reich (1897) and German-born Erikson (1902) endured tumultuous social upheaval resulting from the 20th century's two world wars. While Reich's writing focused on the human body and repression by family, religion, and state, Erikson opened conceptual doors on childhood learning and progression through psychosocial life tasks that allow for the individuation of identity and integration within the fabric of communities and the larger social and cultural frameworks of which they are a part.

How did childhood development and its challenges look to Erikson?

Poetically, he describes the infant's "adventures of the senses" (1950/1993, p. 247): "A tiny human's awareness of their own body in feeding, sleeping, movements of bowel and bladder." Willingness to let "mother [or other caregiver] out of sight without undue anxiety" (p. 247) supports explorations, first wriggling on the belly, and then crawling on all fours.

As a toddler, a child next learns to integrate "inner states" with awareness that they are "observable by others" (Erikson, 1950/1993, p. 251). The child is more conscious of an "environment that encourages him to stand on his own feet" (p. 252). Practicing "holding on" and "letting go" (p. 251), the toddler begins to emerge as a social being capable of greater mobility. But what happens when a child may not have completed an early developmental step?

Many of the young people I see in my practice are in what early 20th-century psychotherapists, starting with Sigmund Freud, called the "latency" age. A period of psychosexual development occurring roughly between ages 6 and puberty, where a child's attention shifts to their performance and how it may be observed in the outside world. Erik Erikson says, "the danger at this stage is the development of a sense of *inadequacy and inferiority*" (1959/1994, p. 91). As children absorb into their minds and bodies the frowns, the confusion, and the growing desperation of parents and teachers, a nagging expectation that they are failing to excel takes root. Lacking in the joyful confidence that grows when a child trusts in their competence, these children struggle.

Even as some children display their disquiet in dramatic fits of blustery protest or feigned superiority, inside they know their behavior doesn't look good in comparison with the surrounding kids. Sensing and often fearing their inferior performance in the eyes of others, they act out as a cry for help. If a child is lucky, responsible adults notice and begin a search for assistance beyond what they can offer.

As stated in the introduction to this book:

> Embodied Play Therapy offers individual children active movement-based sessions with an adult practitioner to build awareness of breathing and feeling using equipment

> designed to enhance full self-expression. Through play using pillows, a large foam cube, lightweight bats, protective punching gloves, along with clay, drawing, and a deep sandbox with an assortment of play figures to place in its depths, a child gets in touch with what's inside them. Along the way, they tap into their innate creative abilities to construct self-affirming stories reflecting positive visions for themselves and their world, while building connection and having fun.

The method adds a family systems lens from my training in Marital and Family Therapy, involving parents/caregivers in play with the permission of their child. My approach also includes the use of music, as I add soundtracks to enliven periods in the session when a child is drawing. I may also move outdoors, beyond the therapy room, for both in-person and online live video sessions. I've written in the 2021 *International Handbook of Play, Therapeutic Play, and Play Therapy* about a germ-phobic child joining me in heaving sticks and stones into a roaring stream as part of an Embodied Play Therapy exposure-therapy-like challenge to his fears as one example of such an outside-the-office excursion (Brodsky, 2021, p. 267). Another tale from an outdoor Embodied Play Therapy Online session with my remote client, Molly, can be found in Chapter 10: Live Video!

Finally, my training in film, television, and photography supports me in exploring the "...notion of sensory, rhythmic, and dramatic playfulness" identified by Sue Jennings as a key part of healthy early childhood development (Holmwood, 2021, p. 168). Because of its variety in use of the body, in use of materials, in the use of guessing games using sight and sound (see Chapter 9: Toolbox about sound effects tools and music), Embodied Play Therapy seeks to expand a child's sensory experience in the context of both relational back and forth and fun. Rather than be so serious about symptoms, it's often better to let a child craft in sand, clay, and story. I'm still repeating the brief poem by Ogden Nash that I heard as a child and still enjoy as one motto to inspire my play with children: "In the world of Mules, there are No Rules" (1930/1987, p. 20).

Yet, in his book *Toys and Reasons*, Erik Erikson speaks of school-age young people as concerned with "rules of performance" (1978, p. 114). And because I find many parent-child relationships are painfully rule-bound, I like to play with turning rules upside down. Inflexible rule structures in family systems, including overly relaxed rule regimens, often contribute to why a child is sent for therapy. So I gently encourage parents to question rules and approaches to discipline, which sometimes have the opposite effect parents intend. Speaking about the role of the parent-child relationship as a contributor to childhood anxiety, Alexander Lowen (1975) says:

> Parents, unfortunately, are not just a source of pleasure: they become quickly associated in the child's mind with the possibility of pain. The resultant anxiety is, in my opinion, responsible for the restlessness and hyperactivity so many children show. Sooner or later defenses are erected to diminish the anxiety, but these defenses also diminish the life and vitality of the organism. (p. 136)

Before these defenses harden, parents can help and often lessen symptomatic behavior in children by attuning themselves more closely to their child. Before enforcing a particular code of behavior, it's useful to take a few deep breaths. To reflect on what your life was like when you were a child. To focus on creating boundaries that enhance rather than restrict a child's exploratory nature. In practice, this means putting a pause on parental attitudes that could cause entrenchment, which often allows a child a moment to relax, rather than respond reactively, letting down energetically into a more flexible state. Before things spin out of control, remember the power one has as a parent over a child. To be curious as to whether that power is being exercised with a semblance of consistency and whether that exercise can be softened by a parent's own embodied sense of self. In a physical sense, a parent is very large and a child quite small. Parents who allow a little laughter at themselves and over what seems absurd or painful in family predicaments can often lower the temperature, helping turn children away from intransigent response before the family relational dance turns toward the traumatic.

In cases of neglect and trauma, psychotherapists Pat Ogden, Bonnie Goldstein, and Janina Fisher zero in on the physical and behavioral effects: "Some children, driven by tense bodies which are hyperactive and hyper aroused, feel out of control, anxious or aggressive. Others have collapsed or frozen bodies that fuel helpless and powerless feelings" (2013, p. 229). The authors "propose that a bottom-up approach that targets the body, in addition to the verbal narrative when available, can produce changes that will influence resolution of symptoms and increase the capacity for relatedness and adaptive behavior" (p. 230).

My caseload is not focused on cases of trauma and neglect involving sexual and physical abuse of children because I believe these are best handled in a clinical context that allows for group therapy with other children and a level of cross-disciplinary collaboration that such a setting fosters. I hope readers will take the approaches suggested within this book, adapting them as they see fit within a variety of practical, growth-oriented, educational, and service environments. But a bottom-up approach, which starts with somatic awareness of the body, is where I choose to start because that is where we begin as beings and where growth can best be grounded for longer-term health into adolescence and adulthood.

A central component of Embodied Play Therapy with children, and my view of a bottom-up approach, involves support at a somatic level for "creative aggression" and "assertion" of individuality as a cornerstone for the identity children will need to construct as adolescents. Playing with such assertions is immensely valuable for these pre-adolescent children because they are less burdened by the intense counter-spins of adolescence and the potential role confusion that plagues so many young people as they move into their later teenage years. A prime rationale for doing therapeutic work early with children is the important factor of time as it relates to anxiety formation and persistence. As Lowen (1975) says,

"...the earlier in life that anxiety arises, the more pervasive it is and the more deeply structured the defenses against it become" (p. 136). The second imperative to take on the work with children rather than wait is the "unconscious striving for a *continuity of personal character*" (Erikson, 1959/1994, p. 109) that will be part of the monumental task of the emerging adolescent, who must also face intensified peer group pressures, the need to grow ideological perspectives and resist "identity diffusion," where a clear sense of self, values, and goals becomes difficult to maintain (Erikson, 1959/1994, Appendix; Jackson & Hogg, 2010).

Starting in early childhood, where discrimination of good and bad is part of the learning process, Eric H. Erikson (1978) says that "As the ability to crawl and eventually to stand serves increased self-reliance, it also soon leads to play with the boundaries of the permissible" (p. 92). Think of the infant who screams or the two-year-old who may bite, kick, or scratch, and then consider your own childhood. I was taught to be a "good boy" early on and suffered for it in later years, as positive assertion linked to now-underground aggressive impulses kept me in a dance of ambivalence with achievement and relationships with others.

In charting the necessity for bounded expression of aggression in childhood play, Dennis McCarthy (2012) draws our attention to several theorists and therapists. Noting first that Konrad Lorenz in his book *On Aggression* posits that "aggression erupts spontaneously and requires some form of regular discharge" (p. 81), along with Konrad Lorenz's second finding "that the ability to form something of a personal bond occurs to the degree that aggression is felt and expressed between human beings" (p. 81).

Writing about aggression in the book *The Way to Vibrant Health: A Manual of Bioenergetic Exercises*, Alexander and Leslie Lowen say that "The word itself means 'to move toward.' People use it to denote 'going for what one wants.' An aggressive person is one who moves toward the fulfillment of his wants. The lack of aggression means passivity – waiting, not reaching out" (1977, p. 117).

Brian Gleason, co-creator of Embodied Relational Work with couples speaking to me of his own childhood, said:

> There was no space in my family for high-pitched emotion. It was a stoic Irish approach. Opening up to a wider range of our human emotional field is a component in developing a sense of agency. When I started to pathologize my inner process, I exiled emotional parts of myself, which led to constriction of my energy. (Brian Gleason, personal communication, 9/12/25)

Linking the role childhood emotional constriction plays in creating relationship anxieties later in life, limiting fuller self-expression in adult couples, Brian and Marcia Gleason, co-authors of the book *Exceptional Relationships* say:

> As children make the shift from a life of seeking pleasure and comfort through contact and exploration, to a life of seeking validation and acceptance through performance and 'should,' their worlds change. ...The goal shifts from being an 'alive self' to an 'acceptable self'. (Gleason & Gleason, 2012, pp. 37–38)

An acceptable self may play well for a while in the short term. Yet if we are hoping to foster aliveness and fuller self-expression to maintain future long-term adult partnerships, supporting a broader emotional range in these early years, including aggressive impulse, needs to be in play.

Erikson (1978) speaks of "aggressive aspects of play – as well as the playful aspects of aggression" (p. 56), saying

> A fundamental and almost innocent 'aggressivity' informs every act of being alive – and thus also of being playful. It simply belongs to a growing organism's very existence in space and time – and, indeed, *aggredere* means first and foremost to *go at* things and people in a way that may invite playful mutuality but may also

> interfere with your leeway without being antagonistic in either intention or affect… [it is] of playfulness confirmed by mutuality. (pp. 56–57)

McCarthy (2012) further enjoins us that "our task with children vis-à-vis aggression is to welcome it, contain it, ground it for them via ourselves and play, and help children both express and regulate it simultaneously" (p. 88). Here's my example:

> *My client, six-year-old Kyra wanted to beat my clay monster, and she had a plan. Her monster had a mouth so big, it stretched from clay head to its foot. No matter that I raised the pitch of my voice to that of a bird. Who was the child? Kyra or me? My monster got crushed, gobbled up, and incorporated into a great glob of clay. The winner was clear from Kyra's squeals of sheer pleasure. And we had become allied, attached human-to-human with less regard to how our physical size and knowledge of the world's workings might have separated us before.*

Speaking of monsters created out of clay or drawn by children, McCarthy says:

> These monsters of ours are an early effort at expressing aggression in the sublimated manner of which Lorenz speaks. They express and contain the 'bioenergy' that Reich and Lowen wrote about…and the Chi that in Asia forms the basis of physical health and power. They are early manifestations of Prana, of the basic life force and our struggle amid the demands of society, family, and our own developing egos. (2012, pp. 89–90)

McCarthy speaks of an in-session encounter bat attack from a child, realizing that:

> in his attack he was not trying to knock me over or destroy me, but rather…He was affirming both himself and me as separate beings. The contact the attack afforded

> was delineating where he stopped and where I began. It solidified our boundaries as well as confirming his own. (2007, p. 103)

I've never had a parent tell me that the assertive and creatively aggressive play in the sessions I offer has encouraged violence in participating children at home or elsewhere. In Embodied Play Therapy sessions, children play with the boundaries of their own aggression as a contribution to their own growth. Negative aggressive tendencies acted out before therapy often decrease (Brodsky, 2015; Brodsky, 2021), and regressed behavior becomes more age-appropriate, especially when parents listen to the deeper messages their child's symptoms may imply.

A parent tells me a story of their ten-year-old child who urinated on the walls of his room at home. When I heard the story, I felt hopeful, noticing the outpourings of the body as a cry for help. Another child, age 9, stuck in a school that did not serve her, would walk around the home without clothes like a two-year-old would. These two children both needed to leap beyond their regressive behavior while also signaling parents of changes that needed to be made. What might happen if the parents of these children did not seek therapy for their family system? Symptoms over time could metamorphose into different forms, perhaps opposition to school demands or later, defiance within the work world, substance abuse, or other imbalanced behavior. Messaging a "cry for help" in more dramatic ways.

When a parent answers the call of their child's symptom for help by seeking an Embodied Play Therapist, the choice is a bold one, a choice to build expressive capabilities they themselves may not have been allowed as children. As a family and play therapist and Core Energetics practitioner, I want to address any possible misunderstandings about emotionally expressive techniques on what we are doing in Embodied Play Therapy. While we lean toward releasing withheld feelings in session, this is done within a careful process that both honors an individual family's and child's emotional and relational reality. Stressful family situations may take time to play out beyond the therapy office, and Embodied Play Therapy needs to be a sensitively crafted vessel to hold multiple influences. If the therapist has doubts or questions about what is being observed in session, the default is always to consult with the parent and, with parental permission, seek to learn more. It can be illuminating to speak with a child's teacher or collaborate with other professionals serving the family, such as pediatricians, occupational therapists, or psychiatrists.

Throughout, we are prioritizing the building of bridges both to parents and the child presented for treatment (see examples, especially in Chapter 4: Parents In the Mix). In essence, what we are doing through play modalities within the process of Embodied Play Therapy is unearthing and exploring new ways of looking at things, feeling things, and promoting fluidity, self-awareness, and self-responsibility in relationships with others. Through story, substance (especially clay and sand), and through other expressive methods demonstrated in this book by participating children, we are acting to prevent what would show up in later life as blocks to feelings and consciousness. Energetic blocks, once hardwired into tensely held teen and adult bodies, can influence how they will behave. Whether that behavior is fleeing in fear, freezing, collapsing, or even, in extreme cases, fainting when faced with difficulties in challenging environments such as school (Brodsky, 2015, p. 155). As children move into their teen years and adulthood, blocks become more difficult, though not impossible, to challenge. I see this clearly with the adults, couples, and groups I've worked with and have had the privilege to participate in both as a client and as a professional (see especially "Afterword: Inner Children Surface in an Embodied Play Therapy Group for Adults" in this book).

While not a prescription for how a child should behave outside of the therapy room, Embodied Play Therapy guides children and parents to be curious about their reflexive responses that may be hurtful to others and simply do not work. To be most effective, the process of building consciousness often needs to be a family affair.

Case in point, my sessions with a seven-year-old client, Stevie, who was instigating fights with his sensitive older sister to blow off steam, leaving her to stew in her riled-up emotional juices, while my client cheerfully moved on to his next activity, relieved from emotional baggage that he'd just dumped. The issue is that, unchecked, this dumping pattern would repeat like a broken record, driving the parents into increasingly harsher punishments of my child client, taking away this privilege and that. No screen time today. No trip to the mall tomorrow. No visit to see your friend. Or your Grandma. And none of this top-down authoritarian approach was working. The parents' disciplinary wheelhouse was empty because the emotional expression behind this diminutive seven-year-old steam engine was the upset over his parents' divorce.

After Stevie's parents told me he had impulsively thrown empty plastic containers from the recycling bin at his older sister, I brought three things into his next session: A three-foot length of bubble wrap for him to stomp on, a few glossy magazines to rip up and toss on the floor, and brown wrapping paper for him to punch through. I emphasized that this was just for his play sessions with me and that my job was to do the cleaning up after the session. That led to a big smile of pleasure from him and an unbridled, joyous few minutes of stomping every tiny plastic bubble until there were no more, ripping magazines to carpet my floor in a blanket of shreds, and a final blasting through of fist through the sheet of brown paper I held for him.

When I suggested to Stevie that he might have some thoughts about people in his life as he was doing all this, he told me about how his overworked dad never listened to him and how his older sister, the human closest to him in his parents' separation, would shut him out with a smirk when the sister's older same-age friends were around.

Stevie might have been small, but he was no dummy. He was hurt, and he was showing it by acting out in the only way he knew – misplaced aggression. A play therapy session where he had permission to experience the sensation of aggressive impulse in the context of fun allowed Stevie to contain and own, rather than disown, that impulse.

While my client Stevie was angry with his parents and his sister, and perhaps justifiably so, he was also afraid. Letting his parents out of his sight had become an issue. Any time he went to the bathroom, whether in my office or at home, a parent would need to be present just outside the door. And fear of insects had him startled and scooting off at any sign of anything flying or crawling near him. But what was the underlying fear?

That he would be left defenseless and alone in his parents' divorce. Anger, hurt, and fear spiraled around him, and the sand world he made that day showed it. Two evil queens point at a married couple. A shark appears that eats both water and sand. How could this child integrate his unpalatable mix of strong feelings? These feelings get projected outward in Embodied Play Therapy rather than torturously held in a small body. Difficult at times for a seven-year-old child to express in words, they often can be decisively worked through in play.

Former Director of Education at the Institute of Core Energetics, Core Energetics practitioner and teacher, Lisa Loustaunau, says:

> As we begin to work with feelings that were previously perceived as 'dangerous' within the safe container of a supportive relationship, [we] reclaim the energy that has been trapped in the previously denied feelings. This life-force, this energy, is now freed and available for our creativity, our well-being, and a powerfully enhanced experience of our aliveness. (Loustaunau, personal communication of class handout, 2015)

Certainly, some feelings are seen as dangerous. For a young child, no feeling is more dangerous than the double bind of seeing your parent hurting and knowing your own rage and terror could upset them more. So, a child acts out both to retrieve the attention of a broken family system and to tug on one or both parents' fixations with their own hurt in the only way that the child knows how. A futile and wasteful task at the crucial stage where the constructive "industry" described by Erikson meets the destructive specter of their possible "inferiority" (1959/1994, p. 87) in handling their conflicting feelings and sometimes conflictual relationships.

Do you have an inkling of what happened with seven-year-old client Stevie after this session and a few more? The Embodied Play Therapy had him headed in some very good directions. As we allowed his aggressive impulses to be more fully felt, he tortured his suffering older sister less. Stevie even made a gesture of repair, drawing his sister an image of their cat for her room. As he played through his feelings about his parents' separation in the sand, there was less fear of being without them. The bugs that were bugging him bugged him less – a possible phobia nipped in the bud at an early age. More aliveness is available for productive purposes, and for a seven-year-old, we're looking at a lot of potential for production! As I say to parents, "better to invest in your child's growth now rather than spend more money on therapy later."

Sometimes, we track the progress of young clients in the sand, through their willingness to engage in encounter bat battles with me or with a parent, and most often through novel narratives of their own invention. Stories imagined, then spoken, drawn, sculpted, or sung, which impart life to internal places where pain may have ruled. Energized movement helps a child's body to relax, the mind to open, and may prod a child, and through them, their family system toward productive change. Productive play grows when a therapist opens up to anything and everything. As I tell my clients, the only rules for our sessions are for safety: "Don't hurt me, don't hurt yourself, don't hurt the room." EVERYTHING ELSE is fair game for play.

In Embodied Play Therapy sessions, I take on an active role as a co-player with a child. D.W. Winnicott, in the book *Playing and Reality*, says that "psychotherapy is done in the overlap of the two play areas, that of the patient and that of the therapist" (1971/1996, p. 54). Co-play converges the four pillars of Embodied Play Therapy: Movement, Breathing, Feeling, and

Play into a workable and enjoyable template. Within any given session, that template remains in the inner recesses of my mind, a flexible guide to use or not while I follow what a child needs in the moment.

This is like the wonderful picture book Stone Soup (McGovern, 1986), which my parents read to me as a young boy, where, beginning with a single stone thrown into a kettle, a savory mix is created of colorful and tasty ingredients. Embodied Play Therapy sessions build a tasty mix of fun-filled activities that meld together, spurred on by the forward momentum of a child's imagination, the shifting sands of a child's inner experience, and the narratives they string together within their play.

As Winnicott says:

> It helps us to understand our work if we know that the basis of what we do is the patient's playing, a creative experience taking up space and time, and intensely real for the patient…to think of the *preoccupation* that characterizes the playing…the near-withdrawal state, akin to the *concentration* of older children and adults. … Into this play area the child gathers objects or phenomena from external reality and uses these. …Without hallucinating the child puts out a sample of dream potential. …In Playing, the child manipulates external phenomena in the service of the dream and invests chosen external phenomena with dream meaning and feeling. (1971/1996, p. 50–51)

The concept of such external phenomena takes on special excitement for me in this era of burgeoning teletherapy services. When I host tele-sessions, clients direct me as their "construction manager" to help build, unearth, and fight through what's just under the surface in heart, mind, and body. Thoughts and dreams coalesce into narratives that hold healing potential, whether a child's play with me occurs in-person or online via live video.

Ari, an 11-year-old star basketball player who couldn't play during the COVID-19 pandemic, began acting out in online school, cheating on tests to assuage his competitive streak that couldn't be exercised in-person on the court. While a part of him was ashamed to be breaking the rules, his parents were desperate to have some rules enforced and this turned into a battle over whether Ari was allowed to leave the table before finishing everything on his plate, and how long he'd have online each day to play Minecraft and be on TikTok. In essence this was a battle around the insanity of a grown-up world going mad in pandemic lockdown, with rules and roles suddenly unclear. What's a kid to do if a large part of them just doesn't want to obey?

I decided to take this theme of flouting rules versus abiding by them (school and parental) and play with its monstrosity to get to the core of Ari's issue. For the online session, I had Ari connect three pieces of paper with cellophane tape to make one giant piece. For that single sheet of paper, he dreams up and draws two monsters.

Ari – Monster #1: The Purple-ator monster can turn things purple and freeze things in time. He's trying to take over because his planet turned purple and he needs to take over ours.

Monster #2 (Ari makes loud slurping sounds): The Purple-ator has one leg shorter than the other. He is very, very big and can take over the world. He's on a mission to help his boss, ten times the size of him!

This led to a discussion of how people become determined to accomplish certain missions. Ari tells me his parents are determined that he stay at the table and also that he is determined to get as good a grade as his friend who is earning all "A's."

Ari sits on the bed in his room and hits the mattress again and again with his fists. Next, he stands, discharging and grounding the energy he's built up, swinging his hands and arms up, over his head, with fingertips reaching toward the floor in a standing forward bend.

Was there a full resolution of all Ari faced? No, there wasn't. Ari would continue to feel competitive and continue to feel frustrated, but the dialogue had begun, and Ari's body, emotions, and thoughts had been nudged by Embodied Play Therapy into motion.

In his quest to define play and its value, Winnicott has us consider its earliest manifestation in infancy, where a baby finds their first significant "not me" or "transitional object" (1971/1996, p. 1), investing it with special meaning. Such investiture continues as children grow to incorporate wider spheres of experience and human interaction into their expanding neurological and energy systems. As an organizer, instigator, and validator of play experience, I pendulate between my adult self and younger self, mirroring for my young client, early experiences of attachment with caregivers. Making such attachment secure as we "play" with roles, returning in raucous humor from the wilds of monstrosity, playing in and through attachment breaks, mock, and otherwise. Turning assumptions of adult dominance and power aside. Experimenting with child-centered heroics and victory.

Acknowledging the work of the pioneering play therapist, Virginia Axline, Winnicott says, "The significant moment is that at which *the child surprises himself or herself*. It is not the moment of my clever interpretation that is significant" (1997/1991, p. 51).

I remember playing "Indian Hand Wrestling" games with my father where, toe to toe, we would lock hands and try to knock each other off balance, surprising each other with sudden moves. As I grew, I practiced this game with my younger brother Paul, almost seven years my junior. To this, we added games of tackle football (as played in North America) on an indoor "field." A hallway connecting our small NYC apartment's dining room and bathroom. What I remember was not winning and losing. I remember the crazy fun of doing this and bouncing off walls.

Focusing on the "location of play," Winnicott says, "play is in fact neither a matter of inner psychic reality nor a matter of external reality" (1971/1996, p. 96) and asks, "If play is neither inside or outside, where is it?" (p. 96). He locates it in the early experience of an infant and mother (for us more broadly, a parent or significant caregiver) "…at the point in time and space of the initiation of their state of separateness" (p. 97). In a therapeutic context, even as we play lightly, or in jesting spirit, we enter an invaluably rich realm. That of "the experience of relating to objects" (p. 98). We play with our experience of what Winnicott identifies as "contiguity" (p. 101) or, more exactly, *proximity with another human being*.

As Brian Gleason has said, in speaking to me about Embodied Play Therapy, where a therapist (and/or parent) actively engages in play with a child: "This is proximity as opposed to parallel play, it becomes an engagement. Engagement in itself is healing, dancing with emotions that come up between us. There's a joy of interaction here that often may not happen at home" (B. Gleason, personal communication, 9/12/25).

For the child participating in Embodied Play Therapy sessions, the therapist is a larger human who models fluidity and flexibility – a playful adult offering safe and proximate contact who is connected with parents but is not the parent. Through play, the therapist provides practice in the relational skills a young person will need to employ as they grow into adolescence and adulthood. As sessions continue, the active therapist will need to continuously track the child, discovering where the client wants to go next. To maintain awareness that any child in pain needs us to stick around with them for a while. To know we won't abandon them even as we see what they consider "bad" in themselves. Places where they may have been shamed and blamed by parents, by friends, or at school. A prime reason we play with creative narrative and shifting identity in Embodied Play Therapy is to create a more durable sense of self that a child can more reliably depend on. As Winnicott indicates, the dilemma of the symptomatic adult is reflective of their often earlier troubled youngster: "…I either crawl out of the muddle or else try to put things in order so that I may, at least for a time, know *where I am*" (1971/1996, p. 104). Locating one's viable self or selves in the greater universe that surrounds and sometimes seems to pound us is the ultimate endgame for the play we find ourselves in. A place where Embodied Play Therapy can serve.

The Process – What It Looks Like Today

As an adjunct "player" attached by an implicit therapeutic contract to a family, for the most part, I provide weekly 45- to 50-minute sessions for individual children, plus a monthly parents-only session. Preferring to meet with parents together, even when they are separated or divorced, it is sometimes useful to hold separate parent sessions either because two separate households are influencing behavioral patterns differently or because the parents have issues getting along and might tend to clam up in the presence of a former partner or spouse. When I see parents with their children in-person (see Chapter 4: Parents in the Mix), I do it with one parent present, although a couple and other family configurations may pop in during online sessions due to the informality of therapy occurring in a client's home.

Mediated Touch in Embodied Play Therapy

As much as possible, touch initiated by me is "mediated touch." Meaning that there's always something protective between a child and me to convey a clear message and a tangible reality of a safe space. This sense of safety gets supported when a child puts on padded boxing gloves, and I hold a padded shield for protection from the onslaught. Encounter bat battles are bat-to-bat and never body-to-body. Aggressive encounters between clay monsters or figures in the sand focus physically on the creatures and don't devolve into wrestling matches between me as a therapist and my young clients.

In my role as witness to the vulnerability and power of embodied play, I'm also aware of my bigness and the power differential this can convey. And that Embodied Play Therapy builds an intimate give and take between me and a child, reminiscent of a parent-child bond. With this in mind, I take special care to model and maintain appropriate boundaries, setting the stage for a child's return, safe and sound, to family and home.

Activities fall into four general categories: *Movement, Breathing, Feeling, and Play.* I have adapted these from the "Breathing,

Movement and Feeling" template developed by Alexander Lowen, M.D., originally presented at lectures he gave in 1965. In my adaptation, I have built in more on the possibilities of play (Lowen, 1991, p. 1).

Pillar I – MOVEMENT (Jumping, Bouncing, Rolling, Hitting, Punching, Crawling)

One of my first observations when seeing a young person walking into therapy is a visceral impression of how they move and hold their bodies. Do shoulders appear tight? Do I notice shallow breathing in a stiffened belly? Are jaws clenched? Are their knees hyper-extended so a push would topple them over? When they walk, does it look like they'd trip over the next object in their path? In essence, we would say this child conveys an impression that they have lost their ground. That they are, in the words of a body-centered clinician like me, "ungrounded." Here's what one of my Core Energetics colleagues says about grounding:

> A child, in biochemical and emotional relationship with its parents, finds his ground by growing into it, by learning to stand on the earth and move with his feet on the ground. Anyone watching a child walk can see whether it's secure or insecure. Just as the tree interacts with the earth, grounding itself through its roots, the child interacts with his parents, and sends down his own roots, called legs. The biochemical interaction is also a social and linguistic interaction. If the soil poor or the weather harsh, grounding, may be poor or too sinewy, too tough. (J. Nabb, personal communication, 1989)

> *Lynette, an 8-year-old soccer player, is nevertheless subject to falls when not on the playing field. She gets shamed by her older brother for falling all the time and being a "crybaby" when she does. Lynette's parents are really pushing her to be a star in sports like her brother, and she knows it. I think Lynette's feeling a lot of insecurity under all this pressure, which knocks her off any safe place to stand, speaking metaphorically. So we*

start to work on balance. For her tele-sessions, Lynette's parents buy her an exercise ball, and Lynette practices balancing on her belly without hitting the floor. At the beginning, she can only go for 4-5 seconds. But she gets better with time.

Next, I convince her parents to get a heavy punching bag at a garage sale that she can go at while standing and wearing boxing gloves. That's because she wants to slam her brother for criticizing her, and that wouldn't end well. In her Embodied Play Therapy, we've started at a place a part of her body remembers, balancing before she learned to stand, and then move to age-appropriate assertion through standing and punching to build experience of what it feels like to hold her ground. All this movement, once metabolized at a body level will need translation into how she can handle the pulls towards a particular identity that may be more her brother's than her own, and standing/maintaining her ground in the face of her brother's "crybaby" taunts. She's not going to be punching anybody outside of her sessions, and I make sure she knows that. Lynette's getting closer to the core of who she is in the moment, building a stronger sense of herself and firmer ground beneath her feet.

Embodied Play Therapy Sessions Most Often Begin with Movement

Children coming to sessions in the afternoon or evening after school usually want to release built-up inner tensions, jumping on a mini-trampoline or bouncing on a large inflated exercise ball over which they can also roll forward and back. Kids will often jump until exhausted, especially if they attend schools where they sit for long periods. Jumping on the mini-trampoline also connects a kid to their legs and feet, bringing energy down from the head, where mind loops of anxiety or depression linger. Energized movement of body and mind creates jolts that return a child's body to relaxation, allowing the mind to open, prodding a child and, through them, their family system toward productive change.

For kids who will move, even those who are at first reticent, I point them toward my mini trampoline, bringing it outside on the "play patio," where I put out all my Embodied Play Therapy equipment for sessions in Connecticut when the weather is good.

> *Ten-year-old Jimmy completes his three minutes of jumps on my mini trampoline and says, "My legs feel like jelly!" Hearing this, I know his muscles have relaxed.*

> *Seven-year-old Paulina, spying my exercise balls of varying colors, jumps on one, bouncing then rolling forward and back, a smile of pleasure across her face.*

With each of these children, oxygenated blood flow is now nourishing neural networks, and each is more readily available for therapeutic play activity with clay, paper and pen, or with miniature figures in a deep sandbox. For access to expansive places where the healing potential of narrative lives.

Before parents sign their kids up for therapy, many begin by asking them the question: "Would you like to talk to someone?" Because I always meet with parents alone first, I give them an in-person or live virtual video tour of my Embodied Play Therapy setup. I tell the parents, "This will be about play. For your child this will be fun." And if they ask what to call me, it's "Neal." I'm looking to remove any stigma or shame a child might feel about being brought to a therapist. The first-name basis with me also sets an expectation for a more level playing field so a child can begin what's ahead with a relaxed, open attitude.

Opportunities for movement vary from what I've presented above to crawling through a mesh play tunnel to just resting there for a spell. For many children, emphasizing movement in their Embodied Play Therapy is a major priority. Movement may be highly energized as a child grabs a lightweight hollow plastic bat or a padded "bataka" to whack a large foam cube placed on its side for kid convenience or, if it's an online session where parents don't have a cube, pillows stacked on a chair. When hitting in this way, I encourage a child to let loose with a loud "NO!" if they're thinking about something they don't like or want to release. If I sense that a child is just enjoying themselves as they hit, the word that gets repeated is a resounding "YES!"

FIGURE 2.1 Child hitting a foam cube with a hollow plastic bat.

Some children exercising their competitive streak may decide to take a few or more shots in a "hitting contest" like the one written about by therapist Dennis McCarthy in his book *Dynamic Play Therapy* (p. 149). My clients count out loud the number of times they hit. Currently in the lead is a 12-year-old with 1,350 hits. Or I may suggest that a child try another contest, balanced belly down on an exercise ball. For these competitive kids, I point out the "top secret" initials of past contestants, other children whose scores are recorded on a paper sheet taped to my therapy office wall. Or a child may don boxing gloves to punch an appropriate kid-sized heavy bag or a padded shield I'm holding as a target. If online, the child may be wearing similar protective boxing gloves and punching a pillow, which, if large and padded enough, may be held by a parent.

In my balancing contest, I count how many seconds a child can suspend their torso belly down on one of my exercise balls, before they surrender the arms-length distance back down to earth, roll off if it's an in-person session with me to my office carpet or, if online, to the carpeted surface of their bedroom or whatever space I've agreed on with parents will be safe for active Embodied Play Therapy movement.

> *Seven-year-old Hanna's parents said she didn't crawl much as a baby, housed in her Pack and Play crib within shouting distance of her parents' verbal battles that echoed against the walls of their tiny carriage house in a quiet suburban town. When brought to me years later, she was now often dysregulated at home, throwing herself onto the floor and her schoolbooks into the garbage. Hanna's parents were telling me of urgent phone calls from their daughter's otherwise flexible Montessori school demanding they leave work to calm their daughter. Too much to handle without support, for even the most caring parents.*

As Erik Erikson says, many kids Hanna's age would "rather be the baby at home than the big child in school" (1959/1994, p. 91). While parents and teachers might reward them for good performance, the "steady attention and persevering diligence" (p. 91) they need to complete required tasks are in short supply when a child's desire to stay young collides with their sense of inferiority about producing at the levels expected of them. My sense with Hanna was that she had skipped over the integration of earlier developmental steps. As a toddler, doubt as to her abilities may have crept in, and even earlier, mistrust of attachment figures may have developed as her parents fought. In preschool, she had begun receiving negative feedback for acting out instead of having her initiative noticed and rewarded.

Knowing that Hanna spent a great deal of time in her crib earlier as a baby and even as a toddler during the COVID-19 pandemic while her parents worked remotely in their home, during her first sessions, I encouraged her to roll and crawl on the carpet. Next, I dropped onto the floor and demonstrated how to lie on your back for support and kick against a soft foam cube with both your legs. This energizes the body as taut muscles release.

FIGURE 2.2 Kicking against a large foam cube.

As part of her Embodied Play Therapy movement, I had Hanna experiment with positioning her body onto her hands and knees. Pausing for a moment, for Hanna to feel the ground on all fours and take a few breaths there, I roll an inflated yoga exercise ball that's about half her standing height slowly towards her. Toes tucked under, she propels herself into a full-body head-first thrust forward. Because the ball is so light, it flies across the room, rolling to the nearest wall. Hanna experiences integration of her entire body as the forgiving boundary of the lightweight ball responds so easily to the child's swift motion and fully embodied power.

In his book *Emotional Anatomy*, theorist, clinician, and educator Stanley Keleman says:

> Muscles give the sense of containing and controlling ourselves as well as others. When muscles and their pump function are rigid with fear, dense in defiance, swollen in false pride, or collapsed from lack of support, our self-mastery is weakened, our self-esteem is diminished and our mastery of the world is affected. (1985, p. 39)

Exacerbated by stiffened musculature, disturbing emotions fester, including terror, helplessness, and rage. Linked with thoughts, images, and memories of abandonment or rejection, real or imagined, disturbing thought patterns, and reactive behavioral cycles can get entrenched in a child. For children who manifest dysregulated emotions and behavior linked to issues with neuro-motor development that influence performance at school, such as the ability to "sit still, focus attention, or hold a pencil correctly" (Blythe et al., 2021, p. 2), the kicking move pictured above is useful.

Such children often work with an occupational therapist to build competence on challenges in areas like fine motor skills, while I focus on emotional and relational areas in Embodied Play Therapy. Sometimes a developmental or other delay becomes frustrating for a child, especially a bright one like Hanna, who had trouble sitting still in class and needed the combined narrative-creating power of sandplay with active movement, such as depicted above, to break through.

After these experiences of kicking the cube with her legs and butting the ball forward and away from her in a move that assertively activated her whole torso, I sensed that Hanna (mentioned above) was building a better command of where her body began and ended. Would this lead to positive movement with the issues she faced? Her parents seemed pleased because she seemed calmer, and this led to a conversation and an agreement with her teacher. When Hanna needed additional support at school, rather than running out, she would raise her hand and given a nod from the teacher, would quietly walk down the hallway to her school counselor's office, where she could sit a while on an exercise ball I convinced her counselor to make available there.

Pillar II – BREATHING

"Fill your belly like a laughing Buddha!" I say, showing a child a miniature full-bellied joyful Buddha. To build awareness of their breath, I teach a child to drape themselves face down over a large exercise ball, molding the front of their body over it. They can then feel the give and take of the ball's soft surface against their abdomen as it expands and contracts with inhalation and exhalation, noticing how this calms the body and mind.

As therapists Nick Totton and Em Edmondson say,

> Watch a small baby breathe, and you'll see how the whole of her body is involved, committed, swept up in the smooth wavelike expansion and contraction that reaches from top to toes…As we grow up and confront this difficult world, however, a *voluntary* element soon creeps into our breathing, a hesitation, a holding back. (1998/2009, p. 13)

Building awareness of breath can improve conscious contact with inward changes of attitude. An angry or anxious child who's held their belly taut to control emotion re-discovers the natural skill of deep breathing. A balancing contest, a bout of punching or hitting, opens the breath, expanding a child's accustomed and increasingly limited capacity for inhaling and exhaling. With practice, a child learns to use their return to deeper breaths as a recovery tool in stressful situations at school or at home to regain emotional balance. Sensing the inner release as pumping lungs expand, the diaphragm drops, and the entire abdominal container with its rich neural network relaxes into a gentle rhythm and flow.

Among likely shallow breathers are children presenting with anxiety, depression, high sensitivity, obsessive/compulsive and rigid behavior patterns, and those who've experienced or witnessed traumatic events. For these children, I work to find opportunities for oxygenating and enlivening their bodies and minds through the deepening of breath.

I usually don't have to prompt a child to flop belly-down on top of a giant exercise ball because most can't resist the opportunity to glide forward on it, like a fish swimming freely. This is frequently followed by sitting and bouncing with abandon, as a child uses feet and legs to catapult their body up to almost an arms-length off the inflated ball. I witness, smiling in silence, a child's joy suspended in the air, free of gravity and the energetic rush of descending into the cushion of a compressed sphere, which will spring them up again and again in a cycle continuing as long as a child is willing. After some minutes of this, even highly energetic kids need to rest. That's when I invite them to check out their heightened breath from their bouncing or gliding maneuvers. I model how to place both hands on our belly and "push the air out" followed by taking deep staccato-like puffs of air through the nose. Just that noticing helps relax abdominal muscles.

Using the diaphragm to initiate a deeper cycle of breathing supports some beneficial things for a child's mind and body. Stimulating the parasympathetic nervous system helps us:

- Navigate the world with safety and flexibility
- Explore options
- See possibilities...

(Dana, 2020)

Returning balance to the sympathetic nervous system, which regulates blood flow and heart rate to balance, helps us:

- Energize to meet the demands of the day
- Mobilize in play
- Move with passion

(Dana, 2020)

For many children, deep breathing and the ability to recall that skill become critically important to building navigation skills in a world where life sometimes feels hard. But if children harden their stomachs against potential slings and arrows that may come at them from their environment, in school, or with family, they're operating in a de-energized, de-oxygenated state. Mobilizing yourself for productive engagement is difficult when the basic process of bringing fuel to your cells is disengaged. Recovering and re-integrating such a basic function as breathing helps children step out of states where they feel jittery and fragmented inside. A child learns to turn to their own body and breathing as a recovery and reintegration tool.

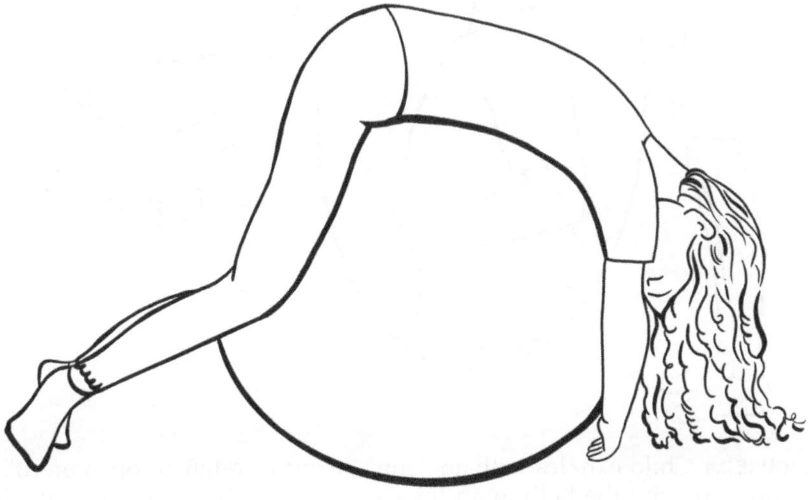

FIGURE 2.3 Child draped over a large exercise ball while deep breathing.

Ten-year-old Charlie looks a bit tense as he enters my office for one of his sessions. He hates the high-stakes tests that will be coming up at school soon, and he tends to freeze up when the papers are handed out in class. There won't be an exercise ball there that he can flop onto, so I teach him a method he can use for about ten seconds before he steps into the test room. He places his hands on his belly and pushes out the air, then relaxes his hands and lets his belly expand with his inhale. I let him watch me as I model this. First, to exhale, I gently press in my own belly with an open-mouthed "ahhhh" sound and then inhale through my nose as my belly rises, pushing out my hands.

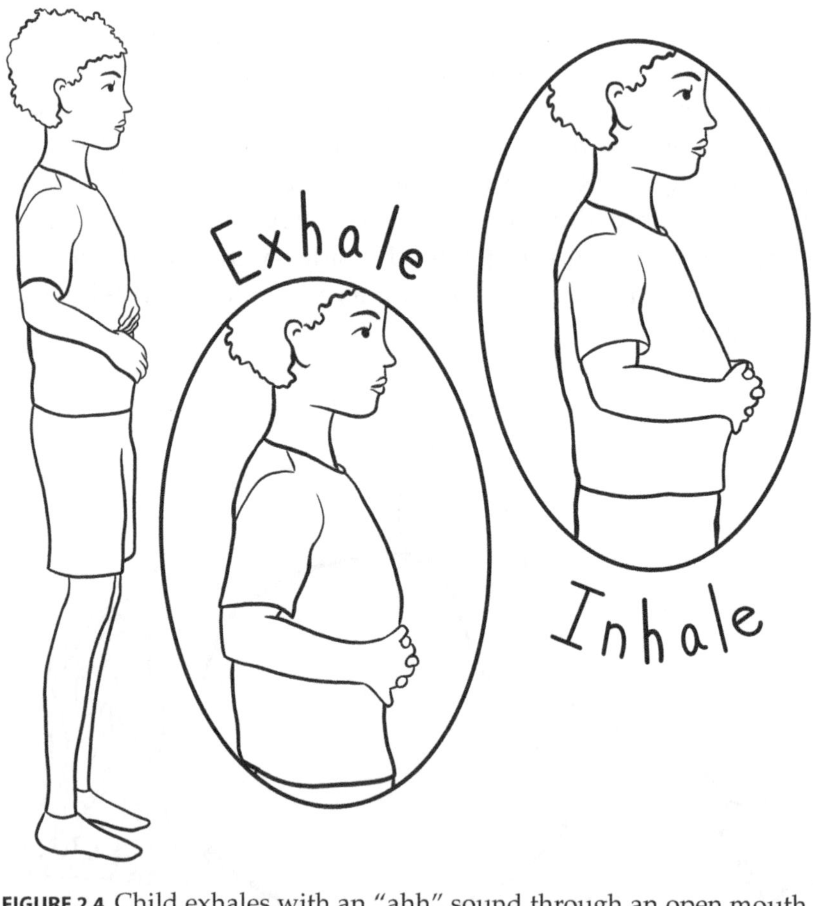

FIGURE 2.4 Child exhales with an "ahh" sound through an open mouth, gently pressing the belly with their hands. The child inhales through the nose as the belly rises, pushing out their hands.

> *Charlie's not used to this, having lost the habit of belly-breathing, which he did easily as a baby. At first, he wants to push his belly very hard. But when he pauses for a few moments, slowing the process down enough, he gets it. After the test day arrives the following week, Charlie tells me he didn't need to use his hands to get the deep breathing going. He just imagined them there. That was enough to calm him down and take his tests with a little more ease.*

Alexander Lowen points us to what's behind a focus on breathing in body-centered therapy,

> Chronic muscular tensions prevent full respiration and so decrease the energy level. The person may get enough oxygen for ordinary activities…However, his breathing difficulty will show up in situations of stress either as an inability to get sufficient air or more likely as an inability to cope with the stress. (1975, pp. 144–145)

As John Pierrakos, the founder of Core Energetics, says, through breathing practices, we help to create "integration" (J. Gotlieb & J. Pierrakos, personal communication, March 4, 1999). By bringing awareness of how the body breathes to a child, we are helping that child learn or re-learn basic processes that support fuller function, integrating these as a resource they can use now and in the future. As a child settles into deeper breathing, their behavior is also given the space to settle, often into more peaceful places where they can relax, let their developing brains think, and let their energy flow. For these reasons, throughout a child's time in Embodied Play Therapy, I will return them to awareness of their own breath and the simple practice of deeper inhalation and exhalation, which, when used in times of need, can help them live with a bit more ease amid the demands of their days.

Pillar III – FEELING

Children tune their brains, bodies, and emotions to inputs from family, school, social media, and gaming environments. Minecraft is a highly popular video game where you might die at the hands of a "mob" or from hunger. *Suraya, a 10-year-old master Minecraft world creator, hated it when one of her playing partners spawned a hundred zombies to attack her.*

Holding the paradox of a "friend" who also "attacks you" tends to tie a young person up in knots. How to unravel it? I ask kids what their body responses say. The flush of heat in the head and neck. Clenching of muscles. An impulse to run. A collapse in the chest and deflation of confidence.

I help kids increase their awareness of emotions by tracking where they feel them most strongly in their bodies. Do you feel a drumbeat of anger in your head? Is fear doing somersaults in your stomach? What happens when you exhale some of that, blowing it out of your mouth and into the wind?

I also teach youngsters to feel what it's like in your body when you stand up for yourself. For a kid who feels hemmed in emotionally in life, slowly giving way to their forward momentum as they push against a padded shield that I'm holding is a good lesson that progress is possible when you move from stasis to motion.

Symbolically pushing away people or their behavior you don't like with your arms while saying, "Get away!" or "Stop!" helps a child get in touch with the need for a healthy boundary.

> *Nine-year-old Bobby was getting spanked by his mother at home and being bullied at school. Rather than block the emotional impact of this, hearing himself speak the words above, accompanied by movement in session, helped Bobby feel the boundary he longed for to keep him safe. Subsequent parent-only discussions helped this family verbalize the inter-generational roots of their background, where spanking a child was normal. The spanking at home stopped, and the needed conversation to end the bullying happened.*

Reaching your outstretched hands to forcefully demand, grasp, and bring in what you want is another way to get in touch with feelings. *Ten-year-old Goldie was battling her father over more screen time. Getting her to symbolically pull that demand in with her hands while loudly saying "Give it to me!" had her smiling rather than staying stuck and pouting, as reported by her parent after her session.*

> *For more vulnerable emotions like longing, I invited 13-year-old Ben, stuck at home for months during the pandemic,*

to extend his arms out from his chest while imagining and reaching toward what his heart yearned for, helping him open to his pain over the physical separation from his girlfriend as his family isolated during lockdowns.

Having worked for some time with Ben during the lockdown period allowed him to trust me with these tender feelings.

Among my primary jobs as an Embodied Play Therapy practitioner is to help a child become consciously aware of repressed emotions that, if expressed, could be judged unfavorably because these feelings are seen as "negative" by friends or family.

Six-year-old Hedda's mom was six months pregnant with a baby who would need some of the love and care Hedda wanted for herself. She threw tantrums whenever one of her parents left for work. Hedda eagerly put on a pair of boxing gloves to bash the red punching bag dangling from my ceiling. The first figure she pulled from my shelves was a miniature baby carriage, which she buried in the bottom of my sandplay box, a beatific smile on her face.

Children rarely express tears of rage as an adult client might in therapy with me. More commonly, kids will "out-picture" their feelings through animated, aggressive interplay between sandplay figures; battles between a monster we each have drawn or molded in clay; padded encounter bat duels with me; or in a relational session with a parent present. When a parent holding a padded shield demonstrates willingness to absorb the full impact of their child's emotional energy as their kid charges at them with boxing-gloved fists, an encounter bat, or just a push, it can be freeing for both child and adult. Experimenting with higher amplitudes of embodied emotion in session can be satisfying for a child, and that satisfaction often leads to enhanced containment for kids who tend to act out. A child's prior explosive or risk-seeking behavior outside of therapy often begins to recede as a result.

Eleven-year-old Cal hated that his father was rarely home and kept taking risks to get dad's attention. A skateboarder, he liked flying off from heights. Parents fearing he'd hit his head against the NYC pavement got him into therapy with me. Alternately passive and explosive, Cal had also been reported to have hit one of the bigger kids at school, who then hit him back. Was his emotional oscillation and acting out symbolic of something deeper, perhaps underlying grief about his father's absence? That grief might be a challenging emotion for him to feel and contain.

According to Core Energetics teacher Lisa Loustaunau, quoted earlier in this chapter:

> TO CONTAIN…means to be able to tolerate and hold within us the discomfort of certain feelings without collapsing, acting-out in reaction, defending, or denying… With Proper Containment, a person can:
>
> - Enjoy a strong sense of oneself
> - Have healthy boundaries
> - Does not project or deflect strong feelings away from themselves
>
> (Loustaunau, personal communication of class handout, 2015)

I can work with kids like Hedda and Cal to express and contain an emotion by embodying it, to experience the freeing that happens, for example, when we do a "Get Off My Back" move. A standing child raises one arm at a time, bent at the elbow, raising it up to shoulder height and back down hard behind their shoulder blades in a repeating circular motion. One arm, then the next. When a child adds words or sounds to this action, like Cal did, saying "Get off my back!" or yelling "No!" or "Uhhhhh!" the emotional jolt received can help that child reorganize underlying and sometimes conflicting feelings into greater balance.

FIGURE 2.5 A standing child raises one arm bent at the elbow up to shoulder height and back down hard behind the shoulder blade in a repeated motion, one arm after the next.

As Loustaunau says:

> We support a client to find clarity in their emotions through use of interventions that employ *charge* – those that add energy, and *discharge* – those that support release. Proper use of these interventions re-pattern the lost wave action that dynamic emotions are meant to follow. (Loustaunau, personal communication of class handout, 2015)

From the perspective of Embodied Play Therapy, the opportunity to feel such a wave through the building up and release of "charge" (often pent-up, disowned, and unconscious emotion) happens as children participate in dynamic movement. The dynamism of such movement can be supplied spontaneously when a child hits a cube or charges toward me with an encounter bat, or it can be facilitated when I suggest a movement like "Get off my back" to get in touch with and release an emotional charge being held inside. Doing this work in childhood, where emotional capacity and containment are first built, helps to expand the emotional container, and the circulating energy-in-motion within, that will define and hopefully cohere much of their later lives.

> *In Cal's case, seeing it was fine to get strong feelings off his chest and off his back helped him to act out less and stop projecting his grief and hurt into situations where he and other kids could get hurt. His dad also needed to hear and act positively on what was troubling his son, to build more time for connection. That helped the waves inside Cal to crash less and put him into better shape for positive encounters with others.*

Emerging from the shrubbery-bordered pathway to my outdoor "play patio" where I give sessions during good weather, a child sees two giant, brightly painted wood letters mounted high on the table where I keep my encounter bats, clay, and rubber mallets for Embodied Play Therapy. Together they spell a word I encourage kids to yell out as they punch a heavy bag or flatten clay with a mallet. That word is "NO." The shortest complete sentence in the universe, as some like to say in the recovery movement.

Nine-year-old Gabriella, looked up at a second set of giant "NO" letters next to my indoor office. Once inside, she started a sand world, grabbing what she called a "chunky dinosaur trying to get to the top of a mountain." Helping her ascend was a dragon "breathing fire straight into the sky." Under the surface and unspoken, Gabriella was touching into her inner "No" about her parents' divorce and the frequency of shuttling back and forth between them that this entailed. While she couldn't control everything about her difficult situation, she could express some of the fiery feelings being held in her heart that were dangerous to express with parents she knew were in pain themselves. The drawing she made for me of the "NO" she felt inside was a big-bellied monster sticking its tongue out, with the word "NO!!!" emblazoned across its chest.

Gabriella's problems were based on the troubles of her parents and she acted her conflicts out at bedtime, where her refusal to sleep was couched in a whiny "I can't." But there's scant energy in "I can't." Frequently cloaked in the frozen failure of "I can't" is an attitude holding higher intensity and greater promise on the emotional tone scale. In Core Energetics, we call it the "I Won't!" Refusal to engage in life's challenges is something I want to nip in the bud before it calcifies into all of the ills inherent in repressed rage and frustration we see in adolescents and adults who become locked into patterns of behavior that are unproductive at best and destructive at worst. Better, in my view, to support a child during Embodied Play Therapy sessions to express their "NO" as part of a wider emotional vocabulary they can call on when that's what's crying out to be expressed.

How does this play out with different types of children? For many kids I've seen, I find the "NO" held back and repressed. Especially in households where rigid, authoritarian parental responses in present or past generations have been a key part of the equation. Of course, some kids exaggerate aggression, using combat with parents or peers as a warped way to build boundaries around their underlying, fragile sense of self. Sometimes this is the only way they know to connect or disconnect. Taught this way of relating by observing the dysfunctional behavior of adults around them, through exposure to mental, emotional, or physical violence, and exacerbated by the intolerance and hostility of our fractious times. One way or another, the cumulative effects do damage to the dreams and day-to-day functionality of many a child.

Yet there is hope. "Finding your NO" constitutes the beginning of a path to transport pained hearts toward peace. If suppressed and held back, that "NO" often results in anxiety that can build up to explosive proportions or depress the nascent potential of a child. When a child can play with an adult who relishes rather than refuses to hear "NO," a wider range of behavioral and parent-child relational possibilities often opens.

For nine-year-old Gabriella, presented earlier, a part of finding answers was negotiation with parents who wanted her to go to sleep at the same time she did when she was six. Understandable from an exhausted parent perspective, but Gabriella hated the early bedtime. After getting into better touch with her "No," this child had an idea. Reading one of her favorite books in bed with a flashlight until she nodded off. A solution both she and her parents could live with.

Finding your NO and playing with the feelings behind it is a key we can use to unlock a treasure house of creative potential and thoughtful progress for children and parents alike.

Pillar IV – PLAYING

Deborah Vilas, Director of Child Life Programs at Bank Street College of Education, says that "When children are playing, they act out scenarios and show us what they're feeling" (Child Life Council, 2015).

Eleven-year-old multi-ethnic Paolo speaks four languages and could run circles around any therapist who tried to reach him just through talk. Brought to online therapy because he lashes out, yelling in anger at his younger sister and rushing most weeks between an apartment in Manhattan and a second home in New Jersey. His parents scream at each other in front of the children, and are considering their own need for couples therapy.

Paolo draws an "Acid Dragon" during one of his first sessions. Acid bubbles out of the Dragon's mouth. "Burning hot acid," he tells me, "can defeat ANYONE...Dragon's legs are made of lightning...His body makes clouds so opponents can't see."

Paolo is confused, and he's acting out in response. Playing with aggressive imagery on paper and in a deep sandbox is a way kids like Paolo can make contact with deep, conflicted feelings. I wanted to mobilize his "protest" through his own creativity. A fitting frame for this was provided for this as Paolo drew his "acid dragon," displaying not only the depth of the fires burning inside him but also the potential for harnessing and rebalancing that power.

With this initial image guiding both of us, highly verbal Paolo began releasing his pent-up energy, bouncing and sliding on the exercise ball. Entering a deeper cycle of breathing helps a kid begin to better navigate his world. Learning of his competitive streak, I mention that other kids are contending in my contest to see how long they can balance, sitting on an exercise ball. I tell him it's also a good way to handle anger. He's all in. "Pent-Up Paolo," as his parents call him, still hasn't fallen off as my counting slowly aloud reaches ten. With practice, his balancing acumen will increase substantially, and I tell him he's made a great start.

There's a method to my madness with such balancing contests as one way to promote emotional containment. Everything is moving: the ball on the floor, the child's body on the ball, and the breath inside the child. In the play between movement and breath, the child's attention is also drawn to feelings, including the fear they'll fall off! Yet if they give in to the fear, or split awareness from the focus required to stay balanced in the present and on the ball, falling is likely. We're not cutting off feeling in a balancing exercise, or movement, or breath. On the contrary, we are building sensitivity to the multiple inputs and interactions that are part of being an embodied human in a world of moving objects and other beings. It makes sense then that enhanced balancing skills built on an exercise ball in Embodied Play Therapy often build a child's awareness and toleration of complex, amplified inner states that contribute to their history of acting out. A step toward building balance in the face of the unpredictable flux that is childhood.

Still, being a child often entails contending with forces bigger than oneself, including one's family, parental decisions, and the frustration a child may feel in facing what may restrict them from getting what they want. Sometimes a child feels like kicking! Alexander Lowen, the founder of Bioenergetics, says, "To kick means to protest" and that "most children… [are] denied the right to protest" (1975, p. 268).

Paolo certainly felt a need to protest his feelings of entrapment during the COVID-19 pandemic in houses where his parents bitterly fought. Instead of repressing this boy's need to assert himself, I suggest an Embodied Play Therapy activity to ground the amplified energies he's been acting out. I call it a "Standing Tantrum."

With my motto of "Safety First" I've spoken with Paolo's parents about how a tantrum as part of Paolo's play could be useful in getting that energy out in session rather than held in to the point of explosion with them. They like the idea and agree that below his feet, for throwing his tantrum, will be a thick carpet or a foldable thick gym mat. The parents later decided that the carpet in their living room, supplemented by two yoga mats, one on top of the other, would suffice.

As an online Paolo stands before me in video, I show him what a standing tantrum looks like. Flopping my limbs in a random and unrestrained rhythm at my sides, alternately raising and stamping my feet, and turning my head from side to side. As the tempo of my tantrum increases, I open my mouth and add some sound. For some children, it's a word like "No" but for most who don't initially feel comfortable with or have had the "No" word driven from their vocabulary it's just an "Uhhhh!" or "Ahhhhh" sound so that's what I do. I'm watching the rapt expression of Paolo's face on the large monitor I use to view my online clients. I ask whether he wants to try a tantrum. He asks "for how long?" I answer, "15 seconds?" At 30 seconds he's still going, arms and legs flailing away. And he's yelling. I think he likes the idea that his parents down the hall might hear him!

Paolo's parents have a trampoline in their backyard. When they tell me he almost landed on his younger sister's neck while bouncing together, I tell them to put joint jumping on pause and buy a mini-trampoline like the one I use for in-person sessions. He and his sister can use it one at a time. That way, until Paolo gets a handle on watching out for his sister's safety, no one gets pushed off or hurt.

Paolo's pushback against his parents, seen in his flouting of their wish that he treat his younger sister with care, probably had an additional source, namely his bottled-up energy during the COVID-19 pandemic, but my family system lens drew me toward getting his parents to notice their own contribution to a family problem. Their bickering was putting Paolo on edge. No wonder Paolo followed suit, disregarding his sister's safety on the big trampoline she was sharing with him. Finally, the willingness of the boy's parents to enter couples therapy and work on their conflicts had things settling down overall with Paolo and the whole family.

I also recommend that Paolo's parents provide a large hunk of earth-colored plasticine clay and a wood-handled rubber mallet for our video sessions. Better to smash clay than his sister. As our sessions progress, Paolo's clay pounding turns into sessions of quiet, peaceful sculpting. He carefully shapes the face of a young girl in clay. She has a third eye that can see through walls, he tells me, "Even when her eyes are closed." Paolo has manifested a "third eye" as a new way of seeing. An additional organ for perceiving intuitive wisdom in his clay girl. Perhaps that feminine, intuitive side of him needed more presence within his play with me so he could learn to care more in his play with his sister. With such expanded sight, the doors of empathy and connection with others open.

During our sessions, Paolo also begins to have me deploy dragon figures in the sand worlds he has me build for him remotely. One dragon guards a treasure chest filled with tiny, multicolored glass jewels. A zebra, with its black and white stripes, is buried in the sand and then unearthed as mom and dad begin weekly couple's sessions with a therapist I recommend. The parents tell me Paolo's making progress at home and has become less combative with them and with his sister as they work on their own "black and white" thinking and conflictual style of relating.

In another session, Paolo says, "Everyone wants to eat fish because they're small.... a big shark finds the fish.... a dragon attacks a stingray...a snake attacks a mother and baby..." Using his natural storytelling talents to create and descriptively narrate his sand worlds helps Paolo play with competing urges toward raw power and the possibility he might choose to pull back and modulate his energy when dealing with those less powerful.

Paolo's inner struggles continue to emerge in the dynamism of his sandplay narratives, reflecting his home life, where his emerging bigness crashes into a parental demand to tone down his power with his little sister. He was entering new emotional territory where recognition of mutable "dragon" energies inside him, sometimes fire-breathing, sometimes slow and placid, could coexist and moderate acting out of the fiery side against his sister.

In a follow-up parent session with Paolo not present, I recommend that Dad, a martial arts expert who fears that his strength would scare his children, try wrestling with his son. The two practice this in a raucous tele-session, which includes me sharing the blaring ending of Ravel's Bolero as an energizing soundtrack for what looks like a lot of fun for father and son.

I see Paolo's progress reflected in his final sandbox. There's some natural kid aggression in the bared teeth of a Tyrannosaurus rex that he's chosen, balanced by a gorilla standing guard at the plastic edge of a "pond" he's filled with water in one corner of the box, and spiders resting peacefully at the bottom of the pond.

I feel an emerging sense of softening, energies moving into balance. Near the end of an eight-month course of therapy, I see a maturing young man, less prone to lashing out. With a twinkle in his eye, Paolo tells me that for his Halloween costume, he's asked his parents to buy him a dinosaur suit.

As therapy wound down for Paolo, I taught him something that had been helpful to me as my life turned topsy-turvy in the early weeks of the pandemic. In yoga class, my teacher of many years, Brooke Stewart, had moved our in-person sessions online. Focusing on restoration, relaxation, and centering our fragmented energy and frazzled spirits, she had us doing the seated "hero pose," where you cross your legs and hold each of your feet with the opposite hand. The "keyed up" kid in me needed something more, and my hands floated up to my shoulders. I hugged myself. Brooke's online class began calling this pose, "The hugging hero." I taught this pose to Paolo. As for me, it calmed him down.

Since I started using "Hugging Hero" with dysregulated children, I've become curious as to whether this may help to soothe the polyvagal system, which regulates, as part of the autonomic nervous system, so much within the human body, from digestive health to neuroception. As explicated by neuroscience pioneers and therapeutic innovators like Stephen W. Porges and Deb Dana, neuroception is defined as "the subconscious detection of safety, or danger in the environment" (Porges, 2021, p. 90).

In his seminal book *Polyvagal Safety: Attachment, Communication, Self-Regulation*, Stephen W. Porges says:

> Play is a natural and powerful therapeutic tool. From the polyvagal perspective, play can be conceptualized as an efficient neural exercise that uses social engagement to actively inhibit fight-flight behaviors. A sensitive adult can attune herself to a way of communicating that recruits a child's social engagement system and downregulates defense. Therapists who work actively through playful modes consciously leverage this process. (2021, p. 201)

From my perspective, Embodied Play Therapy delves into areas bridging body, mind, emotion, will, and spirit as a child explores a therapeutic space with a variety of play materials and body-centered activities geared to express and release energy. Whether it's rigidity held in place by repressed feelings and muscular tension, scattered executive function, the inevitable rages of approaching adolescence, or the influence of parental dysfunction, we aid growth when broadening the play space to emphasize embodiment. Such play brings winds into the sails of a child's therapy and moves that child forward because it is so active on different levels, bringing breath, movement, feeling, and a child's spontaneous addition of narrative to playful interaction with a caring adult. Whether that adult is the therapist, the parent, or both joining the child in play, the crucial element is an atmosphere of ongoing acceptance. Supporting awareness in the child that all will be welcomed amid the inevitable twists and turns of their therapeutic journey. Making the goal to enhance balanced expression of life force for a child is both possible and probable.

Child and family trauma specialist Lorri Yasenik and clinical child psychologist Ken Gardner (2021) say:

> The thing that differentiates play and expressive therapists from those primarily using talk therapies is that play and expressive therapists use their whole body

> when engaging in therapy. Additionally, entering into fantasy play or a drama requires the therapist to be both in character *and* maintain an overview and direction of the overall process. This extension of use of self is complex and requires multiple uses of self in order to remain helpful and not get lost in the process or interactions. (p. 342)

Entering into play with a child can be exciting and exhausting for a therapist who needs to stay on their toes to keep up with a fast-moving child. You'll see more of how challenging this is in the following chapters. During one in-person session, you'll find me jumping from my sandplay room to my office where the child has declared themselves king and I must tread on a path of pillows he's laid down on the floor. In tele-sessions, you'll find me juggling wooden blocks, building a tower to the exacting specifications of my remote client. Then, we move outdoors where I am the cameraman capturing a close-up of a tree. Next, we move back indoors where a guessing game begins. I make a sound, unseen and offscreen, and the child guesses the source. Keeping embodied play flowing demands an ability to shift roles and rules, remaining flexible as a therapist and active play partner.

The four pillars of Embodied Play Therapy conceptually anchor for me as a provider, the often high-speed antics of a child let loose in a play space with a range of possible activities. The movement, breathing, and feelings generated as part of the back-and-forth of co-playing often create a highly charged space as a freely child-centric session dips into new depths and crannies like a roller-coaster headed back to its resting berth. In the descending quiet and peace after a child closes the door or logs off our video session, I am most usually drawn to taking my own deep breath or two, feeling the powerful impact and reflecting on what's just transpired with a child going all out in Embodied Play Therapy. It's usually been strenuous and, more than often, sublime. Definitely worth the energy expended in the service of building a bridge to a child whose life has just taken a step forward toward a little more happiness.

References

Blythe, S. G., Duncombe, R., Preedy, P., & Gorely, T. (2021). Neuromotor Readiness for School: The Primitive Reflex Status of Young Children at the Start and End of Their First Year at School in the United Kingdom. *Education 3-13. International Journal of Primary, Elementary and Early Years Education.* doi: 10.1080/03004279.2021.1895276

Brodsky, N. (2015). Emergence: A Tale of Two Boys. In D. McCarthy (Ed.), *Deep Play: Exploring the Use of Depth in Psychotherapy with Children* (pp. 143–164). Jessica Kingsley Publishers.

Brodsky, N. (2021). The Color of Play: Breaking through Walls within a Child's World. In S. Jennings & C. Holmwood (Eds.), *The Routledge International Handbook of Play, Therapeutic Play and Play Therapy* (pp. 263–270). Routledge.

Child Life Council. (2015). *That's Child Life*. YouTube. https://www.youtube.com/watch?v=daysNIDgSAw

Dana, D. (2020). *Polyvagal Flip Chart: Understanding the Science and Safety*. W.W. Norton.

Erikson, E. H. (1978). *Toys and Reasons: Stages in the Ritualization of Experience*. Marion Boyers Publishers.

Erikson, E. H. (1993). *Childhood and Society*. W. W. Norton. (Original work published 1950)

Erikson, E. H. (1994). *Identity and the Life Cycle*. W.W. Norton. (Original work published 1959)

Holmwood, C. (2021). Neuro-Dynamic-Play and a Hero's Journey: A Play-based Approach in a UK Junior School. In S. Jennings & C. Holmwood (Eds.), *Routledge International Handbook of Play, Therapeutic Play and Play Therapy* (pp. 167–178). Routledge.

Jackson, R. L., & Hogg, M. A. (Eds.). (2010). Identity Diffusion. In *Encyclopedia of Identity* (Vol. 1, pp. 363–365). SAGE Publications, Inc. https://doi.org/10.4135/9781412979306.n117

Keleman, S. (1985). *Emotional Anatomy*. Center Press.

Lowen, A. (1975). *Bioenergetics*. Cowar, McCann & Geoghegan.

Lowen, A. (1991). *Breathing, Movement, and Feeling: The Basis of Bioenergetic Analysis*. The International Institute for Bioenergetic Analysis.

Lowen, A., & Lowen, L. (1977). *The Way to Vibrant Health: A Manual of Bioenergetic Exercises*. The International Institute for Bioenergetic Analysis.

McCarthy, D. (2007). *If You Turned into a Monster: Transformation through Play: A Body-Centered Approach to Play Therapy*. Jessica Kingsley Publishers.

McCarthy, D. (2012). *A Manual of Dynamic Play Therapy: Helping Things Fall Apart, the Paradox of Play*. Jessica Kingsley Publishers.

McGovern, A. (1986). *Stone Soup*. Scholastic.

Nash, O. (1987). The Mules. In *Ogden Nash's Zoo*. Henry N. Abrams. https://www.goodreads.com/author/quotes/41339.Ogden_Nash?page=3

Ogden, P., Goldstein, B., & Fisher, J.. (2013). Brain-to-Brain, Body-to-Body: A Sensorimotor Psychotherapy Perspective on the Treatment of Children and Adolescents. In R.E. Longo, D.S. Prescott, J. Bergman, & K. Creeden, (Eds.), *Current Perspective & Applications in Neurobiology: Working with Young Persons Who Are Victims and Perpetrators of Sexual Abuse*. Neari Press.

Porges, S. W. (2021). *Polyvagal Safety: Attachment, Communication, Self-Regulation*. W. W. Norton.

Reich, W. M. (1983). *Children of the Future: On the Prevention of Sexual Pathology*. Farrar, Strauss, Giroux. (Original work published 1950)

Totton, N., & Edmondson, E.. (2009). *Reichian Growth Work: Melting the Blocks to Life and Love* (2nd ed.). PCCS Books. (Original work published 1988)

Winnicott, D. W. (1996). *Playing and Reality*. Routledge. (Original work published 1971)

Yasenik, L., & Gardner, K.. (2021). Therapeutic Use of Self and the Play Therapy Dimensions Model. In S. Jennings & C. Holmwood (Eds.), *Routledge International Handbook of Play, Therapeutic Play and Plan Therapy* (pp. 341–359). Routledge.

3

Building a Bridge to a Child

Before I became a child therapist, I was a parent myself. An adoptive parent in my first marriage, then a divorced and single parent, and finally a stepparent. Someone who didn't want to mess up like me needed to spend extra thought and care on how to build and come back into connection when the inevitable breaks have us all fearing everything is lost. Sensitivity to the sheer energetic power of relationships became a cornerstone of any success I had in supportive endeavors with clients – adults, couples, adolescents, and children.

Brian and Marcia Gleason, the creators of Embodied Relational Work, rooted in Core Energetics, speak of a "shared energy field" as a "flow of emotional and sensate energy that is perpetually occurring and shifting within and around us" (2012, p. 30). In the presence of a child, that "shared energy field" often vibrates at a fast clip. My job as a child and family therapist is to keep up in a fast-moving field that includes the added complexity of families in motion and growth. Whether parents think this or not, I know from life and professional experience that life can change for the better, especially when we allow our hearts to open and resonate with our children. Such resonance, in its pendulations between contact and distance as a relational field that includes multiple systems – couple, parent, sibling – comprises what I call a "family energy field." One I'm privileged to enter and one which I need to

DOI: 10.4324/9781003328186-5

navigate in and out of as I work with a child in Embodied Play Therapy.

The imperative to "join" with those I am in a therapeutic relationship with, to develop some security of attachment and some common language, becomes the first order of business. As with adults in my life and therapy practice, so with children. I view the bond between humans from multiple lenses, where interactions of body, mind, and spirit converge. The format of Embodied Play Therapy sessions adapts to the needs of a child and their family. Factors including level and speed of activity, boundaries and rules, or need for repetition within and between sessions constitute, for the therapist and child, a balancing act. What we create together are enactments drawn from impulse – those of the child, my own, and those of the parents, whose influence is always present even if a parent is not.

I am also often looking to build a healthy in-session attachment that can be transferred to parents whose child's behavior has them thinking something is amiss in their parent-child connection. As one parent asked me: "Why does my child seem to love me one minute and hate me the next?" As a therapist, I need to build my own containment capability for not always being the perfect adult. Answering multiple demands, even if unspoken, to provide safety, pleasurable and novel experiences, inspiring play partnership, and ongoing validation that a child is both special and worth every ounce of adult attention. Not to mention the daunting task of dropping all adult concerns to get in touch with what it was like for me to be a child in a smaller body who wanted to do nothing but play non-stop. It's a tall order for me to meet as a participant in a few Embodied Play Therapy sessions each day, let alone for a parent who's called on to connect in their every waking hour. Here are some examples of how one of the most creative children I've ever known began to progress in his sessions, building attachment, experimenting with independence, playing with and muscling through to solutions for his challenges that only his fertile imagination could design.

Six-year-old Ricky

Session #1: In-person

Three months from his seventh birthday, an unstoppable ball of energy blazes at high speed into my office. His primary issue: struggling with self-control, hitting other kids at school, his parents, and his two-year-old brother. After one of these incidents, he said to his parents, "I want to punch myself because I'm bad."

Ricky's parents tell me he's seen more than his share of struggle. Born pre-mature, his mother in the hospital recovering for weeks after his birth, his early contact with the world mediated by a helmet designed to re-position his skull was just the beginning of frustration with his own creatively brilliant brain and the compromises required to flexibly fit it into school routines and the cooperation needed by his parents.

Ricky's parents said their son would "never take no for an answer." Aggressive with his younger brother, he would yell if any of his toys were touched, frustrated that he had to contend with playing second fiddle to a brother who required parental attention, too.

Stomping through the main section of my office, whose giant windows face out to 88th Street near Central Park in Manhattan, he traipses into a windowless vestibule between the main room and an adjoining closet-size space which houses a foam cube as high as the top of his head and storage shelves containing blue-padded "batakas" he can use to hit that cube.

Reflection: A client like Ricky will loft a bataka high overhead and smash it down hard on the cube again and again. This helps to ground emotions like anger which the developing child may otherwise use to target others (Kegan, 1982, p. 82). As a child exhausts themselves by "taking it out" on the cube, their energy re-centers, offering access to vulnerable places that may hurt inside.

Casting a doubtful eye on my "hitting room," Ricky exits to the adjoining space, crouching arms down like a sumo wrestler preparing for battle before my shelves of carefully sorted sand play figures. Using one hand, he sweeps half a shelf into a pile on my pink carpet and flings the figures hodgepodge into my sandbox. "Neal," he yells, "Get out!" Raising my eyes with exaggerated alarm (which I hope he'll see), I tiptoe away, closing the two-winged folding door to my sandplay room, leaving him alone. For a minute, the only sound I can hear is beeping car horns outside in the street. And then, a muffled "Neal!" from behind the door. "You can come in!" When I fold the door back open, Ricky is sitting, centered like a king on his throne in my sandbox.

"Where are all my sandplay figures?" I demand in exaggerated alarm. "Buried!" he says, in triumph. "Now you guess what's in the box!" Flashing him a conspiratorial smile, I begin. "Snake! Dinosaur! Elephant!" I'm getting it wrong each time, screwing up my face in shock and surprise as he unearths his hidden figures one by one. This child is getting the biggest charge from my hammed-up struggle with his guessing game and my total failure to identify what he's buried.

Reflection: I'm noticing Ricky's strength as a leader, along with a powerful photographic memory for what he's buried beneath his own body in the sand. My intuition tells me this child will be guiding me every step of the way on his path to healing.

Session #2: Ricky

Ricky tells me a story as he stands with his bare feet in the sand. There's a war between him in the sandbox and me outside the sandbox because I "hold the treasure." He plunks his bottom down in the box and drops a black three-headed dog and ferocious brown wolf, his allies for battle, close to his body. He points to who'll be assisting me: a red, blue, and creamy white snow leopard tiger hand puppet, plus a pink and white plush unicorn owl. "Oh no! You're not going to defeat me!" I tell Ricky in a high-pitched voice, bobbing and weaving towards and away from him as he lounges, protected by the wooden walls of the box that rise to half his standing height.

I'm feeling a bit anxious for him to have an early win, so I hand him two finger-length wooden treasure boxes containing plastic replicas of jewels and gold coins. Too easy for him. Ricky yells back an order, restoring him as the one in charge – "Cook the unicorn owl!" Pausing a beat, he softly confides that "unicorn owl tastes like ice cream when you cook him."

I grab an empty blue plastic pail and plunk the owl into it, making a swirling motion with my hand like the bird is getting stirred in a pot. Ricky says my snow leopard feels sad that his friend has been cooked. He hops out of the box, looking down sheepishly at his sandy bare feet and the white grainy aura on his new therapist's hand-tufted New Zealand wool area rug. I snatch and toss a dry washcloth to him from a stack of yellow, blue, red, and purple ones on my shelf. Catching it in both hands, he brushes sand off his feet, then vaults out, trotting into the adjoining room to discover what's next. Grabbing my "tug of war" rope and casually tossing one end to me, he pulls me across the room, laughing so hard, his small body shakes.

Reflection: I am following this child's directive flow in our play narrative, allowing my impulses to inject intensity in our connection, surrendering to the trajectory Ricky is exploring for his session today. And while I'm very pleased with the initial high level of trust Ricky's elevated-energy interaction with me shows, I'm also aware of the exhaustion inherent in Ricky's processing style and imagine this presents challenges for his parents, who must balance their care responsibilities for Ricky and his younger brother with their work lives, creative endeavors, and relationship as a couple. In my weekly 45 minutes with Ricky, I can afford to go all out, letting him "rule the roost." While essentially, I'm letting him win, I'm also testing to see whether he can trust me enough to fight me, permitting the power of Ricky's energy cycle to play out as fully as possible.

In session, Ricky reins himself in to rest and reflect. He empathizes with my "cooked" unicorn owl ally and connects with sadness, projecting regret onto my snow leopard helper, witnessing the fate of his friend. I am in awe of this child's ability to drop into a wide range of emotions through his embodied play.

Session #3: Ricky

Ricky jumps into the sandbox, this time for a battle featuring his new champion, a silver-gray plastic figure of a knight. He assigns me assistants, once again unicorn owl and the snow leopard tiger. After a few minutes, Ricky's battle moves outside to the larger adjoining room in my office, which has two faded oriental carpets, so large they nearly cover what I consider, by NYC standards, a pretty massive room. Ricky takes one carpet as his base, and he says I'll have the other as mine. Grabbing two red padded encounter bats, he flings one to me. At the edge of our territories where the carpets meet, Ricky fights hard, knocking the bat out of my hand. From his base carpet, he transforms into a character who can touch the carpet with his bat and create electrical storms. I tell him, "When I touch my carpet, I can create ice and snow!"

Ricky grabs and throws pillows at me (his electricity storms), and I throw pillows back as ice and snow. My assistants, unicorn owl and snow leopard tiger, get buried in a pile of pillows that come from his electricity storm. Deciding he's won the battle, Ricky tells me he's now "The King" and plops into my black leather recliner chair, his throne. The King also has my nearby couch where he can rest. He instructs me to create a pathway of pillows stretching from his throne to my couch. If a visitor like me wants to visit the king, they must first be scanned for safety by a red ball that Ricky perches on top of my Core Energetics roller. You only need to be scanned once, and then you are safe to come over. My snow leopard, tiger, and unicorn owl approach via the path of pillows towards the throne. I give Ricky two "award certificates" (clean, colorful hand towels). One award for his kindness and another for his fierceness.

Reflection: Dropping into forgiveness, he constructs a soft path of pillows so his therapist and revived allies can approach him. I sense the healing held in Ricky's narrative as he ties and then loosens knots of aggressive impulse and dominance, returning to flowing communication that builds our connection.

Session #4: Ricky

I'm interested in having Ricky deliberately build conscious awareness of his energy and how he can settle it. Standing, I show Ricky how to put some of his weight, one foot at a time onto a fuzzy yellow tennis ball resting on the carpet. Standing also in my socks, I let him mirror my actions, rolling one foot and then the other over my own tennis ball, experimenting with different positions as each of us wraps toes over our balls, pressing an arch or a heel firmly on it, noticing body sensations as we increase or decrease the amount of downward force we're using. After about a minute, I tap my tennis ball away toward the closest wall. My young client knocks his ball in the same direction, and he's off.

Moving to my shelves, Ricky pulls a plastic snake and a crab and buries them in the sand so unicorn owl and snow leopard tiger can't find them. This accomplished, he moves to the big room where my unicorn owl and snow leopard get defeated by a long-armed power figure he's brought from home. Seeing my vanquished team, Ricky hands me an additional ally – an orange Bengal tiger.

Reflection: I'm impressed by this child's ability to stop and to notice the impact his actions elicit and touched by Ricky's generosity in bending what could be strict rules of conflict, victory, and defeat for someone new in his life, like me, whom he may not initially trust. Yet children need a right to their own boundaries, just like grown-ups have. A place where they can say "It's my toy" and NOT share. An arena supporting the development of self-agency, where sharing from caring rather than a need for approval becomes possible.

> *I let my tiger drop from my hand, and as we watch it motionless on the floor, I tell Ricky my tiger just fainted. Ricky asks what it means to faint. When I explain how you lose consciousness, he wants to see the tiger faint again and again.*

Reflection: I've seen children with big energy cycle profiles like Ricky move into silence where they gather themselves for the next upwelling of activity. So I'm not surprised at this boy's fascination with my tiger fainting. In losing consciousness there is the possibility to regroup and for the attack to stop. What Ricky doesn't know is that I'm thinking of another client, a few years older than him, who, when faced with a strict teacher and an upcoming test, fainted, turning all adults from their focus on discipline toward concern for him.

> *Ricky turns the couch in my office into a mountain from which boulders (pillows) come to crunch my unicorn owl and tiger. Putting on boxing gloves, Ricky grabs my multi-colored rope, like in his first session, for a tug of war with me. I pull harder this time, and after trying and failing to move me much, he falls to the floor and takes a break.*

Reflection: I wonder how exhausting Ricky's desire to win so much may be for him. Are his struggles in play with me emblematic of Ricky's issue at home with his younger brother, who usurped his former position as first and only child? I know this place. In my own family of origin, I was the first son suddenly called on to share his toys, time, and the love of his parents with my younger brother. Why should Ricky have to box up feelings that may include anger and confusion? Must he perform as a "good older brother" all the time?

I want to support Ricky's ability to express a range of emotions that are better felt than repressed and acted on unconsciously, spurring possible regret and parental recrimination. It is better to entertain one's naughtiness in Embodied Play Therapy sessions than play them out at home when everyone's nerves are frayed, and no one's enjoying what's being tested.

I feel the impact of Ricky's difficult-to-resolve situation, and I'm not surprised by the pattern from home that's being explored symbolically with me in therapy: An explosion of energy in service of his demand to win, followed by a collapse of that energy. At home, Ricky would blame himself after hitting his dad or mom, saying, "I'm bad!" I feel compassion for this boy and his longing to reclaim his treasured position as the much-loved baby in the family – something he intuits is an unwinnable task. Ricky needs to stand on his own two feet. The grounded feet of a boy growing into his true age, not that of a baby and not an inflated bigness of a "boy-king" which is unsustainable if it's the only role he'll allow.

Building a bridge to a child in Embodied Play Therapy allows children to get charged up and learn to release or discharge energy that's been activated. Feeling what it's like to cycle back to a sense of one's center. At home, pushing a parent or sibling's buttons may temporarily fulfill a need to release pent-up energy, but such cycles are not without cost. In sessions, pressing the "play" button to a fuller volume can allow a child whose energy is spent to return gently back to earth.

While Ricky may need to rest a bit from his battling between his minions and mine, we have less than 20 minutes left of his 45-minute session. To ground Ricky and bring his body into fuller expression of the frustration he feels, I ask him to push with all the leg strength he can muster, lying on his back with his feet against the front of the couch. Ricky gives a few cursory pushes against the immovable couch, but I sense that he needs to continue to let loose. Lying on the floor, pondering what he wants to do next, Ricky asks me to set up an obstacle course for him. I create one, using a pop-up tunnel made of gauzy multi-colored fabric held taut in a wire cylinder frame. I lay the tunnel horizontally on the floor, with a Core Energetics roller at each end. I scatter pillows around this to embellish our installation with more obstacles for Ricky to zip around and blow past.

Ricky: Close one side of the tunnel so I can be like a rocket ship! *(I hold one end of the tunnel closed with both my hands.)*

Over the next few moments, I let him feel what it's like to be sandwiched in what I call, when I teach Embodied Play Therapy to other therapists, a "second skin." Offering the safety of a see-through tunnel from which he then escapes, he scampers out more like a little boy than the giant projectile he may have envisioned. Capping things off, Ricky destroys his obstacle course, throwing every pillow we've used from the carpet onto the couch. As one final act to ensure those previously vanquished remain that way, he stuffs my unicorn owl and snow leopard tiger firmly into the center hole of the Core Energetics roller.

Reflection: So far, I've been able to afford Ricky the opportunity for a sense of completion and victories over me in these initial Embodied Play Therapy sessions. While most of the time there are repetitions of action and narrative – hiding and being found, losing and winning – we are exploring, moving in and out of connection at this earliest stage of therapy, where a child's trust in my acceptance of them is a crucial factor in the depth of play they will bring to future sessions. Each session represents a chapter of a child's endeavor to dig into ever deeper realms of the body and the multiple selves contained within. Completion of an early a chapter, while satisfying for the child and for me, also builds the child's confidence that their therapist/play partner holds threads of continuity that can be picked up in the next session or later down the line.

Therapist: Remember when you busted out of the tunnel like a rocket?
Ricky: Yeah, that was great. I fit in there, but you're too big to do it!

Reflection: As weekly sessions progressed, Ricky tired of guessing games. And he began to risk building narrative into his sand play…

(More on Ricky's play in Chapter 4: Parents in the Mix, Chapter 7: Deepening Narrative, and Chapter 8: Completions.)

Eleven-year-old Petra

According to her parents, this grandchild of Middle Eastern immigrants was obsessed with two things: germs and money. They also said she hated to sleep alone, which meant she slept in their bed, plus she was driving them crazy with the amount of hand sanitizer she used. And Petra insisted that any family member going outside of the house, parents and her little brother Norton, four years her junior, squirt a liberal dose of sanitizer on their hands when they returned, which she monitored closely. Because both parents mainly worked during the day, Petra arrived for her first session in an Uber. What had me questioning the accuracy of the parents' diagnosis of obsessive-compulsive disorder (OCD) was the interesting fact that Petra, when questioned, told me she didn't need to use sanitizer after handling the doors of the Uber. So, what was all this sanitizing activity about?

Petra – *Session #1*

It's a wintry day in Connecticut, and Petra exits her Uber wearing heavy rubber boots, which she flings off into the plastic shoe tray near my office door. She tells me she's worried that she'll forget them when she leaves.

Petra seems excited by everything I have to offer. When I tell her about the "hitting contest" I have going with other kid clients, she picks up a hollow plastic bat and hits my foam cube 25 times. Not bad for a first time, but she's seen the hundreds of hits recorded next to the initials of other kids on my record sheet taped to the wall and doesn't look like she wants to compete.

Petra walks over to the sandbox, into which she pours a copious amount of water from the filled plastic pail I keep next to the box, molding a ridge of sand with her hands. She tells me a story about the figure of a queen after she places it behind the ridge.

This queen, the ruler, is very self-centered!

She asks everyone to be her slaves.

Everybody teams up to fight her.

Neal: *(Pointing to the completely empty box except for the queen and the ridge between her and the emptiness)* Where are the slaves?

Petra: Next time I'll put all the slaves in.

Petra: *(Looking at her box)* Is self-centered the same as self-absorbed?

Neal: *(Takes a photo of Petra's box with his phone)*

Petra: Try to make the picture you take big! *(She hears footsteps in the room above my office)* Will other people come in the room?

Neal: No, it'll just be us. My wife's upstairs.

So at your home, Petra, it's mom, dad, and Norton, right? *(Petra's younger brother with whom she shares a room, even though she doesn't ever sleep in it.)*

Petra: Norton wants my things. He takes forever to choose them.

Petra: *(Looking up again at the staircase)* How many rooms are there here…and what did you pay for this house?

Reflection: An auspicious beginning for a girl struggling with boundaries around space, determining value, and who's in charge. At home, Petra is trying to be the boss, but some part of her is uncomfortable about how enslaved her family is to her demand that they constantly cleanse their hands with sanitizer.

Session #2: Petra

> *Petra tells me about the dream she had when she was five about a tiger that looked at you with purple eyes and walked like a soldier, stiff-legged, marching in goose-step. She says she likes to be clean, especially at night. We talk about what she can do if she has any fear or anxiety. I show her how to breathe deeply, practicing by having her drape her body over a large purple exercise ball so she can feel the rise and fall of her abdomen. I tell her that if she wakes up frightened in the middle of the night, she can calm herself by placing her hand on her belly, slowing and deepening her breath by allowing that same rise and fall. Standing, I model this for her, and she practices for a few breaths.*
>
> *I show her how to be the thing she is scared of, and we walk around the room together like tigers. Growling at the sandplay animals on my shelves.*

Reflection: I am working to relax this child's rigidity, which lives in the body. First I slow things down to focus on the breath, moving from the memory of Petra's dream where soldiers march in lockstep (mirroring a rigid demand that family members conform to her hand sanitizer regimen) to noticing the rise and fall of one's abdomen that happens with deepened breathing (inhalation and exhalation shifting the body into a slower rhythm, a place where receptivity and connection become possible). Finally, I invite Petra to embody what she feared as a younger child, the tiger with purple eyes, so that she can embody and enjoy her ferocity directly with the approval and participation of her adult therapist. I'm not only a guiding presence with whom Petra can step into big, possibly scary energy but also a co-conspirator with her in manifesting what had been feared, bringing the feared from dream space into playful consciousness. Through embodied play, we pierce the bubble of what could otherwise be just a talk about a dream, tapping into mobilizing energy, entering it together in a co-created shared space that is both safe and a lot of fun.

Session #3: Petra

At home, an email from Petra's mom informs me that Petra is still insisting on sleeping with her mother in the parents' bed while Dad moves into the next room. Arriving at therapy, Petra wants to draw a "private yacht." We make a "monster drawing game" out of it, where I draw a yacht too, she knocks my drawing hand away from the page with her hand (as I've told her she can do), surprising me at three different times. I'll need to incorporate the squiggles that result into my yacht, making it more monstrous! She loves that she can have that power to shift what I'm drawing. When we finish, I notice my ship, while more than a bit warped, is complete, but her yacht is a half boat without a stern.

Reflection: Petra continues to experiment with bigger energy, but it's still half-baked like her boat, with no self-guiding rudder in the rear. An illuminating image for a girl trying to plow forward, dragging her whole family behind her. The entire enterprise could sink, I think, with a few storm-tossing waves.

Session #4: Petra

Smiling and seemingly thrilled to be back, Petra bounces on the exercise ball with impressive energy. She picks up a ball of clay from a flattened sheet of cardboard on the floor and throws it down hard against the cardboard, telling me that next week she wants to throw clay against the wall. I tell her I will bring in a sheet of plastic so she can do that. At home, Petra and her younger brother Norton have been fighting about whether Norton will be allowed to come to Petra's upcoming birthday party with Petra's same-age friends. She draws their conflict where Norton calls her a "tushy face." After throwing clay and drawing, she tells me that while she doesn't want her brother to come, if it's that important to him, then he can come.

Reflection: Petra is taking more risks and getting bolder in her willingness to allow for outrageousness as she becomes more comfortable in her relationship with me. The walls of my office become a sounding board within which her bigger energies can reverberate.

Session #5: Petra

Mom has driven her daughter to her session, and they are 20 minutes early. Petra is eating an ice cream cone in the back seat of the car, and Mom looks nervous. I ask Mom to speak with me inside while Petra finishes her cone in the car. Mom reports that "nothing is better" and that Petra is still sleeping in Mom's bed every night. Mom exits, and Petra comes into the therapy room. As she bounces on the green exercise ball, I remind her of her interest in throwing clay against the wall and that I brought some things so she can do that - white plastic garbage bags and silver "gaffer tape." We can tape the bags together and create a place to throw the clay so that it won't make marks. I select my wooden office door for maximum reverberation potential! Petra wants to draw a target for her throwing, which she does on a piece of paper. We tape the target to the plastic and connect the garbage bags. This action of taping the plastic is done very carefully and in silence. I notice again that Petra is not afraid to touch anything. No "germ phobia" that her parents have spoken of when she is with them.

Petra shapes a hunk of clay into a throwing ball. She winds up and slams the clay hard, making a very loud sound against the wooden door. She says, "Can I stand on something to be higher to throw this clay?" I look around the room for something, and realizing that the sand tray is on wheels, I move it into position for her. When I turn around, I'm amazed to see that she has climbed into the sandbox, standing in it in her goofy socks imprinted with a design...green mummy feet. Earlier in the session, we discussed how great her socks are. I told her that when I was her age, I was afraid of mummies, but she's not.

Reflection: I'm surprised that this kid, who is reported as suffering from OCD by her parents, is willing to wear socks displaying the gangrenous green flesh, however cartoonish, of a mummified body. There is a disconnect between what they are reporting and what I am seeing in session.

As Petra stands up in the sandbox and throws the clay. I encourage her to make some sound. She asks, "Why make a sound?" I explain that it's the same thing as the belly breathing – moving energy through her body, so she can connect and feel more energy.

Reflection: This girl doesn't seem the least bit concerned about all the sand, including that it's all over her pants, feet, and hands. I'm the one who has to encourage her to dust herself off as she exits the sandbox.

Petra wants to be even higher as she throws the clay. Placing the wooden sandbox cover on for more height, she climbs up and throws ball after ball, enjoying the fact that the clay is getting softer and softer. Marveling at the sand granules impregnated in the clay from her time standing inside the box, she wants to tell me a secret. She wants to drop out of school and be a musician in a band. I ask her if she's told anybody else. She says, "Well - I lied to you, it's not a secret…I told Mom and Dad, and my saxophone teacher. "But really, I only want to do this, being in a band when I'm 30 years old."

Reflection: Petra is beginning to trust me with some of her secrets. A part of her wants to grow up, but another part is afraid of what that might mean. Among other things, people might not approve. I know her father is a doctor and her mother a professor. Dropping out to follow a dream and be a musician could be unpopular at more places than just home. But at heart, Petra is a drama queen currently orchestrating some painful scenarios in her house, maybe side-stepping away from what she truly wants. What if she started playing more with her identity, independent of what she believes her parents hope she'll head toward as she moves into adolescence? Taking a "step outside their bed" into places where she can rest on her own?

I ask Petra whether it's OK to talk about her wishes when I meet with her parents. She says, "Yes."

Over the next few weeks, I begin speaking to Petra's parents in parents-only sessions about the value of their daughter being able to sleep in her own bed. That their decision to support such a goal could help her make what I think of as a clean break from the high expectations of her two professionally accomplished parents. (More on what happened with Petra and her family in Chapter 4: Parents in the Mix.)

Invariably, a disconnect between parent and child has prompted a parent to entrust a child into the care of a therapist even as that therapist acts as a proxy for the parent. Given the reality is that something in the "family energy field" likely is in need of adjustment, I often move into the role of advocate for a child whose influence and voice need bolstering or, at the very least, explaining. A child in treatment may be seen as providing a bridge toward change for the whole family system. When that system's other members (especially parents, any siblings, and grandparents) empathetically respond to the child rather than react punitively to childhood symptomatic behavior, growth through the Embodied Play Therapy process is supported. Think of the family energy field as comprised of individual streams running smoothly into a larger flowing river. If the separate streams (individual family members) have their flow blocked by the rigid judgments and reactivity of others, the streams will either swell to the point where they break through their banks or dissipate and trickle out. Empathetic response of all family members to each other allows for easier flow of family energy, helping a child feel better within a family more capable of processing its own ebbs and storms.

Still, a child's symptoms represent a challenge to family function, especially in the early stages of therapy. Symptoms add drama, and within the drama is the possibility of reluctance and resistance but also forward propulsion, gathering momentum, and change. Change to the rules and roles that family members play with each other. Change to the shared stories about each member that families tell.

Embodied Play Therapy provides context for change as a child, with their own pleasure in play foremost, naturally begins to add story, often multi-leveled, many times humorous, to the dramas playing out in clay, on paper, and with figures in the sandbox. Drama is deeply felt in the body and mind of a child as they dive into the richness of relational role play with the co-playing therapist, parent, or both. The word *drama* is originally from the Greek "*dramatos*" meaning "action, deed; play, spectacle" (Etymonline, n.d.). Indeed, building bridges to a child and family requires "actions" and "deeds" in play space. The child's behavior, originally seen as the problem, becomes a primary source of productive change and flexible function of a "family energy field" that may have been stuck in uncomfortable homeostasis.

The initial bridges being created with a child involve building trust in increments between therapist and child and therapist and parent, motivated with the end game always in sight. Return of the child to the primacy of family influence, minus the therapist. As much fun as therapy with children can be, the risk is that the therapist in long-term child-oriented therapy is elevated to the level of an expert to the point where the parent withdraws, "letting the therapist take care of the problems of her child" (Haley, 1987, p. 118). In contrast, the goal of a potentially powerful modality like Embodied Play Therapy is to embed the possibility of change not only for the problems presented but also for future ones that may arise.

This involves empowering the parents, either through direct experiences in play with their child or through active consultation with the therapist in a give-and-take on how a parent may return to the top of the family hierarchy where they can more easily serve as the authorities in charge rather than being cornered into authoritarian stances that provoke rebellion, if not now, then later as children navigate toward adolescence. As Marshall Rosenberg, the founder of The Center for Non-violent Communication, writes: "...anytime it's our objective to get another person to behave in a certain way, people are likely to resist no matter what we are asking for. This seems to be true whether the other person is 2 or 92 years of age" (Rosenberg, 2002, p. 4).

Sessions like the ones presented in this chapter offer a child an opportunity to challenge adult authority, to occupy their own energy field more fully in the presence of someone bigger. To swim in and out of connection with an adult play partner. To craft inner locations of embodied power that feel steadier. To find places they can relocate later at home amid the shifting sandstorms of "family energy fields" they were born into and within which they will grow. Places of power they will need to call on, as demands of school and society for their performance call them to strive for individual identities that, even when buffeted by harsh winds and weather, may stretch beyond the most prescient parents' dreams.

References

Etymonline. (n.d.). *Drama.* https://www.etymonline.com/word/drama

Gleason, B., & Gleason, M. (2012). *Exceptional Relationships: Transformation through Embodied Couples Work.* iUniverse.

Haley, J. (1987). *Problem-Solving Therapy* (2nd ed.). Jossey-Bass.

Kegan, R. (1982). *The Evolving Self: Problem and Process in Human Development.* Harvard University Press.

Rosenberg, M. (2002). *Raising Children Compassionately: Parenting the Nonviolent Communication Way (Pamphlet).* The Center for Nonviolent Communication.

4

Parents in the Mix

Every child who comes to therapy does so as a representative of a multigenerational family system. I view each family as a wavelike pool of strengths and stressors, reacting to behaviors and cycles that disturb or maintain family function. Difficulties of adults are felt and deeply absorbed into the minds and bodies of young people and can trigger intrinsic neurobiological tendencies that feed recursive, problematic behavioral patterns. These patterns become magnets for family attention. This leads families to pursue therapy, often with their child as the "identified patient." This often masks underlying problems within the family, ranging from inherited intergenerational trauma to unresolved childhood wounding in parents and the conflict between parents that often results. Keeping in mind possible functions of symptoms within the family unit, I ask parents to stop self-blame but be curious about how their behavior may contribute to their child's difficulties. As parents experiment with altering roles, communications, and their expectations, a child is often freed to change and grow.

In most instances, parents hope for speedy relief from difficult behavioral patterns in their children that they've noticed building over time. It is a rare parent who will jump at the opportunity to opt for therapy, even play therapy, as a holistic prevention tool. For the most part, patterns have festered for some time before I get the call. Because somatic psychotherapy in the form of Embodied Play Therapy for children sounds innovative and

DOI: 10.4324/9781003328186-6

promising, client families may expect too much too soon. Most parents want to ease any suffering a child is experiencing and move behavioral patterns into what they consider an acceptable range. Some parents ask me, "What's an example of a favorable outcome in a case like our child's…and how long will that take?"

I tell parents to expect a minimum of six months in therapy with me. My injection into the family system in multiple roles as play partner, parental counselor, and provoking outsider favoring change in the family status quo, will take time to play out (pardon the pun).

A parent's recognition of their past can be a font of positive change when made explicit as part of the intake form filled out for me by parents on behalf of a family's "identified patient" child. I'm curious to learn more about a child and their family before I begin seeing a child, and my intake form reflects this. Was this child planned? Were any fertility measures taken? Was the birth vaginal or by C-section? Was the child carried by a surrogate or adopted? Were there any particular prenatal stressors, including relational difficulties, illnesses, or deaths, as this child was carried in the womb? What was childbirth like from the standpoint of ease or difficulty, and was medication used to induce or delay labor?

I want to have some basic information about the background of each parent and caregiver in the family system. This includes whether any adult or anyone in that parent's family of origin has experienced substance issues or abuse of any kind and whether the parent has done any prior therapy or personal growth work. I have found that many children, especially sensitive ones, look to comfort unhealed parents. The primary "help" that the child offers is their own symptomatic behavior, which moves focus away from the parent's difficulties. In such cases, I increase parents-only consultations to learn whether a child's symptoms have a protective function, masking unresolved issues of others.

I remember one child opening my office door, heading to the bathroom, and bumping into their Mom as she stumbled back to her waiting room chair from where she'd just been standing with her ear close to the door. That parent, a victim of childhood abuse, admitted she was eavesdropping on their child's in-person sessions because she was afraid that behind the closed door, I might be abusing her child. In a parents-only follow-up session, we discussed the mother's fear. This became an entry for me to invite Mom to join sessions with her child. While this eased the mother's concern, seeing her child's shocked face in the above incident helped the Mom consider how her anxiety might be affecting her child and to accept my reference for individual adult therapy with a colleague.

Intake with Parents and How I Assess Whether Parents Will Join a Child in Session

I hold at least one parents-only "intake session" before seeing a child. In addition to answering questions parents may have about the Embodied Play Therapy process, I ask each parent present to describe what they think the parent-child relationship felt like from their child's point of view. What would it have been like for your child to have you as a parent at age two, at five, at eight, and at ten? What emerges is a parent's fluency or difficulty in sensing their child's perspective. Did a child miss and yearn for a parent who was working or distracted due to other commitments, worries, or conflicts? Did a child feel the benefit of special activities shared with a parent, or perhaps with other caregivers? When might a child have felt neglected? This inquiry often leads a parent to reflect on memories of their own childhood and upbringing. Their joys, their hurts. Where might they have felt loved as a child or abandoned? Were they heard by parents? Were they criticized? While our focus is on intake for the child being presented, I am preparing the ground for parental involvement and commitment to a process that will need their active involvement to succeed.

In cases where a parent has had a tough childhood themselves, I notice one of two tendencies. In the first, a parent minimizes the challenges facing their child because the parent's own childhood trauma seems so much greater to them. I find this minimization especially present if a parent hasn't processed their childhood experience with some depth in their own therapeutic work. It's very important to take the temperature on such minimization because such parents often pull their children out of therapy before they're on solid enough ground. The second tendency with parents who've had a tough childhood is high anxiety over a child's symptoms. When combined with their own self-judgment that they are failing as a parent, maximization around how bad things are, often way out of proportion to reality, sometimes breeds a panic that a child can feel. Not helpful while Embodied Play Therapy is working to bring a child and family system into balance.

Throughout a course of Embodied Play Therapy, I collaborate with parents in their young person's work via regular parents-only sessions to share observations and plan. These parents-only sessions are scheduled at least once for every three or four child sessions and often happen online. In addition, I often recruit and encourage parents to participate directly in some play sessions. As highlighted by therapist Risë VanFleet (2011, pp. 153–169) and others, it integrates parents more powerfully in their young person's progress, helps a child and family make lasting changes, and it's also just such fun!

Early on in a child's therapy, I assess whether and when we have parent-joining-child sessions on a case-by-case basis. First, I know that a child's play removed from parental observation is often more freely expressive. While parental involvement in Embodied Play Therapy sessions offers me a window into parent-child interaction and possibly larger family dynamics at play in a child's presenting issues, I need to weigh this against other factors.

It can be stifling for many children to have an anxious parent in the room, especially a parent who has a hard time playing. The addition of a parent to the session creates a triangle. Two adults and a child. What is one potential issue? Visualize a child's family system, also a triangle, no matter the number of parents. One corner of the family system triangle is the developing child. Another corner represents the social ecosystem containing prescribed rules and preferred roles. The third corner carries a family history replete with value-laden narratives of what it is to operate as a failure or success in life. The key takeaway is that the family system triangle and the moment-to-moment energetic movements within it – the "family energy field" – is highly truncated in the direction of organized adult power. I do not want to replicate such an imbalance of power in Embodied Play Therapy.

Further, the cycle that often brings parents to the point of reaching out to a therapist for their child often begins when a parent feels out of control. Frequently, a child encountering such parent(s) feels that they can't rely on them to set boundaries. Such children often act out to get parents to create boundaries where they feel safe. Or, especially in family systems split by separation, divorce, and substance use, a child tries to act as a parent, confidante, or partner to their parent. Such "parentified" children often benefit when parents refocus on their adult relationships and resources and free their child to draw strength from the creative wellsprings of childhood and the peer relationships that this child will look toward for sustenance in adolescence and adult life.

In substance, I want to engage a family system in shaking out limiting beliefs and problematic behavioral cycles that have brought that system to my office door in the first place. If I notice a child modifying their in-session behavior, vigilantly "on watch" to see whether a participating parent approves, I know it's time to talk about the value of sessions where a child can play, freed from their gaze. My ability to see through to what's really at play under the surface in a child's life may depend on a healthy mix of therapist-child one-to-one sessions, parent-therapist sessions, and, when it will benefit a child, putting parents into play.

As a first step toward building comfort around play for a parent, I recommend they purchase the slim volume *Floor Games* (2016), published originally by writer H.G. Wells in 1912, which chronicles the games he invented along with and for his own two sons. At least one version in print as of this writing (Andesite Press) contains photographs and drawings of the characters, cities, and islands built on Wells' family floor, conveying the delights imaginative play can hold for both parent and child. (Cautionary Note: Wells uses racially pejorative terms to describe some play figures.)

I am certainly not expecting families to create the elaborate scenarios for home-based play that Wells did. It's the atmosphere of play that I'm after and what Wells called "the ordinary joys of playing with the floor" (p. 17). That's because parents will be dropping down to child level either in my office or at home if it's an online session to engage as their child takes the lead in a play process, which many parents would do well to remember. Embodied Play Therapy with parents in the mix often mercifully transports the bodies, minds, and hearts of both child and family away from the problems that have brought them to me and moves the family theater of operations into a place where play rules.

Among the factors I use to determine parent participation in a child's sessions are as follows.

Age of the Child and Child-Parent Relationship

While I've worked with children as young as three, my primary audience for Embodied Play Therapy begins at six years of age. Erik Erikson suggests that a key task of such school-age children is winning recognition for "producing things" (1959/1994, p. 59). While the sandplay worlds, molded clay beings, block structures, and similar creations are the "products" of our Embodied Play Therapy sessions, the value of having the creation (and destruction) process witnessed and even joined by an attuned adult represents relational gold from the standpoint of fostering secure attachment for a child. In these days of parenting marred by multiple distractions, screens or otherwise, slowing down enough to play with a child beyond their infancy and preschool days sends an unmistakable message of caring for that child. For the parent, Embodied Play Therapy participation, which finds them creating alongside a child or co-creating with them, can re-invigorate "inner child" places within a parent, mirroring the joy, tenacity, and pleasure felt by their child within the play process.

What we're looking to do in Embodied Play Therapy is loosen the narrative around the classic family relational battles – control battles fought over screen time, food, sleep, school, siblings, and more. A parent learning to let go of judgment and be more playful can go a long way to defuse wrangles in areas such as these and help a child settle down. But this does not mean a parent has to show up in a therapy session as another kid. When parents do participate in a session, is the adult putting aside their parental stance to show up in a conscious, accepting, and mindful way for their child? Going beyond just being a bigger body in the room and to interacting with spontaneous, playful power is thrilling to see for so many children. This level of commitment to a child is healing beyond any technique or method I might offer in these pages.

Loss in the Child's Life and within Their Family

For a child affected by traumatic events such as separation or divorce, family illness or death, abuse, or wounding inflicted when neurodiverse learning and other special needs have not been met at school or within the home, the opportunity to play with a parent under the beneficent gaze of a caring therapist becomes particularly valuable. For a parent whose own childhood entailed some less-than-effective parenting, the opportunity to see something different modeled can inspire more positive parent-child experiences. The roots laid down in session can continue growing well beyond the hour spent with the therapist.

Filial therapy, as delineated by Cetin and VanFleet (2021), is structured specifically to emphasize that the client is the relationship, not the individual (p. 251). As a family therapist, I am open to shaking up communication patterns, especially where existing ways of operating reflect wide differences between what a young person wants and parental preferences. In Embodied Play Therapy sessions, we often tackle these intergenerational gulfs through play with the parent or in direct dialogue between a child and a parent in my presence. Throughout the process, parents become more consciously aware of how they might unwind from family enmeshment and organization around symptomatic behaviors in kids ranging from stomach aches to school refusal.

I focus my play therapy sessions involving parents on creating an in-session experience of what Cetin and VanFleet (2021) call "child-centered imaginary play," which occurs at the invitation and leadership of the child (p. 250). "Parents follow the child's ideas for the direction of the play so that themes of importance to the child can emerge and be worked through" (p. 251). Collaboration and family strength are inspired by values such as empathy and acceptance.

Parent attendance in their child's Embodied Play Therapy can move the direction of play forward as these adults contribute their creativity to our process. Additionally, such participation helps in growing the alliance between parents who have sought these sessions and me. When a parent joins in play sessions, I'll often inject some humor as I foster the competitive dynamic between the generations because I want to lubricate the intergenerational communication field and build tolerance within the family for differences in perspective. The funniest thing here is that kids are often the dominant players as we initiate parents into the zaniness of Embodied Play Therapy because they are native to and fluent in play and because it's their symptoms that got things rolling to begin therapy.

Here are some case examples of how families began moving into new ways of being with each other through parental participation in Embodied Play Therapy.

Ricky – Age Seven. In-Person Session with Mom

(See Ricky's earlier play in Chapter 1: Children in an Anxious Age and Chapter 3: Building a Bridge to a Child.)

Initially, Mom sits in the waiting room.

Entering my office, Ricky jumps from the foam cube to the couch, calling me "Poopoo" and "Doodoo," testing to see whether I'll react. Afraid he'll hit his head on the hard plaster wall behind the couch, I prop a thick pillow nearly as big as his body between Ricky and the wall. I match his high energy. "What's that you're calling me?!" For a minute more, I allow him to jump over and over again before calling his mother in to discuss what we've been doing. She agrees that he's been testing both his parents at home, and they're worried he could hurt himself. I suggest mother and son move to the sandbox where Ricky creates what he calls "a conflict" in the sand, each picking dragon figures to fight each other. I encourage Ricky's soft-spoken mom to raise the enthusiasm of her vocal expression, matching her son's high energy level. As Mom gets more boisterous, Ricky settles down and heads towards my box of wooden blocks, dumping them all onto the floor. Sitting on the floor, Mom builds a small square of blocks around herself, saying, "This is protection from Ricky's big boy energy." Eying his mom, Ricky begins building a similar square on the surface of the foam cube. Changing course, he takes all his mother's blocks, starting a larger enclosure on the floor, which mom then helps him complete. Smiling with pleasure, mother and son survey their successful collaboration as they sit together, corralled in a wooden cocoon.

Reflection: Ricky needed to feel into his mixed emotions around being a young human benefiting from his mother's nurturance and, at the same time, experimenting with a tangible boundary for himself as a boy growing his own independent identity. Within Ricky's family, as in all families, times of transition such as these are best accomplished when a child can play between what seem like states of being in opposition. Ricky and Mom's co-creation that pendulates between Ricky's movement from the high-energy "big boy" who has his own space (as seen in his separate block structure on top of the foam cube) and his returning to togetherness with Mom in a jointly built block cocoon portends the possibility that the boy's growth can include both. (See how Ricky played through this further, taking the next step into an independent safe space later in this chapter.)

Ricky had been unhappy at school and had punched his father to express his dissatisfaction when his Dad came to pick him up as planned at the end of the school day.

Ricky's In-Person Session with Dad

I tell Dad privately of my intention: "Let's connect Ricky to your power and create a new story between you!"

At my suggestion, Ricky and Dad try wrestling with each other on my large soft area rugs. Dad, who I know is a dedicated body-builder, cradles Ricky in his arms as the smiling boy wriggles and laughs. When Ricky escapes, he makes a beeline for my box of wooden blocks. I suggest Dad and Son each build their own structures on two adjoining area rugs, which have a space between them. On the edge of his rug, Ricky places a long single line of blocks as a border separating his work from his dad's. At intervals along this wall demarcating the separate play areas, Ricky places single vertical blocks and miniature figures – a wizard casting a spell with outstretched arm, and an armored medieval knight – as sentinels to mark and guard his territory. In his area, Dad silently stacks a tower of blocks. Three horizontal platforms supported by columns.

Ricky, who has been carting blocks into his territory, now steps into dad's domain. He brings miniature figures to fight. Seated facing each other, father and son battle each other with a figure each hold in their hands. Ricky adds sounds to the battle. "Kaaaaa!" Kiiiiii!" and Dad adds his own sound effects. As the battle heats up, Dad has an idea to protect himself. He will turn into a character who wears an "invisible cloak" and cannot be seen. Ricky protests, "Noooooooooo!" but then cracks up into the biggest laugh, clearly delighted with his dad's "cloak" idea.

Stepping back to his own side, Ricky builds a small rectangle of blocks, placing figures inside – a tiger, a growling three-headed dog, and the armored knight that had been on guard at his border that kept his dad and he apart. Ricky dubs this enclosure "The Healing Place." Neal whispers to Dad as Ricky heads to the bathroom: "Maybe use your idea of the cloak and come to school to pick your son up in a costume. Maybe even….a cloak?"

Reflection: The backdrop for this session is Ricky's recent episode, where he punched his Dad, picking him up from a school day that Ricky might have wished were shorter. Their in-session interchange begins with the tenderness of Dad's holding, receiving, and wrestling with his son's big energy. Dad then taps into his playful side and allows his son to take the lead in play – So healing for a son who thrives and revels in opportunities for expression in Embodied Play Therapy. We witness Dad dropping into resonance with his son. A son who has strong feelings, including frustration with school and helplessness that he couldn't be picked up earlier. Unlike other children I work with, Ricky was not engineering scenarios where his parents would have to collect him before the scheduled end of the school day, but he must have had powerful emotions boiling inside to exit school as soon as possible. Emotions like these are hard for children to feel. Sometimes hard to the point where you might hit your father.

In this session, we are not talking about "the problem" – Ricky punching Dad – which is in the past. Father and son are playing in the present. And in this arena, Dad responds with a dramatic flourish, wryly suggesting the "invisible cloak." How do you battle an invisible adversary? Might the cloak (or even the thought of it) serve as an invisible boundary, protecting Dad from a flying fist? Dad has engaged the problem by garbing it in mirth!

Ricky's father could choose to show up at school pick-up time in his "invisible cloak" or not. The point had been made. Engaging playfully with parent-child dynamics and offering opportunities to deepen parent-child relationships through embodied play. In the months that followed this session, I learned that Ricky lashed out at his Dad less. While in a parents-only session, I re-framed Ricky's occasional pummeling behavior, pointing out that the son felt safe enough to bring his fists to his father. That we'd need to continue working on boundaries, conveying that no one, including Dad, should get hurt. (See how this turned out in Chapter 8: Completions.)

Gemma: A Nine-Year-Old Girl

Her diagnoses from a prior clinician were dyslexia, anxiety, and depression.

I wondered whether reported problems in school could also involve additional factors and advised her parents to obtain a learning profile from the Yellin Center for Mind, Brain, and Education near their home in NYC. Many parents of symptomatic children who've been having problems at school tend to initially simplify what their kids are experiencing or blame themselves. The Yellin Center offers support for students starting at five years of age and their families, offering interdisciplinary assessments focused on a young person's strengths and challenges. Part of this assessment is a full evaluation of family function.

Gemma was being bullied at her New York City public school, and she'd been refusing to go, staying home and comforting herself with video games. During her early in-person therapy, she frequently used a miniature wooden treasure chest big enough to contain another smaller one nesting within. She told me no one could open these but her. Knowing that both her parents and older brother were mightily burdened with childcare duties as they stayed home to watch over Gemma, I asked her whether she would agree to other family members joining her in session, which she did. Inviting first her older brother, her father, and then her mother one at a time over the ensuing weeks into the session, Gemma vigorously defended her treasure box, keeping its contents out of sight.

Gemma and Mom in a Tele-Session

Mom knows that the treasure box resting in the sand has not been opened by any other family member. From the figures on my shelves, Gemma has told me to stop and select miniature figures to deploy into my office sandbox on her behalf who will defend her treasure from Mom. A gelatinous pink octopus almost as big as her head, a rubbery fist-sized brain stress ball, and an orange squid will serve as guards. I tell Mom in a deep, mysterious voice that "all the brain power of other family members has not been able to open the treasure box, SO FAR." Mom asks Gemma about a spire of clear crystal as big as his daughter's hand that Gemma instructs me to place in the sand. Gemma tells Mom that the crystal is "the power."

Mom asks that the treasure box be opened, making the creaking and squeaking sound effect of its lid being lifted. But unfazed, Gemma answers that the treasure box cannot be opened so easily. I offer Mom the opportunity to select a sandplay figure to help her and she picks a pirate ship, which is immediately sunk by Gemma's octopus as together daughter and Mom make the gurgling sound of the ship sinking.

Gemma tells us there's something in the room where they are participating in this remote session that can help. She points up at one of her shelves in her bedroom. Mom objects, saying she wants to stick to one world…the world we are creating remotely or their room at home. I pause, say to Mom and daughter that I'm thinking Gemma can shift between multiple worlds as the game developer she aspires to be when grown up… and (in a nod to Mom) that I also recognize the value at times of concentrating on one world at a time. Hearing this, Mom gives the OK. She's open to playing within both.

What is Gemma pointing to on her shelf? Mom says it's a wooden maraca shaped like a lion. I ask Mom to shake the maraca, and we hear seeds rattling inside. Mom says the shaking of the maraca can open the treasure box. Mom: "Can we see the treasure?" I ask Gemma, "Should the box be opened?"

Gemma "Sure! We've spent weeks trying to open it! Let's see what's inside." First, I open the outer box and then the inner box, revealing sparkling gold. Intoning in my deepest voice, 'No one else in the family has been able to open the treasure box except now the team of Mom and Gemma has done it!"

Reflection: Gemma felt out of control at school, where she was having trouble performing, and other children, perhaps sensing her vulnerability, had been bullying her. Dad and Mom had been arguing over what to do. Should they move Gemma to a different school to meet her learning needs or advocate further for additional services to be provided at the current public school? I sensed both the mother's impulse to exercise some control and her pain in not being able to implement workable solutions in Gemma's life that would keep her safe and more fully deal with her learning needs.

In session with her daughter, Mom became willing to drop the façade of control that some parents concerned with self-image hold onto, especially in the presence of professional outsiders like me. As Gemma and Mom explored the reversal of who was in charge, the customary parent-child hierarchy, a sense of the child's independence was fostered within a loving mother-daughter container. Mom saw she did not have to miraculously create the cure on her own. Gemma had been heard through her dogged maintenance of hidden treasure until her partnership with Mom unlocked its lid. After this session, Mom and Dad arranged to have Gemma's learning needs further evaluated. With the ongoing aid of allied professionals collaborating with the family, strategies to help Gemma build a successful life would be found.

Rivka: A Seven-Year-Old Girl

This girl from a wealthy family was used to getting her way. The issue was that she was challenging teachers at her private school, which, her parents told me, was seriously considering expelling her. Rivka's parents traveled abroad often, and my thought was that rebuilding her connection to them might influence her acting out to get attention at school (which certainly had the effect of getting her parents' attention). After a number of sessions where Rivka played with gusto on her own, she was getting to like her Embodied Play Therapy sessions so much that she didn't want to leave!

Session #1: With Mom's Support at the End

Rivka is negotiating with me. My 45-minute session length is "Not Enough" Rivka says with a broad grin. She wants 100 minutes! Rivka knows I have another client right after her. I invented a "10-minute session ending alert" for her in an earlier session, and it's been eight minutes since she had that today. But she's still hanging out in my play tunnel, refusing to put on her shoes. I text Mom, waiting in the car outside to join us. When the door opens and Mom enters, Rivka is crying. Mom reaches into the tunnel, Rivka smiles, and gives her mom what Mom tells us is "the biggest hug in her life." A simple test of affection created by Rivka. That's all she needed. Reassurance that her mom, temporarily out of sight, would be there for her. Mom and daughter leave, holding hands.

Session #2: With Mom's Support at the End

Rivka's speaking voice, which seemed like that of a much younger child, has deepened into a lower frequency, more appropriate for her age. Still, Rivka is pendulating between her need to leave and her need to stay. I texted Mom that I again need her help. When Mom arrives, I ask if we can carry Rivka out together. Mom supports her prone and giggling daughter under her shoulders, and I follow, toting Rivka from the feet.

Session #3: On Her Own

Rivka refuses my invitation to make a sand world. I bring out a dollhouse that I sometimes use for children who are resistant to sand. From my figures, she selects some horses, which I think of as a strong "power animal" figure, especially for children whose gender expression tends towards feminine. As she places these horses in the doll house, I sense that her refusal to do what I'm suggesting, sandplay, is a positive indication of Rivka's claiming agency for herself. She chooses a different forum for her play. And with her power comes a willingness to experiment with less dependence on parental support. At the end of her 10-minute session ending alert, Rivka opens the door and leaves on her own, walking to her waiting mom in the car.

Session #4: On Her Own

Rivka makes up a story about a horse that protects her, as she returns to using containers of water in the sandbox, integrating an earlier phase of her play with what looks like emerging self-soothing and self-empowerment.

Session #5: With Dad's Support at the End

Dad has driven Rivka to her session and waits in his car. Rivka selects a new horse who is "the Queen of horses." Reverting to playing with figures in the dollhouse, she asks me to help her get animals that she says are "stuck" in the dollhouse out of their stuck places. At the end of the session, I texted Dad to come to my office door and greet his daughter. I tell Rivka we'll surprise him and set up the tunnel with one open side facing the open door. Rivka gets the idea. She crawls in the end farthest from the door and when Dad appears, out the other open end into his arms.

Session #6: With Mom

Rivka is very obstreperous and disagrees with anything I suggest for her to play with – no clay, no sandbox, no dollhouse. I text her mom and ask her to come into the session, and we start a game where the daughter orders her mom around. I've done this before with other children to play with roles in the family that have turned upside down when kids begin ruling the roost. Rivka becomes "Queen Rivka" with Mom bowing down to her. Mom and daughter play along with this briefly, but as I watch, I can see the two of them getting a bit uncomfortable. So Rivka and Mom turn their play into a hide-and-seek game where Mom steps outside to the pathway leading to my office and Rivka secrets herself, first in the closet, then in the bathroom, and finally under a blanket. Each time, Mom discovers Rivka to the tune of laughter.

Reflection: Sometimes I suggest an intervention that uses a humorous dose of the presenting symptom as a step toward curing it, known in family therapy circles as "prescribing the symptom." This is what we were doing in the initial role-play, where Rivka acted as Queen, not far off from the dominance of Rivka's demanding ways at home (and in session with me!).

If it's just me and a child in session, I'll exaggerate a "one down" supplicant stance in a sequence like the one above, where a child makes up the game rules and gets to experiment with ordering me around. When a parent gets into the act, abandoning an authority position can be hard, even if in jest. While I may try to cheerlead the role reversal, this has its limits, especially when the funny part wears thin, too close to that sore spot where a parent judges how they may look in the eyes of others, including me.

I will often say to kids: "Your mom (or your dad) is the boss." But not with Rivka. Instead, I was looking to restore a sense of balance. Where this girl didn't need to always be the one in charge. After I met with Mom and Dad in parents-only sessions, they re-established what seemed like more of a hopeful theme in their parent-child relationship: loving parents who will see your needs. And Rivka, enjoying international travel with her parents whenever possible during vacations, remained in her present school.

The "Family Bed" Issue

Sometimes things get very close, perhaps too close, in parent-child relationships. I've noticed in my practice that a surprising number of parents allow children, at ages that may surprise many, into what becomes a "Family Bed." The question becomes whether family accommodation to alleviate the anxiety of a child (or a co-sleeping parent) supports a child's need to individuate and grow developmentally or constitutes regression into earlier stages of child-rearing.

Many children seek the comfort of sleeping near a parent as protection for themselves and sometimes for the adult whose unhealed inner child needs warmth best provided by a partner or a commitment to parental self-soothing. Sleeping on their own, the child is freed to pursue their next steps into a less-fettered adolescence.

Tanya: A 12-Year-Old Girl

Hailing from a Jewish family in NYC, Tanya's night terrors had started at age eight when her father began traveling, often out of the country for work. This intensified the daughter's role as an all-around helpmate for her stay-at-home mother. Tanya attended a school where stories were read about children in the Holocaust. In a parents-only session, I found out that Tanya, on her mother's side, was the great-granddaughter of a child who had been smuggled out of World War II Poland to safety in South America.

Every time Tanya's father left on a business trip, she would refuse to sleep in her bedroom, and her mother admitted taking comfort from Tanya's nocturnal presence in the parental bed. I wondered, since Tanya and her mom did not want to abruptly end their co-sleeping arrangement, if we could approach her therapy by addressing what looked like intergenerational trauma. I told the parents that we could expand the therapeutic container to include them, and I invited the mom in for a session with Tanya because the Dad would be traveling. Before this, Tanya had been highly resistant to doing anything in session that smacked of conflictual energy. No smashing clay with a rubber mallet. No hitting a foam cube with an encounter bat.

The mother, seemingly shy at first meeting, lit up when I said she could enter a "mother's hitting contest." Tanya, who was brought up to display "modesty," raised her eyebrows in shock when her mother picked up the bat. Proceeding, she smashed down on the cube 120 times, counting every hit out loud as a broad smile spread across the daughter's face. I asked Mom to tell Tanya why she chose to hit the cube. Mom told her she was hitting to express her pain about her childhood in a family that suffered separation. Mom missing dad on his frequent trips held echoes of past generations. But as Mom told Tanya, this was not her daughter's problem to solve. Through the mother's willingness to become a participant in her daughter's therapy, this family took a giant step forward, allowing for expression rather than repression in their present lives within the context of family history.

Reflection: Using the bat here to hit a foam cube was not, as it sometimes is, about mobilizing aggression for a positive purpose. It was about the assertion of the mother's grief from her own childhood and an uncomfortable truth about the present held inside, which her daughter had been expressing as she slept with her Mom in the father's absence. The family energy field was held captive in an uncomfortable behavioral cycle where it had become the daughter's job to be the caregiver. An assignment better left to adults. Using a lightweight plastic bat in a bout of hitting allowed for the bigger energy Mom needed to amplify what Mom held within and the daughter needed some freedom from.

Changes came fast and furious for Tanya. Always a creative writer, she started penning a play, the main character a young girl who escaped the Holocaust. She also decided, with the help of her mom, that the family should collect clothing and toys for refugees now settling in her community.

Tanya began having an easier time staying in her own bed when her father bought her a miniature "home planetarium" that projected stars on the darkened ceiling of her bedroom at night. She also took on leadership in her peer group, moving away from the popular crowd at school to spend more time with what she called "the sensitive artistic set." She told me this group valued both her creativity and her advice. When I asked her if she'd like to grow up to be a therapist, Tanya grinned.

Mark: A Nine-Year-Old Boy and His Two Moms (Tele-session)

We are working on the issue of Mark's fear and why he sleeps in a sleeping bag every night right next to his parents' double bed in their NYC apartment.

In his book *Children's Special Places: Exploring the Role of Forts, Dens, and Bush Houses in Middle Childhood*, David Sobel (1993) says:

> During this period of middle childhood, the self is fragile and under construction and needs to be protected from the view of the outside world. The secretive nature of the hiding place is significant. The self, like the metamorphosing larva of the butterfly, needs to be wrapped in a cocoon before it emerges into the light. Thus, the places that children seek out are places where they cannot be seen, places to begin the unfolding of the self. (p. 70)

I can hardly believe my luck that Mark decided to create a scenario where he was wrapped in a cocoon of his own making to begin the session.

> *A parent's name appears in my virtual Zoom waiting room. It's a bit early for the session, and I'm adjusting the crane contraption I rigged up to hold my cell phone for virtual sessions in the sandbox. It's only our second session, and I'm not surprised when it's both of Mark's Moms appearing on the screen rather than their child.*

Neal: Where is your son? Will you move the camera a bit so I can see different parts of the room?
Mom #1: Mark is hiding.
Neal: Could he be behind the chalkboard?
Mom #2: He'd have to be two-dimensional for that

> *One of the parents redirects their laptop camera toward the pile of plush animals heaped on Mark's bed.*

Neal: Moms, you're both surgeons, what kind of operation could we do to find your son?

Mom #1: *(Looking balefully at the stuffed tower containing Mark)* Maybe we can use a scalpel to cut into the pile and look around!

Mom #2: *(Makes a face)* He could get hurt if he's in there!

Mom #1: *(Using her index finger to cut into the pile)*

A muffled rumbling of laughter erupts from its depths, and Mark jumps out.

The session continues as Mark's Moms tiptoe out of his room.

Mark gets back into his bed. The only part of his body that's visible is his head. Plush animals are scattered around him and on the floor.

Neal: Ready to do a sandbox?

Mark: I don't want to do a sandbox today…just ask me questions.

Neal: So your Moms told me you've been sleeping in a sleeping bag in their room? Are you afraid?

Mark: Yes

Neal: You know, when I was your age, I was afraid and stood at my parents' door for hours in the middle of the night. It was cold. What do you do when you're in the sleeping bag in your parents' room?

Mark: I talk to my Moms. It's easy to do because they're so close.

I make a mental note: Tell Mark's parents to buy one of those intercoms where you can talk from room to room.

Neal to Mark: My parents took me to a therapist when I had trouble sleeping because I was afraid. It was different for me, though. When I was a kid, my therapist didn't have sandboxes or punching gloves or a bat to hit pillows.

Mark emerges, sitting cross-legged on his bed.

Neal: I have a feeling you'll come up with a 'Mark' solution…an experiment to sleep in your room…on your own.

The following day.

A text from one of Mark's Moms to Neal:

Wow! Last night, he slept in his own bed!

Reflection: There's a level of terror for children when they believe or are told they can do anything they want. Even when ruled by impulse, children often sense on some intuitive level that they don't have full control. They need boundaries to relax their own internal terror that screams, "I don't feel safe!" Nine-year-old Mark felt some shame around his nightly sleeping near his parents. Even though this arrangement had its comforting side, it wasn't fully a cocoon of his own making. In the resulting move this boy made to experiment with sleeping independently, Mark was taking a step toward his own unfolding into a more age-appropriate stage.

It's Not Always This Easy

It may take a while for parents and kids to untangle themselves from patterns of co-sleeping. Most often, the child leads the way out of this co-sleeping dilemma. One child started sleeping in the lower section of a bunk bed with a curtain she pulled across to make a "nest." Then there's Tanya, described in this chapter, whose father bought her a light generator to project images of stars on her ceiling. Very comforting.

Ricky, whose embodied play with his parents is also profiled in this chapter, sought the comfort of their bed on many nights. One afternoon in an Embodied Play Therapy session with his mom, where we had begun talking about how he could experiment with sleeping on his own, Ricky came up with an alternative idea on how to build some comfort and a place of rest for himself that would also let his hardworking parents sleep. Calling it the "Tent of Safety," he drew a plan for it with pen and paper as he sat on my office floor. Strung with LED lights by his parents, the Tent that his parents located in the living room away from their bedroom became a quiet space that could ease him into a slower rhythm at the end of the day.

Ricky's Tent of Safety became even more important as a place of refuge for him during the difficult early days of the COVID-19 pandemic, when he was spending so much more time in his family's apartment, now doubling as an online school. At my suggestion, Ricky's parents added relaxing music to his Tent. They read to him there at night before he went to sleep. When he wanted to show me his newly set up tent during an online session, he brought his iPad inside and read to me! Soon after, his parents told me they were impressed when Ricky, in a magnanimous gesture, invited his younger brother one day to come into his Tent to join him in play.

Another single parent whose 10-year-old child was sleeping in their bed took the step of buying a cheap air mattress for their son, placing it on the parent's hardwood bedroom floor. The air mattress was so squeaky that it kept everyone up, including siblings in the next room. After a few nights of this, the son decided his bed was a better bet for getting some sleep.

11-year-old Petra and Family find their way to their own beds… (See Petra's earlier story in Chapter 3: Building a Bridge to a Child.) As you read earlier, Petra may have been enforcing boundaries around hand sanitizer, but her own boundaries were a bit muddy when it came to where she slept. As Mom, Dad, and I strategized together in parents-only sessions, Mom, whose hobby was carpentry, had a thought that she began sharing. To design and build a fully enclosed "compound" within their suburban apartment that would be, once completed, solely Petra's territory. Much to my delight, in the weeks that followed, mother and daughter brought this idea into reality, creating walls and interior components from recycled plastic decking boards. Petra's compound included a loft bed, desk, storage for books and toys, and a door!

In one stroke, the parent, in collaboration with their child, achieves both a parental goal – independent sleeping spaces – and a growth experience for a child who delights in helping to build her private space and then inhabits it. A parent modeling and pointing her child toward competencies children need to negotiate as they move toward adolescence.

These examples demonstrate a successful re-tracing of yet-to-be-completed childhood developmental steps. Among these are autonomy (child sleeping/recreating in own space), initiative (taking an idea and collaboratively moving it forward with a child, as in Ricky and Petra), and then industriously putting it all together. A "problem" is employed as a fulcrum to foster a child's growth. Positive parental action assists their child's forward momentum, vaulting up and through what Erik Erikson defines as a key task for children of school age. Namely, openness to invention, effectively bringing a child through fears of their own "inferiority" into a place where their "industry" (building a sleep/play solution) can tangibly flower (1959/1994, p. 91).

But Embodied Play Therapy has its limits with certain parents who may bridle at my nudging them to make changes to family sleeping arrangements and create clearer boundaries for children as they approach new phases of sexual maturity and the need for independent identity. Setting a parental bedroom up with a door that must at least be knocked on to enter is important in my eyes. A child walking in on their parents having sex is not the best idea in my view on how to educate them. While I believe these are important topics to broach with parents, I am not successful in every instance. The firm stance I took with one set of parents resulted in their child being pulled, I felt prematurely, from therapy. Still, I continue to advocate on such matters where I feel a particular child's growth and development may be hampered by unfettered entrance to a "family bed," which could be contributing to them staying young when it's high time to move forward.

References

Cetin, F., & VanFleet, R. (2021). The International Appeal of Filial Therapy: Values, Methods, and Its Use in Turkey to Empower Children and Families and the Therapists Who Assist Them. In S. Jennings & C. Holmwood (Eds.), *Routledge International Handbook of Play, Therapeutic Play and Plan Therapy*. Routledge.

Erikson, E. H. (1994). *Identity and the Life Cycle*. W. W. Norton. (Original work published 1959)

Sobel, D. (1993). *Children's Special Places: Exploring the Role of Forts, Dens and Bush Houses in Middle Childhood*. Zepher Press.

VanFleet, R. (2011). Filial Therapy: Strengthening Family Relationships with the Power of Play. In C. E. Schaefer (Ed.), *Foundations of Play Therapy* (pp. 153–169). John Wiley & Sons Inc.

Wells, H. G. (2016). *Floor Games and Little Wars*. Monroe ST. Press. (Original work published 1912). See also: Wells, H.G. (n.d.). *Floor Games*. Andesite Press. (Original work published 1912). Andesite Press. (Original work published 1912)

5

Touchy Subjects

Bodies, Butts, and Poop!

Five-year-old Neal: *I'm in the bathroom at the end of the hall with my friend Tamar, and we have our pants down. I'm looking at her butt. I am interested in the smell. Also, her private parts are different than mine. Suddenly, the door opens. It's my mother. Tamar's mother is right behind her. The expression on my mother's face is one of shock. Her mouth turned down in disapproval. Tamar's mother looks scared. We pull up our pants and trudge out the door.*

Reflection: I feel such sadness thinking back to that day, and I can't remember what, if anything, was said to us. But the memory of having my sexuality and joyful interests shut down remained, along with shame. One of my tasks today is speaking to parents about their children's sexuality, the need to maintain a relaxed attitude that supports the burgeoning and beautiful energy of intimate contact with another human being, as well as to teach children a sense of body integrity that will protect them… It's a tough formula to feel we're getting right.

An anxious mother speaks to me about her 10-year-old, who sits beside her with his hands in his pants as they watch television together on the couch. What's she to do? She can tell him

DOI: 10.4324/9781003328186-7

that while touching yourself is something almost everybody does, it's best to do that in the privacy of a separate room.

I felt shame with my own sexual exploration, judged by two mothers. And five years later, under the covers with a flashlight at age 10, I flipped the pages of a book filled with diagrams on the human body and procreation that my parents had left in our living room bookcase. Inside, I held the emotional residue of imagined parental disapproval. So much of my own growing sexual aliveness remained mostly under wraps. I took a risk to express some yearning for friction with another body at age 12, but only when the lights were out, and classmates gathered for slow dancing parties as we played with switching partners in an apartment with no parents in the room.

What Sigmund Freud dubbed the latency stage does not equate to a limitation of a child's early interest in their own body and the bodies of others, just because an egg or viable wiggling sperm cannot yet join to bear fruit before puberty. I believe there is much to be explored in the ground between the sexual freedom Wilhelm Reich espoused as a cure-all for society's ills when he wrote *Children of the Future: On the Prevention of Sexual Pathology* (1950/1983) and the shutdown of sexuality by parents and society. Reich said, "Like other animals, children are born without armoring" (p. 11). Reich wrote of childbirth in his era, where:

> The first greeting is a slap. The next greeting: Take it away from the mother. ...The baby has no body contact after having had nine months of body contact at a very high temperature – what we call the 'orgonotic body energy contact,' the field action between them, the warmth and the heat. (p. 3)

He further went on to decry societal practices beginning with circumcision (p. 3) and the "compulsive regulation of infants" (p. 45), noting "the occurrence of genital masturbation to be a favorable indication for prognosis and its absence...an unfavorable one" (p. 141).

Embodied Play Therapy Steps into the Breach on Bodies and Emerging Sexuality

Children need acceptance for the curiosity developing in their bodies, minds, and hearts. They will be experimenting with language that puts parents on guard because children can be graphic. We adults may squirm when reminded of places in our younger selves where fascination with body parts, bodily functions, and sexual energy first surfaced. Children test our reactions, sense our discomfort, and may shut down. So parents, therapists, teachers, and other adult caregivers need to be mindful of harsh judgments that can surface as we witness the flowering of children into fuller sexual self-expression.

As a child delves into the reaches of their natural-born pleasure within the wilds of embodied play, any adults in the room need to take a breath, reassuring their younger selves that they can handle what's going on. A gesture like a smile or a nod can communicate to a child (or participating parent) that all is well. In a later parent-only session, a therapist can help parents sort through their child's process, bringing any observations from it into the family framework, so the child can be better received and their development nurtured rather than rejected.

This said, most parents I've encountered want their kids to be socialized into a level of containment proximate to the parents' interpretation of what is acceptable to them. But for kids who need to explore what they are beginning to sense and feel, the journey may involve a good deal of "getting down and dirty." My part of the therapeutic bargain is to stay centered and open as these children explore.

"Butt Training" from Seven-year-old Zara

Coming from a strict, Modern Orthodox Jewish household, Zara was described as highly anxious and exceedingly soft-spoken in her responses. The intensity of the NYC neighborhood where she lived had her hanging onto both her parents and often refusing school attendance that would take her away from home. Zara had bad dreams about shadowy figures looming over her. It would be particularly important to create a receptive space for whatever Zara needed to express. We decided in an initial parents-only session that Mom's presence could help Zara feel comfortable in her daughter's first session. With a new baby due soon, Mom wasn't as available to her daughter as before. I wanted to bring these two together early on, reflecting the closeness of their original connection.

First Session with Mom and Zara

Mom seems extremely anxious at the door of my office, so my initial inclination to do a mother-daughter session is confirmed. I want to scope out their dynamic and what Zara may do with the variety of Embodied Play Therapy offerings. She doesn't appear interested in my more movement-friendly possibilities. No exercise ball, punching gloves, or mini-trampoline. So, I hand Zara some markers for drawing. She draws a composite man/woman and tells me, "It's you," and begins talking about "cleaning butts." Mom appears shocked.

Zara moves over to the sandbox, picks horses and a married couple from my figure collection on the shelves, then buries them in the sand. Zara, observing the puzzled expression on her mom's face, wants to uncover the couple she's buried. Mom helps. Is Zara picking up on Mom's anxiety about her daughter's out-there-ness? At the end of the session, Zara wants to step into the sandbox in her socks, and she does!

In the following sessions, Zara explored what it was like to be on her own without Mom, testing whether I'd react to the increasingly visceral and dramatic nature of her play. Crawling on all fours through my play tunnel, then zipping out to engage me in a battle with encounter bats. Pushing every stick of furniture in my office to one side of the room, which she tells me is "my side!" Grabbing my "magic wand" and turning me into a "frog."

While there's more to tell of what happened with Zara, it was becoming clear she was getting more comfortable seeing that, far from being a disapproving presence, I would accept whatever she was willing to bring. That comfort was reflected in the story she dictated to me soon after this first whirlwind of in-session activity.

Zara's story:

> *One day, Neal went to teach butt training.*
>
> *He teaches butt training because he wants his butt to get bigger and his belly to get fatter. And he wants to die soon. And he started yelling at one of the butt trainers. He said, "You need a bigger butt!"*
>
> *So we had to stay at the butt training club all day long. So he did it for a whole day and for 100 days, and then he could be done with butt training and go to the next level. Since he got yelled at, there are 100 classes to go. After butt training, he got ice cream. Then he died because he worked so hard, and he had a fat belly and a fat butt.*
>
> *And that is the end.*

I've been writing furiously as Zara speaks, and after I read it back to her, she wants to hold another battle. According to Zara, it's between "Miss Perfect" and me as "the mean one." Zara is yelling as she attacks, a red encounter bat in hand. As the battle continues, I mirror back her loudness, aligning my energy with hers. She seems to love it and finally knocks the encounter bat out of my hand. Zara then writes a note to me, which she gives me at the end of the session.

"But you have a big butt, you big poop. I love you, stay cool, my yucky poop Neal poop."

Zara likely benefited from a forum where younger places in herself might reign for a time. All this "butt talk," which might have been frowned on at home, didn't lead me to throw her out my door. My guess is that her first battle was an inner one around her fascination with body parts and whether she would be judged as "bad" or not. Once expressed, Zara's impulses needed the reassurance of my acceptance. The final step that Zara moved into immediately was the encounter bat duel with me that served to ground the excited energy she'd generated in all the butt talking, drawing, and affection-filled outreach to me.

In instances like this, I try to have a specific follow-up with parents around the value of a child feeling parental "resonance" with the oftentimes breathtakingly fast-moving ins and outs of children's fantasy lives. Fantasy lives in which they may revisit times past and present and which may find us blushing, smiling, shocked, or stunned in delight. In Zara's case, I failed to get both parents together for this discussion, but I did communicate with the Dad. Later, I advised the Mom to investigate her reactions to Zara's embodied play process with her individual therapist, who was helping her explore restrictive aspects of her upbringing.

While Zara and Mom had other things to process as her therapy proceeded, it looked like Zara and her therapist were "cool." She began to resolve some of her issues. Among them was allowing a teenage sitter to watch her when her mom headed out for work. Zara began using her voice more. She spoke up when noisy, chaotic environments bothered her, and her parents really listened. They bought headphones for her to wear when needed outside in the city. Opening to parts of herself that might have frightened her, partly because they were not easily accepted at home, Zara's nightmares abated. This girl, who'd been battling with impulse and uncertainty around bodies, found some relief. After a few months, she finished therapy and moved on to training in martial arts.

"Pants Alert!" What Children Wear to Embodied Play Therapy Sessions

Parents may fear talking about bodies and developing sexuality with children, regardless of their age. The good news is that Embodied Play Therapy often provides an opening to broach such topics with a child. Because it's so activating for their young bodies, excited kids create in-session scenarios that help a therapist bring discussion about bodies and body integrity into the therapy room – dealing directly with any queasiness that may come up for parent or child in the moment.

> *Six-year-old Eric blitzes in.... and asks me whether I want to see his underpants, pulling his jeans down an inch. An opportunity to have the conversation. I tell him there are things that you do at home that you do not do in public. I pop my head into the waiting room and ask his mom to join us. We talk about safety. Mom agrees that if an adult wants to see your underpants, you say "No."*

One of my colleagues who works a good deal with adolescent kids, Tracey Masella, reminds me about the sexually explicit content children may be seeing on the internet today. Content is viewed, if not in their own homes, then in the homes of other children, which may contain older siblings or have more lax policies on media and screen usage. When sex is objectified, a child's sense of themselves veers away from reality and headlong toward confusion.

I view Embodied Play Therapy as one support for a child to build well-rounded acceptance of body, mind, and their imagination, resources they can use as they seek relationships in adolescence and partnerships as adults. When parents display disapproval of what their child expresses in the realm of body awareness, the parents risk unbalancing that child's already unsteady equilibrium. In any case, it's almost guaranteed that the scales will tilt the other way when peer power replaces parents as a behaviorally motivating force. Intuiting the reality that's coming, parents and children benefit from open dialogue in pre-adolescence about what is present today.

I'm also proactive with parents around issues of body integrity and developing sexuality as it relates to the outfits their children should wear for Embodied Play Therapy sessions. The headline here is: Your children will be jumping, running, climbing up and over, and into things. They need to have maximum freedom to move. I don't think exposing their underwear or parts of their bodies while sitting in the sand or crawling through a semi-transparent tunnel is a good idea. So, send your children to their sessions in gym-appropriate sweatpants or shorts!

But of course, complications inevitably arise, as in the time a girl came in wearing sweatpants so ill-fitting that they were constantly slipping down. I requested that her mother join us in the office, rather than play the part of parent myself. A bit red-faced, Mom began talking with her daughter about the need to keep "clothes on straight." I thought Mom felt guilty in some way for somehow failing to send the child dressed in pants that would stay up. But I didn't want to shame her in front of her child. As I paused, a solution was concocted almost immediately by the daughter, who wanted to continue having fun and had only one pair of sweatpants to play in that day. With her mom still sitting in the session, each time she noticed the loose elastic band beginning to sag, she called out "PANTS ALERT!" and pulled her sweatpants up. She was delighted with her temporary solution. And while Mom had to endure a bit of blushing in my presence, the problem was solved. That child never came in with loose-fitting pants again!

Abuse in the Family System

Multiple children have shown up in my practice, sons and daughters of parents who were themselves abused, either physically, emotionally, or sexually as children. Some parents were slapped or spanked into submission. Some came from households where screaming was a major communication mode or where bodies were violated by adults, siblings, or others. As I work with these families, there's an opportunity to break an intergenerational pattern of unconsciousness or silence. Many parent victims, not having fully dealt with the impact of their past, are unaware of how their child may be enacting a clear call for boundaries around body integrity through play.

I ask in my intake form whether anyone in the family system has been a victim of any kind of abuse. I began noticing how what children wore to their sessions had an uncanny correlation to one of their parents' having had some abuse history. This showed up in the form of girls wearing dresses prone to flying over their heads on a mini trampoline and riding up over their hips in the sandbox, the "Pants Alert!" girl, and the boy who wanted to show me his underwear earlier in this chapter. It often took multiple requests on my part to have a child sent to sessions in clothing appropriate for an active level of embodied play, but this has also, in multiple instances, led to something very useful – a parent-only discussion about how I saw their child enacting an echo of abuse in the system and the need children have for environments where their bodies are respected.

Before continuing, I need to let you know that in my own childhood, there were instances where my father used his belt to "strap" my behind. I remember tears and shame. Today, as a mandated reporter in cases where abuse might be suspected, I have spoken with more than one parent regarding the impact on children who get hit to force them to comply.

Even though corporal means of discipline may be prevalent in many cultures and many households, my stance is to stop such behavior. Children may lack the means to defend their bodies against incursions by larger humans. There may even be debate about the unquestioned primacy of parent power. But I see the impact on adults who were once children in such family systems where perpetrators remained in place because silence ruled. Whenever possible, the cycle ends with the child in Embodied Play Therapy.

> *I'm speaking to the parents of a child, who tell me he sometimes gets spanked when he misbehaves. In this parent-only session, the dad tells me, "You should have seen what happened to me when I was a kid." I advise Dad to work through in his individual therapy what it felt like for him as a child, because he may be minimizing the effects of even an occasional spanking on his son. We talk about how his own frayed nervous system may be at play, along with other repressed emotions, including*

helplessness, when he uses his hands as a last resort rather than his heart. I ask Dad to place his hands on his belly, exhale air out with the help of his hands pushing his abdomen, and take a deep breath in, feeling his belly expand. I've taught this to Dad in a session together with his son before. What's new is the question I ask him now: "What would it be like if you took a pause when your son's acting out and took a breath?" Remember what it was like for you when you got hit. I see tears welling up in Dad's eyes. In a follow-up phone call with Dad, he reports that spanking has stopped. That he's working through his reactions and emotions with his individual therapist.

An Exercise in Boundaries for a Child

I've adapted an exercise portrayed by psychotherapists Pat Ogden, Bonnie Goldstein, and Janina Fisher for children whose perception of safety has been compromised, such that they are subject to hypo-arousal (2013, pp. 236, 239) or hyper-arousal and thus overly aggressive (p. 243). They suggest inviting a child to place a rope on the floor at a distance of their choosing around their bodies (pp. 236, 239). In the case of hypo-arousal, where a child tends to be passive, a large ball is rolled slowly into the circle, and a child can talk about their feelings as the ball crosses the rope boundary circling them. Afterwards, that same child might challenge their low energy by pushing or kicking the ball away. For a child who tends toward more hyper-arousal and "fight" energy, the child might use their voice and arms to deliver the message "Get Out" (p. 243).

Seven-year-old Benjamin is being physically bullied on the bus that takes him to summer day camp. While his parents have spoken with the camp directors, Benjamin's body is pendulating from the fight response that would have him hitting back and the more frozen space that had him entering my office for his session, a bit glassy-eyed, his shoulders elevated in a posture of self-defense. In front of Benjamin, I pulled out a length of blue string three to four times his height and asked him to imagine he could create a "circle of safety" surrounding him. We experimented with the shape and size of the string boundary, and he stepped in. I knew that even though the bullying had stopped and the child who'd hit him had been permanently transferred to another bus, Benjamin was still holding the energy of what had happened inside.

I ask Benjamin: "How could you use your hands to deliver a message to Danny (the kid who'd hit him) to stop? Benjamin held up his hands, palms facing me. "How could you use your voice?" Benjamin says, "Stop!"

It seems for the moment, enough. Last week, when I'd first heard about the camp bus bullying incident in session, we'd discussed what would have happened if Benjamin had hit back. He knew that he'd be in trouble with his parents. Benjamin steps out of the circle and towards a waiting hunk of clay and two rubber-headed mallets. He wants to build "monsters." He tells me I'm to build exactly what I'd created the week prior – "a transmitter." Last week, my "transmitter" was being used to call Benjamin's parents to the bus (my idea of what Benjamin wanted.) This week, Benjamin tells me my transmitter will call his friends. He pounds the clay flat with a mallet, rips it into smaller hunks, and rolls it out into the multiple legs of what looks like a spider.

Reflection: I sense that Benjamin is still processing what happened on the bus, but his processing has entered a new realm where feelings held in the body can be expressed by gesture, by voice, and through crafting something with his hands that will transmit both internal communications from his body and external messages to reach others.

Notes on Gender Fluidity from an Embodied Play Therapist

I write from the perspective of one older cisgender straight male witnessing what I see as growing variety and fluidity in gender expression and sexual preference among the young people I've worked with. In my caseload over the last 15 years, I've noted that kids who came out openly as anything other than straight did so at ages of 14 and over. While adolescents over the age of 13 are not the topic of this book, I'm becoming increasingly alarmed by societal intolerance and what I've observed in parental repression of children's self-expression in these areas. From the standpoint of this book, here's why I'm especially concerned. According to The Trevor Project's 2023 National Survey on LGBTQ Youth Mental Health, the age of "coming out" to share one's sexual orientation or gender identity with other people is getting significantly younger. Further, The Trevor Project said in 2022 that more than half of LGBTQ youth who came out before age 13 (56%) seriously considered suicide in the past year, vs 42% who came out afterwards (The Trevor Project, 2022).

Here's a case example where I believe parental attitudes contributed to distress in a child who presented as gender fluid. The parents were primarily concerned he'd been exposed to sexually explicit media content.

Eight-year-old Jackson and his mom show up in my NYC office wearing the same color nail polish. All of Mom's nails are done up, along with a few fingers on each of Jackson's hands. His parents are very upset because the older brother of his best friend has shown the younger boys some pornography, and now all he wants to do is talk about sex, which the parents say is "inappropriate for his age." Jackson's stomach upsets are constant, and he's been telling his parents that he's evil. The parents aren't telling me what kind of sex their son is talking about. No one besides me is saying anything about the nail polish, and what that could be expressing.

I ask the parents to check in with the parents of Jackson's friends, where he'd seen the explicit internet content. But they don't like that idea. "Too embarrassing," they say. With the parents' permission, I call the school. Seems he's been exposing himself in class, and the guidance counselor tells me he's been having panic attacks at home. Mom and Dad are disagreeing on what to do next because they have different parenting styles. Mom came from a family where "you got your mouth washed out with soap" if you said a curse word, and Dad, more permissive, just wants his son to get through what he calls "this difficult period."

I meet with the parents in person without their son. Mom wants me to help negotiate a deal with Jackson, so he won't say bad words. Dad is concerned that Jackson is playing with Barbie Dolls. I ask the parents about what age kids today get connected with the parts of them that want to explore sexually. Mom says, "14 or 15?" I say, "Age four or five or so is when kids get especially curious." The parents look shocked.

Session with Dad and Eight-year-old Jackson

I hand Dad a padded shield, and Jackson gets boxing gloves. After I explain the rules, "Don't hurt yourself," "Don't hurt me," and "Don't hurt the room," at my suggestion, Jackson punches with Dad holding a padded shield in front of him.

But the son's blows seem lacking in energy. He stops after about 10 hits. Tossing the boxing gloves aside, Jackson and Dad move to the sandbox for what the son says is "Jackson versus the Dad-ians." Jackson brings "a lava thing" (a plastic miniature volcano) into the sandbox and buries it in the center of the box. Dad just wants to "Bring peace to all. Everyone lives in harmony." Jackson dumps a large plastic shark into the box. Dad perches a bird on top of one of the box's sidewalls as "a lookout watching for anyone doing something illegal." Jackson grabs the figures he and his dad have placed in the box. He buries them all and then digs them all up from the sand. Heaping sand in one corner of the box, Jackson builds a mountain.

Neal to Jackson:	What do you want from coming here?
Jackson:	I don't know. I'm here because I did bad things
Neal:	I know you've seen things. High school and college kids have YouTube channels…

FIGURE 5.1 Child punches a padded shield held by an adult.

Jackson:	The librarians at school spy on kids to see what we're watching there.

Dad and Jackson look at each other. Dad looks shocked.

In the next in-person session, I bring Mom together with her son. I show the two how kids hold their breath to control anxiety, and Jackson tries draping his body over an exercise ball to feel his breath and calm. Standing next to my sandbox, Mom and Jackson, and I have a discussion.

Neal:	Kids have thoughts and fantasies. (*To Jackson*) Can you go to your parents to tell them about your thoughts?
Jackson:	Yes
Mom to Jackson:	Did anyone touch you? A teacher?
Neal:	An older kid?
Jackson:	No.
Neal:	Will you tell Mom and Dad if that were to happen?
Jackson:	Yes
Neal:	Parents get worried. *(Looking from Jackson and turning to Mom)* Is it OK for Jackson to come and talk to you?
Mom:	Yes

Reflection: What was really going on here? I wanted to learn more. But the bottom line was that there seemed to be a lot unspoken in this family and a limited desire to dig deeper. After a few sessions, Jackson's parents pulled him from therapy. I guessed that they were too uncomfortable with discussing Jackson's emerging sexuality. Lacking control, they decided to explore other options.

When young people try on different identities that conflict with their parents ideas on how a boy or girl should be, these kids often end up in pain. I've seen kids who want to run away. Kids who end up abusing substances to self-medicate in adolescence. Parents who send their kids away to boarding schools, to psychiatrists, and to hospitals, as the family tries to grapple with acting out behaviors often rooted in the family's own difficulty coming to terms with a variety of human expression in its midst.

At the center of so many family dilemmas is discomfort around bodies, sex, and how we nurture the next generation of humans into fuller function in a world that desperately needs their gifts. All this in a shifting climate of gender fluidity and sexual expression, crashing head-on with cultural and societal norms that haven't kept up. When conflict over change migrates to confusion within families, children can get caught in the crossfire. In the end, these struggles are about bodies. How we use them and who we use them with. Embodied Play Therapy with children opens doors to sensation and links a child to the meanderings of imagination. Such imaginal journeys offer fertile ground for children whose self-expression is subject to change. Therein lies the magic of this work, which allows for deep forms of play. How deep a child goes on the journey of self-discovery has less to do with how many sessions their parents sign them up for and more with how much creativity their bodies will allow to blossom. And, how far their families will allow them to travel. A tale of a child awakening to themselves will happen in that child's own time. Not in mine. Therapeutic presence and parental powers may be accompanying witnesses on the path, but in the end, the child will serve as the leader, pointing the way forward.

References

Ogden, P., Goldstein, B., & Fisher, J.. (2013). Brain-to-Brain, Body-to-Body: A Sensorimotor Psychotherapy Perspective on the Treatment of Children and Adolescents. In R. E Longo, D.S. Prescott, J. Bergman, & K. Creeden (Eds.), *Current Perspective & Applications in Neurobiology: Working with Young Persons Who Are Victims and Perpetrators of Sexual Abuse* (pp. 229–258). Neari Press.

Reich, W. M. (1983). *Children of the Future: On the Prevention of Sexual Pathology*. Farrar, Strauss, Giroux. (Original work published 1950)

The Trevor Project. (2022). *The 2022 National Survey of LGBTQ Youth and Mental Health*. https://www.thetrevorproject.org/research-briefs/age-of-sexual-orientation-outness-and-suicide-risk-oct-2022/

The Trevor Project (2023). *The 2023 National Survey of LGBTQ Youth and Mental Health*. https://www.thetrevorproject.org/research-briefs/age-of-gender-identity-outness-and-suicide-risk-mar-2023/

6

Moving toward Balance through Selected Methods in Embodied Play Therapy

So much of a child's world these days is caught up in outdoing others and competition. This is the reality for our anxious children today in an anxious age, where they must grapple with the twin tasks of what developmental psychologist Erik H. Erikson saw as seminal in building toward adolescence. Be recognized in school or by parents for their "industry" – what they produce, and avoiding the "inferiority" they will inevitably feel should their production not stack up against that of others in their cohort (Erikson, 1959/1994, p. 91). The adults are watching, and the children know it.

The struggle to achieve can be traumatic for many children and for parents who hope to contribute to their success. When you add parental difficulties, including battles to balance partnership and parenthood, self-care, work, and responsibilities for their own aging or infirm parents, you have major challenges on your hands. Into this anxious mix, Embodied Play Therapy offers growth for children, parents, and new possibilities for critically important parent-child relationships that will model what children will choose to do and how they will live their lives in connection with others as they move into adolescence.

DOI: 10.4324/9781003328186-8

First, in an age where children are often more *out* of than *in* their bodies, we are building fluency with what it feels like to be more fully in a moving, breathing, and feeling body. To move for the joy of moving, to breathe deeply because we feel better when we do, and to sense the electric flow of feeling and impulse coursing through one's being. Doing this in the presence of a therapist, parent, or both is to have a felt sense of being seen. And having felt taken in from a heartfelt place by one adult or more, it often becomes possible to move on from symptoms that have nagged at a child or plagued a parent. Then, moving forward to new and productive ways of being that might not have been envisioned if the journeys in play children embarked on, such as those in this book, never happened.

Let's be honest here. Most children are in a battle to produce what parents and schools expect. What these children have been taught is the need to fit a certain version of themselves into the sometimes tight containers of family and classroom. Many children bridle against such constraints. Should we not teach children to "play nice?" Isn't there a risk when aggression is engaged that it will bubble up beyond any control after a child has left the therapy room?

My answer and experience say "No." There is a power for a child in being seen, and children know when a therapist is willing to dive down with them to discover what's underneath the trouble that brought them. When everything's in play, anything becomes possible. What seems mean and nasty in a sand world, or a battle between monsters drawn or sculpted, or a wrestling match between a dad and his son, turns most often into something much more peaceful and valuable because it's been engaged with. That engagement supports connection. Connection with self and connection with others. That is what family is meant to provide and what societies that hope to survive need to promote. Still, we need to hold this lightly because getting too serious about play threatens its healing potential. As a therapist, my goal is to embody a spirit of authenticity, acceptance, and appreciation for all types of zeal, including competitive and destructive impulses which surface in play. Surfaced so they can be felt, accepted, and balanced as part of the full spectrum of being human.

Building and Falling

What is the stance of Embodied Play Therapy for children facing confrontation with their developing selves? Children for whom the only certainty is constant change? All of this sounds so serious! And yet, I believe it need not be. If nothing else, playing with children needs to be fun, and to pull that off, a therapist needs to reach first for some connection with the kid inside themselves and be willing to go full out in joining a child in the wild scenarios they will inevitably concoct.

A therapist may offer lots of varied activities, equipment to move and breathe on, props to play with, and a variety of formats to create in, from drawing to clay to sand worlds, but it's the child's energy and enthusiasm for what's being presented that adds life to what otherwise could be dreary. Let's face it. Part of what drives humans is competition, and Embodied Play Therapy is willing to provoke it when needed. How high we build before our tower of blocks falls down, how long we can balance belly down on an exercise ball before we topple over, how many times we hit or whack a punching bag versus the child whose initials are in the lead on your Embodied Play Therapist's chart – all of this could be grounds for feeling bad about yourself unless the goal is something different.

The goal in all this building and falling is not winning a competition or fight with yourself or with others; it is constructing a relationship with parts of yourself you may not have known you had. A growing fluency with your own breath and body. A joy in digging deep to bury and then uncover treasure in a cave you've created in a mountain of sand. If a child needs to battle to find or balance their own enthusiastic nature, such engagement is more than worthwhile. Worthwhile because all of the activities that have children eager to create something bigger, or taller, or wilder represent the urge toward identity and expression of life force. In Embodied Play Therapy, the impetus is to harness impulse, stir up a story, and give the child an experience of what it feels like to find one's ground and balance one's energy in the moment.

There is nothing like the pure delight of connecting with oneself and others in play. Kids notice the drawings of monsters by other children covering a wall in my office. They often get inspired, vying for the most monstrous. It's similar to the young people who ask if anyone has beaten their record in a particular contest. I respect those kids and parents who don't like to compete, but may challenge certain children who hold themselves back, reticent to engage in competition because they're afraid their growing competence might upset others.

Here are some of the ways it's done.

Balancing on Your Belly

Teaching a kid how to breathe diaphragmatically in the natural way of infants becomes critically important in situations where they have been subjected to trauma. Children learn to hold their stomach muscles tight to suppress painful emotions. Assaults, whether verbal, physical, sexual, auditory, or visual (including observation of another's abuse), destabilize a child, sometimes dramatically. In-session breathing exercises can begin to unstick a traumatized kid from states of hyper- or hypo-arousal and return them to feelings of well-being. Dennis McCarthy, the creator of Dynamic Play Therapy, first introduced me to the practice of timing a young client as they balanced face down on an exercise ball.

> *Ten-year-old Perry, habitually witnessing his parents' pattern of verbal outbursts at each other, learned he could deflect these altercations by hitting his younger sister. Like a lightning rod, his behavior diverted attention from parental conflict. This very tightly wound child took well to the Balancing-on-your-belly contest, in the process learning to feel the breath in his abdomen pushing against the exercise ball. As he balanced and breathed, he began to calm. With his frequent outbursts no longer offering a distraction from the primary conflict in this family system, his parents entered couples therapy with my encouragement.*

Hitting Contest

Therapist Dennis McCarthy, who introduced me to his idea of "hitting contests" (2012, p. 149), has told me that when a kid hits 100 or more times with a bataka or lightweight hollow plastic bat, their life changes. The child in my practice, currently in the lead, has 1,350 hits. While many children like to compete and begin a session asking me if anyone has beaten their record, some veer away from it, especially younger clients. For this reason, I tend to introduce the hitting contest, where competition is with past kids who've participated, to those in the 9- to 13-year-old age group.

As I scan down the vertical column of children's initials who participated in my hitting contest over the years, I remember children heading to my basket of hitting implements, some with deliberation, others with trepidation, to pull out what would soon be held in their hands as they stood poised next to the foam cube before them.

I see hands held together across the handle of what I call their "weapon of choice."

- I see the child who was satisfied with ten solid hits.
- Another who needed 1,350 hits completed over a full 45 minutes to express the pounding he felt inside.
- The proud child who scrawled his initials on my chart in big letters after besting his own record of 300 hits.
- The timid child who asked me to inscribe his initials after 30.
- A 13-year-old boy, criticized by parents at home, who used my heaviest bataka to experience what freedom felt like. This boy who couldn't open his mouth at home but hit again and again, looking down and intoning like a mantra of breath and sound and movement. "No... No...No..." The vibration of the bataka against the cube loosens taut muscles, his words sending healing pulses of energy down from his gyrating arms all the way down to his feet. This boy, who fought back by shutting down in

school, shifted after a few sessions from cutting classes to sticking with them.

- An 11-year-old girl whose divorced parents couldn't agree on much except that she needed therapy walked in with the words "I've just gotta hit something" and found a way to unbottle the helplessness she felt inside.
- A 12-year-old girl failing in school who didn't want to be sent away to boarding school, opening herself to getting the academic help that would amplify her strengths.
- A 10-year-old boy in the shadow of his accomplished high school sister, who needed to find his balance and hit again and again, the sibilance of "YES" like some powerful whisper of his unique gifts and growing confidence.
- A 9-year-old girl who stumbled in, wanting to run away from her anxious parents, and did. She found a way through active movement and story to get in touch with her fears and stay put.

"Try hitting a few times," as I say to the kids, especially the ones who will only hit for a minute or less – "Each one harder than the last!"

Arms pumping together way up and over the head and then down on the cube. Whack, whack, whack…I record the numbers. But it's not only the numbers on my chart that count. It's the integration of embodied movement, breath, and feeling. The impact of sensing oneself in the pulsation of one's own presence.

Mountain and Cave Building (in Sandbox)

Moistened play sand gets stacked up. The only limit is how much sand a box contains!

The mystery: what will the young person place on top? A communication tower to contact a divorced Dad whom a kid yearns to see? A tiger to face down the pain of perfectionism? A crystal-clear diamond to see through to a brighter future? This is also a great technique to build containment and a sense of structure for kids who just want to throw things around. Creating something massive adds a certain weight to things. Think of a kid with untethered energy who, like a balloon, can fly off without something to anchor them to the earth. Mountain building provides a strong base for sandplay figures to defend turf at different elevations, ascend heights, and achieve summits. Mountains also offer fertile ground for caves that can be built into them, for figures to wait in safety until they, like their child creators, are ready to emerge.

Block Building: Cooperation, Contests, and Crashes

Block structures can be built by kids without my assistance while I watch admiringly during in-person sessions. But for live video Embodied Play Therapy, if a child doesn't have their own set of blocks at home, the therapist becomes the builder! It's one thing when the inevitable happens and a block structure a child has built themselves crashes down. It's another when a structure I've built at the direction of a child in a remote session falls because I've placed a block somewhat haphazardly, creating a shaky foundation. For me, it's sometimes high anxiety, especially if the structure suddenly comes crashing down. No matter what, kids seem to love the downfall of the blocks that've been balanced. They love to do the pushing themselves for in-person block building, direct when it will happen, and delight in the consternation on an adult's face when the clumsiness of a therapist or parent is on full display!

One eleven-year old online architect guided me, balancing on a step ladder, to build a tower that reached seven feet before commanding, "3-2-1 knock it down!"

Unbalancing: Turning Things Upside Down and Coming Out the Other Side

If you asked me to consider the seed at the center of Embodied Play Therapy, one of my answers would be that this modality of support for children and parents allows the turning of the way things seem upside down. In play, children are the experts. We adults and parents who cling to authority are often suddenly, and sometimes to our chagrin, knocked down a notch during the process of play. Witnessing a child's growing power as seen in their facility with symbols in sandplay, with mashing clay or attempting a drawing of something monstrous, and even in defeating parents' attempts to mold them into an image that does not fit – these are humbling experiences for any adult, whether therapist or parent. And in that humility is a truth. A truth that children will be moving ahead in directions we can only hope to glimpse.

Will they learn that grabbing in greed, while often satisfying a momentary impulse, produces resentment in others and generates fear that we may not be able to hold onto what we've gained? In Embodied Play Therapy, we engage many impulses, even destructive ones, because childhood growth is often fostered when we assist children to uncover their most unsettled places. It doesn't all have to look nice. There will be other dance steps in play in the lives we are preparing children for. The dance of power. The dance of "me." And the dance of experiencing "us" in play, whether the "us" is child and therapist or child and parent with therapist as ally for both.

As I watch children block-building or creating worlds in the sand, I notice how so many seem so relaxed. I see how my capacity for play may have been limited as I grew further from childhood. Ways of being I am only re-learning now through my work with children. I did not grow up as a "digital native" schooled in the speed and frequent violence of today's video games and combat-rich social media platforms. My nervous system requires recalibration to higher tolerance levels for "crash," so I can help anxious kids better learn to calm down. Staying attuned to fast-moving creative kids in Embodied Play Therapy continues to be a fruitful source of my accelerated re-education!

Taking on the role of assistant to a child, whether that's asking a child whether they want a mountain or a cave in the sand and then fetching the water that will help them build that mountain higher or dig that cave deeper, calms a part of me that felt anxious as a child. Adult cooperation in the building of a mountain in a sand world, or a tower of blocks reaching for the ceiling or the sky, often engenders heightened calm in a child. A structure rises from cooperative effort, with the kid as boss, reversing the more customary adult-to-child hierarchy of instruction.

In any case, a child client experiences the satisfaction of their therapist/play partner working diligently in the assistant role, measuring the height of their block structure with a tape measure, appreciating their innovation and willingness to experiment, no matter the height or stability. When a parent gets involved in play, the willingness of that parent to parry in a sand world battle, to joust in the service of joint enterprise, even when the result is parental obliteration in the face of an unstoppable child onslaught – it can be a vital step toward a durable connection between child and parent. A family therapist's dream.

References

Erikson, E. H. (1994). *Identity and the Life Cycle.* W.W. Norton. (Original work published 1959)

McCarthy, D. (2012). *A Manual of Dynamic Play Therapy: Helping Things Fall Apart, the Paradox of Play.* Jessica Kingsley Publishers.

7

Deepening Narrative

It's not so much the length of time a child spends in Embodied Play Therapy as it is the ability to dive into their own depths that predicts movement toward healing. Birthing oneself anew in ways that parents, teachers, friends, and other family members notice as growth in a good way often sprouts as children seed stories into their play. Characters they invent to populate narratives to accompany their play serve as experimental alter-egos for new selves soon to emerge. Children craft in clay, draw monstrous creatures capable of amazing feats, spawn worlds of figures in a deep sandbox, and battle a parent or their therapist, often in the service of something larger. Mysteries may be harvested from the dream spaces inside a child, keys to a child's future plumbed from the depths of their stories.

Before looking further at school-age children on their journeys in Embodied Play Therapy, let's again consider where they began. A human fetus in the womb floats in liquid, grasping and propelling toward what will, after birth, be air outside. Most often, children presented for therapy are in a regressed state, lacking the emotional balance parents expect for their age. It makes sense then that Embodied Play Therapy permits a child to utilize materials that draw their attention to the power of the tactile, among their earliest senses, which fosters outreach toward sources of safety and sustenance that lie beyond the body.

When a child works with clay or in the deep sandbox, they are engaging the upper torso and neurological transmission

DOI: 10.4324/9781003328186-9

stemming from arms and hands to the heart, abdominal, and thoracic centers, where muscular tension limits inhalation, holding feelings at bay. I believe that much of what I do as a body-centered therapist is about opening closed hearts to a deeper range of emotion and expression. The enlivening heartbeat pumps oxygen into the system, fuel for our emotions, and all we undertake. The transmission fibers of our nervous system spool from the chest cavity outward to hands that touch and shape, hands that bring us what we seek and push away from us the unwanted (Pierrakos, 1990).

As a theorist, clinician, and educator, Stanley Keleman has written in his book *Embodying Experience: Forming a Personal Life*:

> In growing up, we make form by shaping our feelings. When, as children, we are intimidated or criticized by adults, we slump in, withdraw, shrink, become small. We create a form that communicates smallness or humiliation. Or we respond to criticism with defiance, rebellion, anger, or contempt, warning off the attack by stiffening and bracing. Thus, feeling creates our form while form keeps certain feelings intact. (1987, p. 34)

Embodied Play Therapy is a quest to cultivate inner pathways for self-exploration early before access is blocked by habitual somatic-supported defenses. The goal is to have kids better able to sense what feels right to and for them, to reclaim their center in fast-moving and not always friendly environments. To find a connection with the physical core of the body, such that a belly stiffened in rigid response to everyday stressors, can relax and let go into flow, into the give and take, and the rough and tumble interactions that might destabilize an ungrounded child.

As children extend their hands and arms, manipulating and molding clay or sand into newly envisioned forms, they lend their excitement and energy to what was just moments ago, inert and still. The mountain or cave dug into the sand, the multiheaded monster emerging from a brick of soft clay, speaks beyond childhood limitations of vocabulary. The material becomes language. Communication within the body, within the self, and with others grows.

As they gain experience in a therapy that has them moving, breathing, feeling, and going full out in play, sessions develop a rhythm. Sometimes chosen activities are repeated. Other times, a new mood strikes. The molding and battling with clay monsters may not attract them as it once did. A child may suddenly throw down the clay or a drawing and move on to something new. This shift, which can be sudden, often coincides with a deepening of narratives that accompany a child's play. Narratives related to why they came to therapy in the first place. Narratives that may relieve them of burdens they would prefer to process and put down.

Sometimes, the narrative that will cut through to a child's core issues doesn't surface for some time. In other instances, the message in the material rises up in an instant to face down anything in its path.

Getting to the "Meat of the Matter" – A Younger Child Breaks through in Clay

Six-year-old Geraldine spoke with a lisp so severe it was hard to understand her words. But her hands shaped a sharper story. A lump of clay she flattened with a black rubber-headed mallet turned into a monster that was all mouth. As she worked, I sat beside her, making my own monster whose big feet and body were no match for this little girl's monstrous maw that devoured mine in moments, incorporating its entire substance into a massive blob of victory. Geraldine, smiling at me sweetly, glanced up at her mother, who'd been silently observing us from a child-sized wooden stool across the room. I could see that Mom, the family's preoccupied primary breadwinner and newly minted bottlewasher for Geraldine's new baby brother at home, wanted in on the action. I invited her down to the cardboard on the carpet that held the chunked remains of my defeat at her daughter's hands.

As her mom began building, Geraldine made a new monster with two very long arms. I knew Geraldine, shunted off weekdays to her Connecticut grade school, had mixed feelings as she waved goodbye to her mom, baby in arms, from the bus window. Today, witnessing her mom putting the final touches on a heavy-bellied monster, Geraldine asked me for more clay. Amazed, I watched as her small hands powered into the torso of her newly built monster and squeezed it, arms and all, into a single snake, which she used to corral her mother's monster.

Reflection: I told her Mom after the session that I'd never seen a more powerful message of a child missing a parent than what Geraldine had created. Depth of desire clarified in clay. A reaching out to this parent beyond what any words from her child might convey. The drama had its effect. Mom engaged part-time help for the baby so she could spend some quality hours with Geraldine.

Tales of Two Children in Their Own Deep Sandboxes

Often, after a child experiences success in feeling their power to influence and invigorate a parent-child bond, they circle back to core conflicts that still haunt them. Whether it's the loss of status that comes when there's a younger child in the family or the loss of parents who once lived together but no longer do, there's usually a deep desire to dig down into the pain of it all, because, given the opportunity in Embodied Play Therapy, it's just too good to miss the theatrics of a play where you can create the ending!

Ricky, Seven Years Old – Burying a Difficult Attitude in the Depths Leads to Positive Change

(See more on Ricky's play in Chapter 3: Building A Bridge to a Child, Chapter 4: Parents in the Mix, and Chapter 8: Completions.)

Ricky jumps into the sandbox in my office. Pointing to figures for me to throw to him, he catches all I lob to his waiting hands. Then he begins to place them carefully down onto the surface of the sand. When I ask, he tells me the story reflecting his inner conflict: To share, or NOT to share his toys with his interloping younger brother, who also wants to play with them and him.

Neal transcribes Ricky's words about his sand world and reads it back to him in session like a poem.

(As Ricky places a shark, rhinoceros, seal, alligator, and a dinosaur in the sand)

Ricky: These guys are fighting for the "legendary bridge."
They really want it and don't want to share it.

Reflection: Just like Ricky needs to voice his need to NOT share his toys or his room with an interloping younger brother.

Ricky: *(Pointing to a dragon and a tiny turtle near the "NO-Share" group of fighters – the shark, rhinoceros, seal, alligator, and dinosaur)*
The other team **Wants-to-share** *(dragon, tiny turtle)*
The shark tries to beat the tiny turtle, but he can't because the turtle has a shell.
He lands on the shell, and it hurts.

Reflection: "It hurts" like Ricky hurts when called out for his "bad" behavior by his parents or his own powerful inner critic.

Ricky: The shark's face is stuck in the ground.
The seal's butt is stuck in the ground.
The alligator is stuck in the ground.

Reflection: The "NO-share" team is stuck, buried in their refusal to share and the need to maintain that and no other position. Something Ricky is torn about. He tells me: "The legendary bridge leads the bad guys to the death chamber, where they get overheated…."

A part of Ricky believes he is "Bad." But does he deserve to die for his mixed feelings about his little brother, who's stolen his station as "solo son" and now wants to play with Ricky's toys? It's evident to me that Ricky is wrestling with his urge toward empathy for his brother, with whom he might share, and for the part of him that might be "stuck" in his desire to hold the line against his brother's incursions. Has Ricky now dug into his depths and storied himself into a new way of handling things? A week after he crafts and narrates this sand world, Ricky's parents report more tolerance of his little brother.

And he hasn't hit him again – not even once.

Deborah, Seven Years Old – Add Water, Mix, and Stir

Stepping into my sandbox for the first time as the worst days of the COVID-19 pandemic faded, this child of a recent divorce steps into my sandbox, sits down, and doesn't want to get out. Grabbing fistfuls of sand, she flings "clouds" up over her head and onto my carpeted floor. Sandplay figures in both hands get tossed haphazardly around her. Her parents say Deborah only does what she wants to do. She stomps out of her school classroom, announcing, "I'm not reading!" She needs a day or more to settle down after each transfer between her separated Mom and Dad's homes in a small city near my suburban Connecticut home. As each of her parents worked virtually during the COVID-19 pandemic, Deborah's life was largely isolated, with no preschool and few, if any, playdates.

Now, in school, Deborah is having meltdowns, turning her body away in fury. Dad says she ran from the car into the busy strip mall parking lot, and he had to catch her. At school, she's been reported running out of class looking for the psychologist who knows how to handle her outbursts in supportive ways. Clearly, Deborah needs to move from chaos to consistency. At a joint parents-only session, I ask each to pick a word they can remember to inspire them and as a goal for their daughter. Dad picks "resourcefulness." Mom picks "faith."

Reflection: We need to accommodate Deborah's impulse to make a mess. And give her boundaries to suggest the possibility of some "containment."

Deborah's Next Session

In quick succession, diminutive Deborah jumps on what is for her a chest-high purple exercise ball, rolls for 15 seconds, and grabs one of my red encounter bats, bashing away at the red padded shield I'm holding for 30 seconds… and she's off to the sandbox! Tossing fewer figures in than last time, Deborah wants to add water to her box, so I hand her a plastic container to carry water from the bathroom in the hallway. But remembering the clouds of sand from last time, I cover the carpet with a large plastic tarp.

Lugging the brimming container back into my office and balancing it over the sandbox wall and into the box, she plops her sandplay figures in – among them a baby sucking one of its thumbs.

Deborah: No one likes the water.

She shows me that a gray plastic shark flashing white teeth prefers to swim not in water but in the surrounding sand. One by one, she rescues her drowning figures from the water container, placing each back on my shelves.

Reflection: Deborah's play looks like that of a three-year-old. Her narrative is so oriented to survival. I suspect there's something she's trying to resolve from much earlier in her life. Did she have difficulty moving through an earlier developmental stage? Had she learned to crawl as a toddler? Deborah's parents didn't remember because their caregiver role during the pandemic was taken over to some extent by other adults in their extended family. There's a good sign: Deborah is playing with some boundaries by using my plastic water container as a feature in her sand world rather than just throwing water into the box like she'd tossed sand around the week before.

Session #3: Deborah

> *Back into my bathroom to tote sloshing water in her container for the sandbox. An elephant drinks. She says there's a message in a bottle.*

Reflection: Communication established with water may signal a new turn in the story. Could Deborah flow into some new ways of operating at home and at school?

Deborah: *(Yelling so loud I wonder whether her dad, waiting in his car outside, will hear every word through my open office window.)*
We need to find the missing prince who'll save the baby. Don't take any animals to the water, just take them home!

Reflection: Deborah misses her separated Dad. Even though she hopes he'll come back and everyone will once again live in one home, somewhere she knows, as time goes by, living out of two households, this may never happen. I think Deborah will find a way to rescue herself!

Session #4: Deborah

I want to encourage Deborah's storytelling acumen further to promote her growth into a place closer to her actual age. As she lugs the largest container yet of water to the sandbox, I prompt her with "Once upon a time…"

Deborah begins her story:

> *"A shark and emergency truck rescue a baby trapped in the water." (Deborah, digging deep into the sand buries "a hero" – an emergency vehicle.) She tells me solemnly that the Shark is also a hero for gathering "all the other animals to help!"*
>
> *Deborah has another idea on how to rescue the baby. She finds a large plastic bridge among my figures and puts it in the water near the baby.*

Reflection: Deborah is pulling out all the stops, creating more than one rescue character and a bridge to boot! I sense the part of this girl who wants to grow up into her fullness. Sandplay provides her with a narrative frame for progressing.

Deborah brings a horse into her story, which she names "Neigh-Neigh."

Reflection: I wonder if Deborah is trying to unravel inner places where fear and confusion had blended, deploying Neigh-Neigh as a "power animal" who can safely transport her through intertwined mediums of muddy sand and water.

Neigh-Neigh's Story

The bridge was under the water.
Someone was pretending to put up a sign that said "Wrong Way."
(She's placed a miniature street sign that says "Wrong Way" in her watery sand world)
But the shark ate it.
The sign was floating everywhere.
The alligator tried to bite the sign.
Then the hospital truck drove underwater to get some gas because he was running out.
It took a while for the gas to come.
It was the Crocodile– "Roarrrr!"
(Deborah's voice moves into a lower and louder register)
Water creatures live in water
"Neigh-Neigh help me!" (She's looking at the horse. Deborah's voice rising in volume, as she sings Neigh-Neigh's name, high-pitched and tremulous, like the sound of a horse's "Neigh! Neigh!")
Neigh-Neigh, help me!
Neigh-Neigh was hurt.
The crocodile saw Neigh-Neigh was hurt.
The crocodile saw.
As a child, Neigh-Neigh helped everyone, but not me, because I was a crocodile
(Shark to Crocodile) "Show me your roar first!"
Neigh-Neigh can't come back alive.
Emergency truck: I'm still driving no matter what!

Reflection: Deborah is giving me a short course in how to construct a way where previously she had no way. The guiding forces come from her imagination, extending beyond her small body into the world of fantasy. I notice how she projects herself into this with increasing levels of power. A power sourced from a story, carried by inanimate figures into which she blows life. Characters who interact within the variety and structure of her play. The life she imparts includes the vocalized roar of a crocodile that sees that Neigh-Neigh's helping presence is limited by her hurt and that Neigh-Neigh "can't come back alive." Somewhere, Deborah knows a part of her younger self at play today will not survive. Sacrificed in her wayfinding toward maturity.

On one level, Deborah is all she has created. The "Wrong Way" sign, sitting in water-logged sand may relate to Deborah hearing the disapproval of parents and teachers who want her to behave with more decorum. The alligator who tried to bite the "Wrong Way" sign, like Deborah, gnashed her teeth in a confining schoolroom. Running away from Dad, whom she wished (and told) would be better off if he were back together with Mom. The hospital truck that miraculously "drove underwater to get some gas" like Deborah diving deep in play into currents where vision alters and where a child like her can procure some fuel to keep going.

Yet "Neigh-Neigh was hurt" (Deborah's observation of her alter-ego – the horse who carries power and wants her rescue). This is emphasized two more times in Deborah's narration of her crocodile's voice:

"The crocodile saw Neigh-Neigh was hurt.
The crocodile saw."

Reflection: Neigh-Neigh may be a healer, but her abilities are limited, especially in Deborah's present stormy times, where yet-to-be-healed childhood hurts loom large. Now the tides and Deborah's clarifying narrative converge around Deborah's core hurt.

"As a child, Neigh-Neigh helped everyone, but not me because
I was a crocodile"

Reflection: Deborah had been crying out for help for a long time, her dramatic actions drawing attention to her and eventually leading her into therapy with me. She was the crocodile who roared! But here's the dilemma: Deborah wants to resolve the pain of her self-judgment, and she wants acceptance and nurturance from surrounding adults. In her play, Deborah has created a possible way through her pain, via the shark that ate the "Wrong Way" sign.

Shark to Crocodile: *"Show me your roar first!"*

Reflection: Deborah, like the crocodile, wants her *"roarrrr"* of pain heard. The pain of her parents' separation will likely continue, and Deborah needs to integrate it. Embodied Play Therapy sessions have handed her containers to hold the entire sweep of her inner dramas. The chance to express rather than repress it all, including the *"roarrrr"* of protest against what's hard to feel.

In the end, *"Neigh-Neigh can't come back alive."* Some of the younger parts of Deborah will be supplanted by new inner selves in her parliament of personalities, whose life tasks will be of a new and more complex order. But Deborah's not finished yet. She brings back the Emergency Truck, the original rescuer of her baby in an earlier sandplay session. Motoring up with resolve and strength to speak in Deborah's final narration of her Emergency Truck's words:

"I'm still driving no matter what!"

Reflection: At the end of this session, Deborah told me that the alligator that tried to bite the "Wrong Way" sign (but failed to consume/destroy it) had a job: "To protect the ocean." I wonder if this "ocean" symbolizes Deborah in her entirety. A full, flowing constellation of selves that needed to establish inner communication and be validated. A self who could throw fistfuls of sand in the air when difficulties demanded attention and another who constructed tales grounded in sand and water that transported her back down to earth.

Roberta, Twelve Years Old – Battling with School and Parents

Roberta was having trouble paying attention in school and was the subject of much scrutiny from concerned teachers and parents. Her parents admitted they had problems with alcohol, and the Dad had recently returned to the family's apartment from imposed sobriety at a program for substance users. At home, there was a battle going on around Roberta's use of her tablet, and Mom, the disciplinarian of the two parents, was constantly taking it away, her daughter then locking herself in the bathroom to avoid the frequent bickering of her parents. Despite the high level of conflict in the family, I knew that both Roberta and her younger brother frequently slept in the parents' bed. Were the children on patrol to keep the peace or looking for comfort in a home where waking life was extremely uncomfortable? At least in a shared family bed, closed eyes and mouths offered some respite, some relief.

During her first few sessions, Roberta gathered bucket after bucket of water from the sink in my office bathroom, returning to dump and flood the box. In my notes, I wrote: "Testing limits… How much will creativity be allowed? How much pleasure? Where is safety to be found….and flow?" While the parents might need to "dry out," so did Roberta. She was living at home with blurred family boundaries, where so much in the family was out of focus. Roberta and her symptoms were a key ingredient in the glue holding the family mess in place. Parents trying to alleviate pain by numbing it through alcohol were causing problems that I couldn't solve. But paying focused attention to Roberta's issues in therapy could create some boundaries amid a mixed-up family dynamic. We could start to model working things out, therapist-to-kid, through some session rules. Water needed to be in containers. When this young adolescent wanted to shoot hefty clay balls at me as if from a cannon, I said, "No."

Roberta lived at home in a messy intergenerational stew with ill-defined borders and little sense of safety as her parents continued drinking. Because conflict was a language she was conversant in, I thought it would be productive to engage Roberta in experiments where she could battle for space. When she started fomenting fights between her figures in sand worlds, I decided to lean into play with her and provoke active resistance to adult incursion – a symbolic model for what Roberta might need to do at home, where an identity differentiated from her parents would need to come into focus. So I set up something she was lacking at home – a border in the sand between her side and mine – a long plastic fence stretching wall-to-wall across the length of the box. With this boundary in place, my provocation began.

Neal: *(Makes a sound like a dive-bomber coming in for the kill)* What happens if my three-headed monster comes in breathing fire?!

Roberta: *(A grin on her face)* Your monster can't breathe fire! *(Holding up a big-bellied black plastic Buddha figure)* Buddha's patrolling the barrier and he's impartial!

Roberta: *(Pointing to the top of my high-ceilinged NYC office room)*
And the barrier goes up to the ceiling!

Reflection: Roberta was experimenting with how far she could go to stop me, an adult who was symbolically threatening her territorial independence. Might she stretch into a more independent identity if she attended to herself rather than her parents' struggles? Intending to challenge the harsh judgments of her parents and her own self-criticism, I saw another opportunity. A psychiatrist had diagnosed Roberta with ADHD. I wanted to remove the negative connotation of that label.

Placing two squeeze toys, spongy gray miniature brains, on the surface of the sand, I told Roberta that, as it related to her brain, I saw that what she had was "attention possibility." A smiling Roberta immediately buried the brains in the sand. In this quiet moment, I brought up what her parents had told me. She had trouble falling asleep. I knew her parents insisted she be in bed an hour after dinner, something I thought might have been appropriate for a younger child. So, I asked Roberta if she wanted me to bring this up the next time I spoke with her parents. She nodded, "Yes."

As our discussions ramped down, Roberta headed towards my bin of larger Embodied Play Therapy tools, grabbing one foam-padded encounter bat and handing me the other. Taking a stance facing each other, Roberta's attack as she moved towards me seemed tentative. I think a part of her is holding back, scared to emerge. So, I changed the rules. From a basket of fabric blindfolds, I hand her one to put on. I'm measuring her level of trust, and I'm also giving her leeway because I know she can see a bit through the bottom of the blindfold. Everything is quiet. I'm going to try and slip past her before she knows it. If she taps me even slightly with her encounter bat as I move, she wins that round. But of course, Roberta got me every time, and then when I put on the blindfold, she took great delight in getting past me. Something with which I cooperated as we built a connection through our playful encounter.

As the session winds down, we discuss how scared Roberta had been as a younger child when her Dad had been hospitalized with a life-threatening illness. Although it had been in remission for a long time, Roberta remembered, and it didn't help now that this same parent had been away again, most recently in substance rehab.

Reflection: Roberta is returning to the deeper emotion behind her hyperactivity. Masked beneath is a quieter grief. If she can drop into that grief, it could help lessen her agitation and heal a younger self that moved underground when her Dad was ill.

Roberta's Session a Few Weeks Later

We had a break of a few weeks because of summer vacation and Roberta, now returned to school for a few days is already exhausted by the advanced curriculum of her new academic year. She comes into the session, slumping her body down into a snake-like curl on my mini-trampoline. I mirror her body posture, collapsing onto the carpet a body length from where she rests. Roberta tells me about the drama going on at home around her cell phone, which had broken when it fell out of her pocket and dropped to the concrete sidewalk as she attempted a wheelie on her skateboard. Dad and Mom had been fighting about buying her a new one.

Mom had left on a business trip, and Dad, overwhelmed with the care of Roberta and her younger brother, had purchased a new cell phone for his daughter. A pacifier, I thought, to keep his daughter occupied, although this new device came with additional costs for Roberta and her family. Battles escalated as the new phone was taken away when she defied her parents. Roberta's parents wanted her to focus on schoolwork and not her phone. Roberta, like so many adolescents, was drawn to social media and friends calling out to her by text from the tiny screen.

Roberta was caught in a battle with inner impulsivity and the authority of parents she wanted to rebel against. Our next interaction allowed me to place a tangible fence around behavior that could endanger both of us. From her backpack, Roberta pulled out a sparkler, the kind you light with a match. She asked whether she could light it now, right here in my office. I decided not to act impulsively. I told her I'd consider her request with safety in mind and would let her know my decision at next week's session.

Roberta sighed and pulled out a bataka, hitting the foam cube 115 times in a row, a new record for her. I showed her how to "ground" and discharge the energy she'd built up by going into the "bow" posture, softening the knees and pushing the pelvis forward, which often initiates vibration in the legs and lower torso, bringing charged energy built up from the hitting, down from the head to the feet, resting firmly on the ground. Roberta didn't want to do it my way, and I encouraged her to discharge her high-energy state the way she wanted to, which was folding her body forward into what Yoga practitioners call a "forward bend" or "rag doll" and what some Core Energetics practitioners call a "waterfall." I invited Roberta to concentrate on feeling her head dropping and the vibrating shiver of energy that might restore her to a resting and grounded state when she slowly, one vertebra at a time, brought her body back up to standing.

But Roberta wasn't done yet for the day. She moved on to something I use to promote mindfulness and calm, a "Buddha Board" where you draw with a brush using water. Fascinated by the varying textures and shapes, thick and thin as she drew squiggles and straight lines that disappeared as they dried, my thought was: this kid's recovery won't always be in a straight line. I'd need to keep my cool in the process, or at least find ways to return to it as the ride with Roberta continued.

Picking up a tennis racket, Roberta challenged me to a contest. How long could I balance the racket vertically with the butt of the handle on the palm of my hand? Of course, Roberta won. Neal: 3 seconds to Roberta's 55. I thought of the gifts that Roberta's innovation skills provided for her as our Embodied Play Therapy experiments with substance and space went on. I asked her to slow down to notice what was in the room where we were. To find different shapes. To count them. To describe them. Using her language. Letting herself feel the nuance and texture of words as they emerged from her mouth.

As our session came to a close, Roberta asked to use the bathroom in my office waiting room. She spent a long time in there, something many kids do when they've let down into relaxation after a particularly intense Embodied Play Therapy session. She emerged, smiling, back into the waiting room.

Roberta's Last Session before Winter Break

Roberta sank into a soft blanket on my office couch. She told me that she's had it with weekly trips to the family's second home in Maine and tells me she's too tired to make a sand world. I say: "OK, you direct me, I'll be your agent and put what you say in your sand world." But instead, gathering herself from the couch, Roberta began tossing figures into the sandbox, looking completely assured she knew exactly what she was doing. I thought: She reminds me of the artist Jackson Pollack, frenetically dripping paint into a pattern, or a basketball star hitting a long-distance shot from the far end of the court.

Roberta spied a flashlight and turned it on, pointing it at the sandbox. She asked me if I had more flashlights. After rummaging in my office closet, I handed three or four more to her. She instructed me to turn off the office lights and pull the shades as one by one she placed the lit flashlights on the rim of the box and the shelves above. Multiple beams trained on different sections of the box, as sandplay figures she'd thrown in cast shadows on the sand and the sandbox walls. Never having seen this level of ingenuity in a child before, I complimented Roberta on the multi-dimensionality she's created through her addition of light.

Reflection: This girl, caught in the flood of her parents' problems, who'd flooded my boxes, constantly testing parental boundaries and mine, was teaching me something powerful about expansion in the Embodied Play Therapy world. Opening to inner depth through play sometimes needs to happen in the silent places where a young person's individuality and genius reside. In the quiet that had descended as we beheld the luminescence of Roberta's lightscape, I thought: "She's a lightworker in her life, shedding light on her life and the family."

References

Pierrakos, J. C. (1990). *Core Energetics: Developing the Capacity to Love and Heal*. LifeRythmn.

Keleman, S. (1987). *Embodying Experience: Forming a Personal Life*. Center Press.

8

Completions in Embodied Play Therapy

Children and Families as Heroes on a Journey

Since my training in body-centered methods (Core Energetics and Embodied Couples Work) focuses on the complex connection between the intrapsychic and human attachment, along with family system influences, including intergenerational trauma, my preference is to build a longer-term relationship with a child and their family to sort through what's needed.

As mentioned earlier, the range of presenting issues for children brought to an Embodied Play Therapy practitioner's door is wide. Some of these concerns include fears and phobias, screen overuse, hyperactivity, learning differences leading to problems in school and self-esteem, reluctance to self-advocate, limitations on which foods a child will eat, obsessions and compulsive behaviors, and pushback by children on parental needs for cooperation. Such childhood symptoms may be rooted in neurodiversity, gender diversity, learning differences, medical issues, or other factors organic to the child. The roots of symptomatic behavior may also be found in unproductive cycles of interactions within a child's family.

DOI: 10.4324/9781003328186-10

Embodied Play Therapy seeks to work with children and families using presenting symptoms as doorways into fuller individual function for a child, as well as fuller relational capacity for that child with family and in school. These formative environments will set the tone and substance for all that will come later. In-session activities that allow for movement, breathing, and feeling within a framework of flexible play offer a child agency to create new narratives about themselves and their surroundings. Parents and often the children themselves are looking for relief from the ways things have been. Yet, with all the fun, the lessons that emerge for later-in-life use may not always be initially apparent.

When parents notice substantial positive changes in a child, this usually determines when therapy is moving toward "done." Still, in my view, the ideal time for the completion of a child's therapy is indicated when the child says so or does something that indicates "this is enough for now." The child who has completed a fruitful chapter of play may make its sufficiency clear through a narrative, a drawing, or something they say which conveys, in their own style, the closing words we're all familiar with before the final credits of a film roll: "THE END."

Deborah – Age 7 – Final Session

A Child of Divorce Finds Her Way Back to Dad

Deborah began her therapy by throwing clouds of sand in the air (see more on Deborah in Chapter 7: Deepening Narrative) and then experimented with boundaries using water containers in the sand, a symbol of containment for her big emotions in the face of her parents' divorce. Now, she will be having her last session at my home office in Connecticut. She'll soon be away at camp for the summer, and her parents are noting her progress in school. Deborah has had fewer verbal outbursts, and her sudden running out in the middle of class has ceased.

Deborah wants to be "found" by her dad, except she wants her father and me to run something akin to a gauntlet first.

The men will have to work! At the beginning of her session, Deborah hatches a plan that Dad writes down.

There will be four "stations." Tests that Dad and Neal will have to accomplish include a review of activities and objects Deborah has interacted with in her therapy.

- *Dad and Neal put a container of figures back on the shelves*
- *Touch the tissue box (one time)*
- *Punch the exercise ball (three times)*
- *Put a rock in the sandbox and touch it 10 times (with a red encounter bat)*

Deborah has scripted the ending of her last session through a ritual that honors what she has done and the reality of her return to being with her family, minus my involvement.

Then something new happens.

Deborah has always refused to draw in session. She needed to be in constant motion. Drawing wasn't speedy enough for her. But the sessions involving her stories had slowed Deborah's pace to a more manageable one. The girl with so many demands is now finding a place where she can come in for a landing.

Deborah picks up a pen from my desk and begins to draw. Among her drawings:

- *Two Girls. The first has eyes, a mouth, and ears, but no hair. (Is this baby Deborah?) The second, whose long arms reach toward her companion, has long hair but no eyes, mouth, or ears (Is this the older, more mature Deborah not yet fully formed?)*
- *Three castle towers. A flag waves from the top of each tower. The central tower has a door, not yet open, and a small sign next to the door. Squiggly lines on the sign, while clearly words, are not written for us to decode today.*

Reflection: What will be the directions that open doors in Deborah's future next? While this may yet be determined, I am so touched by the details of this girl's planning. She's already confident enough to direct her dad and me to what we'll need to accomplish to help her complete her final moments of therapy. And these allow her to feel, and us to witness Deborah's connection to the allies she'd deployed within Embodied Play Therapy. The figures we adults must to return to the shelves, the exercise ball, and even the box of tissues that she knew could be used if she wanted to blow her nose … or needed to cry. Even the red encounter bat she'd used to bash my shield in an earlier session turns into something that Deborah's dad will use in a blessing gesture that reminds me of what a king would do, touching his sword to a knight's shoulder to invest him with power. The single rock in my sandbox was graced with a final touch.

Flags waving, the two girls in Deborah's drawings, perhaps the one who came initially to Embodied Play Therapy and the one headed toward maturity, will exit today with her father. At the door for the last time, Deborah jumps into her dad's arms. Through my office window, I watch as they walk down my path to their car. Meeting my gaze through the glass, with the bend of a single index finger, Deborah waves goodbye.

Ken – Age Eight – Final Session

Fears ease…

Ken had told his parents he wanted to have a therapist, which didn't surprise them since so many of his classmates in Manhattan had one. They wanted me to help Ken get over his fear of insects, which had limited their ability to go on family outings. What I found out as I got to know more about Ken's concerns is that what was bothering him had more to do with the nature of his relationship with parents who were often too busy during the week to spend time with him. His fear had gotten his parents' attention. I wondered if that fear was connected to the possibility of rejection if he expressed wanting more from his parents. Short of using symptomatic means as a method to attract the human contact he craved, I believed Ken could benefit from putting his foot down in a self-affirming way to communicate his needs more directly. Soon, he'd need to do this without the support of a therapist because Ken's parents had told him that therapy with me would be ending. Still, there was a lot on Ken's mind that he wanted to get off his chest. We'd just have to have his voice heard loud and clear and do it fast.

I sent an email to Ken's parents requesting that he show up for his last session wearing heavy snow boots, even though it was early summer with no chance of snow falling on us. I could almost feel the smiles of the parents who I suspected knew what I might be up to in fostering some bigger putting-down-my-foot energy for their son.

Ken stomps in with his boots, and in the synchrony that often happens between client material and therapist instinct, he tells me that he's angry with a girl at school named Quinn, who he says is annoying him. Moving to a hunk of clay, I tell him I'll be cooking up a "Quinn Monster." What does Ken want to create?

Ken builds a "shape monster." Its body is a circle. Its legs are rectangles, and its feet are triangles. I mold my "Quinn monster" first into a helmet, turn it upside down, and tell Ken it's like a cup or bowl, "to get his needs filled." No sooner than these words leave my mouth, my monster-turned-bowl gets obliterated in a single hand-held leap by Ken's "shape monster."

I look from Ken in his boots to the clock on the wall. Twenty-five more minutes left in our last session. I place a thick rubber pad in front of Ken and tell him he can stomp on it, reminding him he may need to put his foot down with his parents, expressing his objection to their heavy work commitments that keep them away from him so often. Pointing to the two wooden letters standing upright on a table near us, I tell Ken to yell what they spell – "NO." Stomping ten times hard with each foot, the vibration of his voice reverberating through his body, I sense that the point has been grounded into conscious awareness for Ken.

He looks at me and heads toward the sandbox, kneeling on the pad I keep in front so kids don't skin their knees in the excitement of crafting a sand world.

And then something happens that neither Ken nor I could have predicted. As the boy stands next to the sandbox, a black spider descends on a single thread of gossamer filament, right in front of our faces. I turned to Ken. His gaze is steady and calm. I tell him, "I don't think you could have done that when you first came." Ken nods, kneels, and begins digging a hole in the sand, then filling it in and smoothing the sand flat with his hand.

As he places figures in the sand, Ken tells me about his sand world, and I write:

- *There's a hill with something that haunts it.*
- *The crocodile is protecting the "haunter" so it doesn't die.*
- *The tarantula is guarding its tree.*
- *Alligators and snakes are having a little chat that no one can understand.*
- *A dragon stands close to a figure of a human skeleton.*
- *The dragon and skeleton are fenced off by a white wooden picket fence, which curves around them.*

(Ken has placed two wizard figures near each other. The first wizard stands facing an empty black cauldron. The second wizard stands in front of a teepee.)

Ken speaks slowly, as if from a dream.

- *The dragon eats people who are mean to the wizards who own the whole place.*
- *The first wizard is making a potion that can do anything.*
- *The second wizard is trying to get some rest.*
- *The little alligator is trying to get out of the hole.*
- *The hole becomes - a hill.*

I watch in silence as Ken completes his work. Removing all the figures, he puts them back in the places on the shelves to which he's become accustomed. He looks out into the woods outside my window for some moments and returns to the box. Kneeling, he flattens the sand, creating what looks to me like a crater on the moon, a landing pad for his accomplishments during his short course of Embodied Play Therapy.

Reflection: Parents are in charge and make the final decision on whether a child will continue coming beyond the time when symptoms ease in their eyes. And yet a child therapist acts as an advocate for the voices in a child that may require continual amplification. Embodied Play Therapy, with its emphasis on allowance for "big energy," offers outlets for turning up the volume on real childhood needs that might otherwise get stuck in young bodies, minds, and hearts. For Ken, who made himself heard about getting a therapist, stomping around a session in boots provides an outlet to stand up further for himself. On one hand, it's standing up for the part of himself that wants his friend Quinn to stop annoying him. On the other hand, it's about getting his needs met with parents who are sometimes too busy for their son.

For his final session, Ken connects with a protective fire-breathing dragon and conjures up wizards to help him escape from the holes he was in. Ken puts a final period on his play and finds a "landing pad" that I thought likely represented mixed emotions about his therapy ending. But the message was clear enough for both of us to see. When the descent of a spider has become cause for fascination, not fear, it's OK to move on. Especially when you'll be a bit more prepared to speak up and to be heard.

Ricky – Age Nine

A Journey into Self-Confidence Completes a Chapter…

(See Ricky earlier in the Introduction and in Chapter 3: Building a Bridge to a Child, Chapter 4: Parents in the Mix, Chapter 5: Touchy Subjects: Bodies, Butts, and Poop!, and Chapter 7: Deepening Narrative.)

From the day Ricky had blazed into my office as a 6-year-old and kicked me out (Chapter 3: Building a Bridge to a Child) to the sweet times building enclosures of blocks together with his parents (Chapter 4: Parents in the Mix) to dreaming up plans for a "Tent of Safety" in which he now slept (Chapter 5: Touchy Subjects: Bodies, Butts, and Poop!), a formerly jealous Ricky began to share toys with his brother (Chapter 7: Deepening Narrative). Ricky was becoming more sure of himself and more at peace in his own body.

Ricky had worked successfully on building inner strength, harnessing his own powers of imagination and using his own creativity to invent solutions for what bothered him. He was learning to allow the coexistence of mixed feelings and accept his many parts. The part of him yearning to be the one and only son in a family that had given birth to another. A part wanting "To NOT SHARE" his toys with his competing sibling. And still another that began to find pleasure in sharing. A part wishing for the comfort of what had been before, sleeping close to parents. The part that could craft his "Tent of Safety" capable of sheltering his emerging independence. And now a final challenge for Ricky to tackle...

In a parent-only session, Mom, Dad, and I came up with an idea to reward a part of Ricky that was building containment for his impulsive side. After all, he was getting bigger, and no matter how strong his bodybuilding dad was, a punch from powerful Ricky could really hurt. So, as he was now completing Embodied Play Therapy with me, why not reward his impulse control with something he might value? How would the "Not-Punching-Dad" challenge work? He'd need to accrue ten checks on a chart posted on their kitchen refrigerator by his parents for "Not-Punching-Dad." Ricky would even receive a check if he thought about hitting Dad and then didn't!

From the first time I presented the idea of some type of reward for the "Not-Punching-Dad" challenge as a capstone for Ricky's months of fruitful work, it took a few weeks of negotiation to figure out what the reward would be. My initial proposal for a miniature diamond-like quartz crystal was vetoed by

Ricky. The reward Ricky agreed to, as we were all emerging from the COVID-19 pandemic, was what he couldn't have all that time. An in-person session with his therapist. About ten days after Ricky, his parents and I arranged the "Not-Punching-Dad" Checkmark Reward Challenge with Ricky's buy-in, I learned that the requisite ten checks had been completed, and we scheduled Ricky's in-person reward session.

Ricky – Final Session Outdoors on My Play Patio

> *After winning his in-person session as a reward for not hitting his father, it's taken two hours in heavy traffic for Ricky's parents to drive him from New York to my office in Connecticut. He needed to pee so badly as he exited the car, he was holding his crotch. I point him and his dad toward the bathroom. Ricky asks, "Can we stay only for 25 minutes?" He knows my sessions with kids are 45 minutes in length, and my guess is he's exhausted from the ride and thinking of the long car trip home.*
>
> *We walk in silence along the path to my Play Patio, soft cedar wood mulch underfoot. Spying the familiar mini-trampoline rebounder from my old New York City office where he first had sessions, he jumps on it with abandon. With some of his lost energy reclaimed, he heads to the sandbox and asks, "Can I step in?" I nod yes. He runs his fingers through the familiar dry sand that he has not touched for almost two years of remote sessions during the pandemic.*
>
> *His eyes soften, calmed by his contact with the sand, and then he steps out from the box, so much older, and taller than the child I first met three years earlier for the first time. Ricky picks up the rubber-headed mallet and hammers some clay into a pancake on the cardboard sheet. Then, kneeling over the sandbox, he pounds the sand with his fist to flatten it. I say, "Ricky, do you know that expression about pounding sand?" You tell someone to 'go pound sand' because they'll never win. But you just won. You're here, in person!"*

I ask Ricky if he wants a cave or a mountain in the box. He says, "a mountain." I ask him how many figures he wants to pick to put in the sand, "Five or ten?" Ricky says, "Five." But choosing only one to start, he says, "Now you pick." From my shelves chock-full of sandplay figures, I select one of the small turtles. He also takes a small turtle from the shelf. I feel tears welling up in my eyes. Ricky makes connections so easily now. And powerfully.

He needs water to make the sand pliable for molding a mountain, and I hand him a filled plastic pail. In a corner of the box, he palms piles of sand for his mountain, and he says, "I'll bury my guys and you find them." It's like the game from three years ago. Yet it's slower-paced, a dream-like echo of a long-past ritual that he needs repeated so he and I can remember and perhaps so he can let that game from a younger Ricky go. No need for me to make more of this to build our relationship, so I discover most of his figures quickly and tell him I will bury mine for him to find if he closes his eyes. What he uncovers first is not one of my figures but something buried by a child who came a day before that I neglected to remove, a treasure chest. A good sign, I think, for Ricky and his future life without me in it.

Rising from the side of the sandbox, Ricky once again walks over to my shelves. Taking two knights, one in each hand, without bothering to return to the sandbox, he begins a battle between the knights, accompanied by sound effects. The knight mounted on an armored unicorn, he dubs the "unicorn knight." I jump into the action, grabbing a king from the shelves. Ricky confidently retorts, "There are two Kings!"

He doesn't need to find another sandplay king figure. It's sufficient that this second king exists in his fertile imagination. Who is this second king? My sense is – it's Ricky! Ricky trusts I will acquiesce to this new shared authority with him. A privilege we both know he's earned over the years of Embodied Play Therapy, and which makes sense now that his therapy is ending.

In a Russian accent, I tell Ricky, "I have to replenish my energy!" Turning my king upside down, I place him head down into a broken hole on the top of my plastic sandplay figure shelves. It reminds me of the chess games I played with my father, where he would tip his king over to signal I had won. Off with the king's head and off with Neal's! This embodied play therapist is about to become ancient history.

Ricky has accomplished so much through his play, completing much of what was sought by his parents. He's sleeping soundly in his "Tent of Safety" in his own room. He's no longer hitting his brother and his father. He's hosting events at school for other kids. And most tellingly, he's stopped coming down so hard on himself. I've recommended to Ricky's parents that they transfer his work to a therapist who's closer to home for in-person sessions. Everyone knows I'm there if needed.

When Ricky first learned I knew about the new therapist, he told his parents that I shouldn't worry, that next time he saw me, he'd give me a big hug. If he wants to initiate that today, I'll accept, but for now, I suggest an alternative that will actively embody another way we connected. I hand Ricky a pair of large, fingerless sparring gloves, more appropriate to his age than the small red boxing gloves he'd first used three years ago when I first saw him. As I hold the handles of my red padded shield, he delivers powerful punches, one after another, until he tires.

In the quiet that descends, I invite Ricky to choose and bury something in the deep sandbox for another child to find. Ricky agrees and picks the small figure of a dog to hide. A dog who looks a lot like his dog at home. Ricky's generosity is in full flower now, sharing the dog he loves with another child he will never meet.

Like so many children who come to my home office, Ricky is curious about what's inside my house. Looking through the large picture window on my patio into the dim interior, he's shocked to see and hear the gurgling sound of a small lap pool on which floats a retractable plastic cover. Ricky says, "I want to see it!" Because I've been super cautious during the pandemic, Ricky and I put on face masks before stepping inside. His eyes alight, I let him help me pull the hand crank to open the pool cover an arm's breadth to see some of the water below. There are only five minutes left in our session, and although I've considered the possibilities of Watsu therapy in my warm pool for adults, especially for calming the nervous systems of expectant parents, it's not something I intend to offer in Embodied Play Therapy with kids. The only thing Ricky will be jumping into as he completes his therapy with me today is his parents' car.

Turning the pool cover crank a bit more, I take my eyes off Ricky for a moment. As I turn towards him, he's removed his mask and put on my snorkel! Panicking probably a bit too much, I tell Ricky, "Put on your mask!" Pointing to the pool, Ricky says, "I want one! Can I have a pool party here?" Ricky had told me months ago that when he grew up, he would be buying a Tesla for himself one day. I say, "You want a pool and not a Tesla, Ricky?" Ricky says, "Yes, I want this instead!" As I point to the door and we exit, I'm thinking that this boy, like so many, has big dreams for himself. Some aspirations will be material. Others will be in realms where value is measured in areas less monetary and more in the treasures found in self-worth – and in loving relationships.

Ricky and I head up the path that will lead him back to his parents and brother waiting in the car. As we walk, I ask Ricky how he accrued the ten checks and the reward for this in-person session with me. He answers, "I didn't hit!" And in that moment, I realize how big this win is for Ricky. For him to have been able to feel the familiar impulse to use his fists, fighting back against a tide of misalignment rising within him, and to pause. To say "No" to that impulse and "Yes" to a new way of being that will not get him into trouble. Stopping the self-judgment that had him saying "I'm bad." I think of how hard Ricky had been on himself and how guilty he felt after he'd hit his Dad, whom he loved so much.

I ask Ricky if he's talked to his new therapist yet about his big feelings. "Not yet," he says. "OK," I tell him. "You can do that when you're ready."

Reflection: I'm sending off this boy, who has been such a teacher for me, with the knowledge that he has come so far and has completed this chapter of work so well. Ricky has taught me about the sheer power of movement to propel a young body beyond the uncomfortable places a growing mind has gotten stuck in. How self-expression can find containment when we mobilize our big energy in the service of fuller inner connection. How tapping into imagination to engage with another in play can connect us deeply and joyfully.

Across my office floor three years ago, Ricky had set down his first path toward me, a therapist and a stranger. A path of pillows strewn before us on which I might approach him. Reconnection to and reassurance from his parents were found as he built enclosures of blocks within which he could rest in the knowledge of his enduring connection to each of them, even as he constructed a wall between Dad's work and his, an early experiment in the healthy self-identification he must ultimately create for himself. He fought the inner battle for the "legendary bridge" that would lead him to feeling a wider range of emotions amid figures he placed in his sand world. The sharp feelings of a shark who refused to share toys, and the softer feelings of a tiny turtle who wanted to share toys but needed protection for his emerging tenderness, which only a shell surrounding his soft body could provide.

Ricky had taught me how childhood imagination can craft a home of one's own. A childhood den illumined by strings of LED lights, which, while paid for by parents, were envisioned first by his creative mind. A "Tent of Safety" located a distance away from a parent bedroom where adults tasked with caregiving could find their own retreat and rest. A "Tent of Safety" where a boy can be read to, where he can listen to music, and where he can recuperate into a slower rhythm as the day winds down into night.

At a time that spanned such a difficult period in the history of humanity during the height of the COVID-19 pandemic, Ricky had endured and emerged with greater wholeness and confidence as part of his growing journey into manhood. My sense is that he'd had a lot of fun in the process.

There's something of a tradition in the sandplay therapy world to have children complete their therapy with a "Hero's Journey" as a capstone. Often, the child selects a human figure to represent themselves, along with an animal figure "ally." The journey becomes a story spun by the child and may take place over multiple sessions. Chronicled by the therapist serving as scribe, the Hero's Journey is an opportunity for a kid to place themselves in a larger epic of cinematic proportions. Replete with wizards, dragons, explosive confrontations, and treasure, the journey is something I've enjoyed photographing and sharing with kids and parents.

Ricky refused to take a "Hero's Journey." When I brought out a CD of Ellis Paul's *The Hero in You,* a compilation of songs and storytelling about heroes from Benjamin Franklin to Rosa Parks (2012), Ricky scoffed. He didn't want to hear it. And in the months since Ricky's therapy was completed, I've come to understand why. Ricky wanted his life to "be enough." Without the pressure of living into an inflated heroism of someone else's making. A life not his own. The completion of Ricky's odyssey in Embodied Play Therapy didn't require a "Hero's Journey" as a finale. From my perspective, Ricky was finding his way in his relationship with family and his relationship with himself. A journey whose variety of voices was a precious gift well worth the hours of witnessing and listening. A journey well worth embarking on and completing in ways defined more by my young client and less by me.

Some Closing Words on Closure

When I began this work with children, I was told many stories of therapists who specialized in helping kids that stopped working with this population. I believe I understand some of the reasons why. The therapeutic contract for work with children, unless it's mandated by the state or school authorities, is with parents.

While parents may participate, many choose to remain on the sidelines.

Therapy with children shines a light on the rest of the family. The brightness of that illumination is not always comfortable. It may call parents to new choices about themselves, which aren't always easy to make. The need to face the impact of their own childhoods. The need to grapple with relationships and work lives that require rebalancing. The need to see their role in a larger society whose history and ways of operating are likely ready for an overhaul.

When parents decide to terminate therapy for their children earlier than seems beneficial, factors may include financial or time pressures. As children stabilize and symptoms reduce, a child's treatment becomes less of a focus. Often, other problems within the family come to the surface. A parent who has put aside their self-actualization needs as they tend to child-rearing responsibilities realizes they should no longer ignore pressing inner priorities. A struggling marriage may need attention. The competing needs of other siblings must be met. Having little control over the length of time for a child in treatment, I've become more flexible (and less frustrated) in accepting whatever time we'll have.

Wherever it may transpire, whether in my office or on live video, the inventions of children in Embodied Play Therapy and the progress I see are sometimes dramatic and most often inspiring. Yet, there is a side of me that always thinks I could do more. One of the challenges in my line of work is accepting that what's been accomplished by children and parents in therapy is sufficient for now, complete because they deem it so. Enough because the work can continue without me in the relational interplay of child and family over time.

Reference

Ellis, P. (2012). *The Hero in You* [Album]. Black Wolf Records. https://www.ellispaul.com/cds/f/c/5669/

Part II
Practical Matters

9

Toolbox for Embodied Play Therapy

What's a session like with a therapist where you don't spend the whole session talking? It's fun! The first thing that a young person sees when walking into my in-person office or for an online session live on video is a rainbow of color – large green, blue, and purple exercise balls, shelves filled with sandplay figures, red boxing gloves, earthy plasticine clay, and rubber mallets for smashing it just for the joy of flattening something, judgment-free.

Ten-year-old Paul heads immediately to my single-person-sized mini-trampoline to get his energy moving, having suffered seven hours with his butt glued to a school desk. Because I imagine he needed to keep his mouth shut for most of his classroom time, I told him it is ok to yell, letting out a "whoop" to encourage him to sound out his sense of freedom from school. Next, he's bouncing on my biggest exercise ball, "bringing his energy down" from a head full of conflicting thoughts and emotions as he rushed between classrooms, worried about how he looked in front of his classmates, comparing his insides to other people's outsides, and wishing he could escape an educational institution he feels trapped in.

A Toolbox for Embodied Play Therapy needn't vary much whether sessions occur in the office, outside, or online. The main

DOI: 10.4324/9781003328186-12

difference? Parents or caregivers may need to purchase some of these items for use at home during tele-sessions. (See list of items for parents to buy in Chapter 10: Live Video! Embodied Play Therapy Online.)

Important here are the safety rules I tell everyone:

- **"Don't hurt yourself"** (wear gloves; watch out for slips and falls; no punching walls).
- **"Don't hurt me"** (no punching below, above, or around a shield)
- **"Don't hurt the room"** (knocking things over, deliberately breaking things).

Tools for Working with Expression, Grounding, and Containment of Strong Emotion

Earlier in this book, I wrote about the link between childhood aggression and anxiety. Among the roots of such anxiety are overuse of screens, cell phones, and social media, exposure to violence in media and video games, along with parental anxiety in a time of turmoil, both on a worldwide basis and among families who face a variety of stressors. (See Chapter 1: Children in an Anxious Age.)

I've spoken about my support within the scope of Embodied Play Therapy sessions for "creative aggression" and positive assertion in children (see Chapter 2: The Four Pillars of Embodied Play Therapy with Children: Movement, Breathing, Feeling, Play) and comment on mobilizing aggression online (see Chapter 10: Live Video! Embodied Play Therapy Online). I also offer some further thoughts on expanding the limits of "play nice" to include engaging aggression and a broader range of connection with self and others in play (See Chapter 6: Moving toward Balance through Selected Methods in Embodied Play Therapy).

Here are descriptions of the tools I use to help clients move, breathe, feel, and play in more embodied ways.

Tennis Ball

When indoors, children take off their shoes for Embodied Play Therapy sessions and hang out in their socks. This allows me to demonstrate that standing and pressing the sole of your unshod, stockinged foot on the firm yet yielding surface of a tennis ball can help you release a maelstrom of spinning thoughts and impulses. This grounding exercise calms a child's system by focusing them in the present moment and the physical sensation that rolling on the tennis ball sends tingling up their foot. A useful activity to try before a child launches into further movement, grabs some clay, draws with markers, or heads toward the sandbox to engage in narrative play.

When sessions are held outdoors, a child takes off their shoes and uses the tennis ball on a mat, then puts their shoes back on for the rest of the session.

Large Exercise Balls

Exercise balls are used to harness the "forward momentum" of young people, adding energy to hypoactive youth, balance for the hyperactive, and getting a kid's energy moving in body-centered sessions. They are also used to teach the experience of deep, diaphragmatic breathing. (See Figure 2.3 in the "Breathing" section of Chapter 2: The Four Pillars of Embodied Play Therapy with Children: Movement, Breathing, Feeling, Play.) Exercise balls are also great for young people to balance on belly down as part of a more extensive group of embodied activities to work on emotional containment of anger. (See Paolo's story in the "Playing" section of Chapter 2: The Four Pillars of Embodied Play Therapy) Many kids also just like to express their joy and bounce! Note: Buy different sized balls for different sized kids. My exercise balls are either 65 cm or 75 cm in diameter.

Mini-trampoline

Jumping up and down on a mini-trampoline or a large exercise ball focuses a child's energy on the lower body from the belly and pelvis down. The springing motion fosters vibration throughout the body, and the excitement of momentary suspension in the air invariably brings a smile to many a young face. As therapists and parents consider buying one of these, I have two thoughts. First, there should be a durable outer circle of fabric that protects a child from falling through the springs supporting the trampoline. Second, especially for younger children and those with balance issues, consider a mini-trampoline that has a balancing bar. Some parents I've seen purchasing mini-trampolines opt for a bar that runs at belly or chest height for a child in a U-shape across the entire mini-trampoline. While I have no experience with these bars, when I look at bars advertised that are only on one end of the trampoline, they seem less secure.

Lightweight Hollow Plastic Bat

Lightweight hollow plastic bats are specifically **and only** for moving energy by hitting a foam cube or pillows piled up on a chair, couch, or bed (if a child is participating remotely in a live video session from their room) to express repressed emotion and for the simple joy of hitting. I want to be very specific here – this is a yellow lightweight hollow plastic 32-inch bat often packaged together for sale with a white plastic wiffle ball. The impact of these plastic bats is loud, even on padded surfaces, so budding Embodied Play Therapists are encouraged to have some earplugs on hand to protect their sensitive ears and those of clients as necessary.

Bataka (Foam Bat with a Hard Inner Spine)

A bataka is made of durable fabric-covered foam with a polished wood or smooth plastic handle and comes in a variety of widths, sizes, and weights. A bataka is used as an alternate tool (see "Lightweight Hollow Plastic Bat" above) to move energy by hitting a foam cube or piled-up pillows. **Because batakas have an inner hard spine, they should never be used to hit or otherwise engage with others**. Since batakas are padded, they tend to be less noisy than plastic bats when a person hits a foam cube or pillows. More of a thud than a thwack! Nevertheless, ear protection for the therapist and client is still advised as needed, especially where an Embodied Play Therapy practitioner is recommending an extended hitting exercise. (See "hitting contests" in Chapter 6: Moving toward Balance through Selected Methods in Embodied Play Therapy.)

Encounter Bats (No Hard Inner Spine)

Encounter bats, soft, padded and lightweight, with no hard inner spines, have smooth plastic handles. (See stories of therapist-child battles and those between kids and parents throughout this book.) Traditional encounter bats made by Uniquity are now manufactured in Germany and can be found for purchase online.

Gloves to Protect Hands While Hitting Punching Bags, Shields, Cubes, or Pillows

I have a variety of gloves for children of various ages/sizes and for different purposes.

- Padded boxing gloves with high-density foam inside. Before a stint of using fists to slam a punching bag or shield (which I or a parent holds), the adult helps a kid put these on.
- Fingerless boxing gloves, well-padded with foam to protect that area close around the wrist, with wraparound Velcro. Older/larger kids tend to use these for punching.
- Lightweight fabric or batting gloves to protect hands from blisters when hitting with a plastic bat or a bataka. If a child is entering my hitting contest, I always hand them a pair of these, recommending they grip the handle of the hitting implement lightly. It's that twisting friction that causes blisters!

Heavy Bags for Punching

I strongly prefer bags that hang from the ceiling or a sturdy stand. Because my ceilings aren't that high, I opted for a heavy bag (40–50 pounds) that hangs from a chain on a sturdy stand. The stand sits outside on my Play Patio, protected from rain under a balcony.

The alternative is a freestanding heavy bag mounted on a plastic base, which you fill with water and sand. No matter which bag you use (or a parent has their child employ for live video sessions), that bag may require a bit of stabilizing while a child punches and it swings. During in-person sessions, I stand close by to monitor. For live video sessions online, I may ask a parent to stabilize a swinging bag as needed.

Shield for Punching

A rectangular polyurethane-covered hand-held shield is made with a sturdy foam core to absorb punches (or pushes) from a child. In Embodied Play Therapy, I have kids focus on punching and pushing, which activates the whole body and grounds the vibration of impact and muscular torque into the legs and feet. My shield with handles in the rear is approximately 15 inches wide by 25 inches tall and 5 inches deep to protect an adult's body from the torso to the pelvis. (See Figure 5.2. Illustration of a child punching a padded shield held by a parent in Chapter 5: Touchy Subjects.)

Pillows

Large pillows are held up by a parent or me as a soft boundary to receive the impact of a child's body. I encourage children who need to physically express feelings ranging from frustration to sheer joy in forward movement to try being an oncoming projectile. Sometimes I'll encourage a cautious child to take a few steps back and get a running start. For others, it's enough to bump a shoulder repeatedly against the shielding pillow. Important: Teach kids to use their shoulder to absorb the bounce off the pillow and not their face to avoid injury to their eyes or teeth. Note: Two large pillows are also useful for a child to flop down on when exhausted or when in need of some relaxation.

Small pillows covered with fabric are great for repeatedly throwing down to the ground, engaging creative assertion. Advised when frustration over school, a demanding teacher, a bully, a parent who takes your screens away, a friend who shuns you, or a therapist who won't listen to your need to take a nap, or if anything else getting you mad boils over and needs release.

Pillows piled up on a chair with arms that help hold them in place can be used for hitting with a bat or bataka. When pillows fall to the floor as they will inevitably do, the therapist retrieves them (or asks the client in a live video session to pick them up) and lets the hitting continue! Of course, if you have a foam cube (see below), there is no need for pillows to hit. Because I do some of my in-person sessions outdoors on my Play Patio, I pull out a chair and pillows from the adjoining room for outdoor hitting.

Foam Cube (Fabric-covered)

Core Energetics practitioners typically use a foam cube for their clients to hit with a bataka (with a hard inner spine) or a lightweight hollow plastic bat. For in-person child clients in my office, I take a cube that stands higher vertically and turn it on its side so a child can hit without reaching up (we want the energy going down into the legs and feet).

My cube's dimensions standing vertically are 24 inches by 32 inches and 36 inches high. For smaller kids, I rotate the cube (stand it on its side), so it is 32 inches high, and for the smallest kids, I set the cube up so I'm using its largest horizontal surface at the top of the cube (24 inches high, with a horizontal of 32 inches by 36 inches). For uses of the cube, see hitting contests in Chapter 6: Moving toward Balance through Selected Methods in Embodied Play Therapy, plus Figure 2.1 (hitting) and Figure 2.2 (kicking) in Chapter 4: The Four Pillars.

Kids benefit from bouncing their shoulders, hips, or their full body (check for any injuries first!) against a cube positioned securely against a wall or door. Gets the breath going and challenges muscular/energetic blocks in the system.

Plasticine Clay and Rubber-headed Mallets

Plasticine clay can be used for grasping and squeezing (calming through exercising the thoracic neuromuscular pathway leading to the cervical spine and brain), molding, and smashing. Clay monsters created by a therapist and a child and/or parent with their child may battle and get flattened – getting in touch with creative assertion! See stories about clay and how it's flattened and used, beginning in the "Pillars" chapter with Kyra's brief story, followed by a discussion of why I use clay and Paolo pounding clay in that same chapter, Petra who wanted to throw clay in Chapter 3: Building a Bridge to a Child, Benjamin, ripping and rolling clay in Chapter 5: Touchy Subjects, Geraldine who built a monster that could corral her mother's in Chapter 7: Deepening Narrative, and how my monster got soundly defeated by Ken's in Chapter 8: Completions in Embodied Play Therapy.

I use plasticine clay since it doesn't dry out between sessions, buying a few one-pound bricks at a local arts supply store.

Deep Sandbox

I have three sandboxes ready, allowing me to see back-to-back clients, whether it's for in-person sessions (outdoors on my "Play Patio" or indoors for when it's raining or cold) or for live video sessions. For in-person sessions, a child or parent selects from a wide range of sandplay figures. For live video sessions, as I pan my cell camera across the shelves, a child or parent (if it's their turn) says "Stop!" when they see a figure they want to use in a sand world that I'll construct as they instruct.

All of my sandboxes are deep to allow digging, burying, and unearthing of figures, plus the construction of mountains or caves in the sand. **Each is filled with sand at least six inches high.** There is an excellent discussion of sand and sandbox selection in the book *Sandtray Therapy: A Practical Manual* by Linda E. Homeyer and Daniel S. Sweeney (2011, pp. 13–17). As the authors point out, the interior bottom of sandboxes is painted blue to simulate water, and the interior sides are blue to simulate sky. I have worked with many children who delight in digging down to the blue bottom of the box. Perhaps because it's like getting down to the ocean floor, where much that is ordinarily hidden in darkness may emerge.

Each of my sandboxes was hand-built by carpenters over the years in my region. Because I have worked out of shared and rented offices in NYC, often used by therapists who were not using sandboxes, the size and exterior finishes of my sandboxes and how they appeared needed to vary to match other furniture in the shared, rented office. For example, my smallest sandbox is 25 inches by 25 inches in length and width, 12 inches high, has wheels at its base so it can easily be moved, and has a lacquered, blond wood exterior to fit in with the décor of one shared NYC office. My biggest box is 28 inches by 28 inches in length and width and 17 inches high (I had more room to accommodate this size in my office at home). The first box I ever had built when I was experimenting with the depth of sand is again 28 inches by 28 inches in length and width, 13.5 inches high, and has stationary wood feet and no wheels (impossible to move when filled with sand!). That last box had to be reinforced with steel at each corner after the weight of a container of water that I left for a week in the box while I was on vacation ended up cracking the sides of the box. (That story is told in my chapter "Emergence: A Tale of Two Boys" in the 2015 book *Deep Play: Exploring the Use of Depth in Psychotherapy with Children* edited by Dennis McCarthy).

It's important that any deep sandbox can repel water (use waterproof paint or a clear seal) because you need to add a little water to your sand periodically to moisten it so you can more easily shape mountains or dig caves without everything collapsing. Authors Homeyer and Sweeney recommend therapists have a spray bottle of water to add a bit of moisture to sand (2011, p. 17).

Each of my boxes has a wooden cover that matches the box. I leave the covers slightly ajar for moisture to evaporate. My sandbox that lives outside year round on my Play Patio is protected in between sessions with a plastic tarp over its fitted wooden cover. Some stones hold the tarp down to keep it in place during windy weather.

Kneeling (Knee) Pad for Sandboxes

Kids usually reach down from a kneeling position to shape sand into mountains or caves, or to place, bury, or dig out figures. To avoid knees getting scraped if kids are wearing shorts or pants getting torn as battles between figures heat up, I give a child a thick foam pad to kneel on. This also imparts a little elevation for smaller kids so they can reach over into the box! Available for purchase at most hardware or gardening stores and online.

A Note on Water for Use in Sandboxes

Many kids like to flood sandboxes, pouring pails or containers in! It's useful to have a few plastic containers of various sizes handy so that children of various ages and carrying capacities can handle them when they're filled! I often help kids pour water, putting some limit on how much is going in.

Props and Sandplay Figures

Props in my in-person and online sessions range the gamut from puppets to clown noses, along with hundreds of miniature figures for sandplay, varying from both wild and farm animals to sea creatures, dragons, dinosaurs, people of different ages, skin colors, and genders, a wide array of miniature emergency, medical, and fire personnel, soldiers from different times in history, treasure boxes, dollhouse furniture, toilets, baby carriages, cars, trucks, boats, and other vehicles, bridges, fences, gates and vegetation ranging from trees and cactus to mountains and volcanoes. For a thorough listing of sandplay figures for a therapist to offer, I recommend the chapter on

"Miniatures: Selection and Arrangement" in the book *Sandtray Therapy: A Practical Manual* by Linda E. Homeyer and Daniel S. Sweeney (2011, pp. 19–29).

Rope for Tug of War with Your Therapist or a Parent

I use a soft rope with nylon or a similar coating that helps protect hands and won't get too slippery when you sweat. The important thing for each participant is to grip the rope enough so you don't drop it. It is best to have a soft carpet below to catch a kid enjoying the rush of descent as they fall.

Tunnel

I use a multicolored, semitranslucent tunnel that pops open, expanding to a length of six feet. I deploy this with younger children to give them the experience of being in a safe, cocooned space. Many kids love hanging out in a tunnel, resting, and looking out at a parent or me through the color filter of the tunnel walls. This engagement with perception combines functional and flexible armor like a second skin or membrane, which offers security, yet still preserves contact with what is external to the child. This encourages an embodied sense of safety that a child can conjure at will, without the need for a play tunnel, although this may take some time to internalize. (See Ricky's story in Chapter 3: Building A Bridge to a Child and Rivka's story in Chapter 4: Parents in the Mix for instances where tunnels were used.)

Drawing Supplies

I offer a variety of crayons, colored pencils, and dry-erase markers (when using a whiteboard) and a sketch pad (ideally 11-inch by 14-inch heavy paper with perforations so you can easily remove drawings). I encourage kids to leave drawings made on paper with me, taping them to the walls and ceiling of my office for the child and others to see.

Sound Effects Tools

When parents and kids were stuck at home during the long initial months of the COVID-19 pandemic, I began getting more creative with sound and music in online tele-sessions, inspired especially by kids who were musicians themselves or, like most kids, music enthusiasts. I began taking kids for virtual visits to the woods around my house, encouraging some to pick up something percussive at home (two spoons or two books to slap together) and making sounds to indicate what they liked on the journey – two hits for "like," one hit for "no like."

This practice has flowered into sound-based guessing games to build awareness and sensitivity (kids guess what's making the sound). Then it's my turn to guess what they're using off-camera and out of my view. Is it the rustle of paper? The click of a stapler? A door closing? (See Claudine's story in Chapter 10: Live Video! Embodied Play Therapy Online for an example of one of these sound guessing games, and Molly's story in the same chapter for an example of one of my outdoor journeys.)

In my music basket, I have percussion sticks, maracas, tambourines, a small drum, a rattle, a small rainstick, and a kazoo. I'll sometimes initiate a sound game with something from the basket.

Note: I've always asked kids to tell me about music they like. For online sessions, I'll often ask a kid, "Music or no music?" and play something from a genre they've told me they like as a soundtrack while they're drawing.

Paper Ripping and Bubble Wrap Stomping Paraphernalia

Children light up when given the opportunity to rip paper apart, watching the floor of an Embodied Play Therapy space fill up with what you've given them to tear into. Preferably for this purpose, collect colorful glossy magazines, catalogs, or advertising circulars. If you still have access to a print newspaper, you could use this. Kids wash their hands afterward to remove any ink that may have ended up on them. I've invited parents to join in the delight of tearing things up with their child and encourage families to try this at home. During the early years of the COVID-19 pandemic, one family created a ripping ritual, designating a room to rip together. A creative antidote to deal with some of the frustration they held from being stuck together in their apartment for weeks on end. While parents and children at home may clean up the mess together (this can promote productive family dialogue on who handles cleaning chores in general), I make it clear to child clients I see in person that they shouldn't worry about making a mess because picking up and recycling what's been ripped is part of my job. For therapists reading this book, that's part of why I leave 15 minutes between sessions!

Stomping on bubble wrap is another way for children to "get into" and feel their legs feet on the ground while having fun. The sound of popping the air out of bubble wrap provides a multisensory experience for kids. For the therapist, clean-up is a cinch.

References

Brodsky, N. (2015). Emergence: A Tale of Two Boys. In D. McCarthy (Ed.), *Deep Play: Exploring the Use of Depth in Psychotherapy with Children* (pp. 143–164). Jessica Kingsley Publishers.

Homeyer, L. E., & Sweeney, D. S. (2011). *Sandtray Therapy: A Practical Manual* (2nd ed.). Routledge.

10

Live Video!

Embodied Play Therapy Online

During the COVID-19 pandemic, I was forced to work and play exclusively in the teletherapy world. While in many cases, I've gotten back to in-person interaction, I'll continue to do live video sessions where they're most convenient for families. Telesessions, I would argue, because of the safety implied by physical distance, in many ways offer an even greater opportunity to play malleably with relationships and communication because the VERY BIG presence of the therapist is not looming over the client in physical space. Even funnier to me is the fact that our roles are reversed! Most children are viewing me on a laptop computer or tablet while I'm seeing them on my large-screen monitor.

My job as an online body-centered therapist is to play with my communication style, watching the child's responses that may tip me off to suggest modulations in my visual and vocal output. Should I move my onscreen presence emphatically closer or give a child some virtual space and retreat a touch? Cued by occasional changes in the manner of my appearance as well as my unexpected out-of-the-box antics, a child, even one prone to distractibility, begins to watch for my next move and concentrate more on our electronically mediated connection.

I do telehealth sessions surrounded by drawings of young people taped to my home office walls and ceiling. A child's

DOI: 10.4324/9781003328186-13

traced outline of their hands and face is the canopy above my head, reminding me of the ephemeral nature of our mutable bodies.

Choosing the Tele-session Room

A child's creativity is often easier in tele-sessions when they have a say in choosing the room at home where they do their Embodied Play Therapy sessions. I learn so much as I see the spaces at home where kids and families live. Kids want me to know what's important to them, and that often includes showing me some of the items in the room they call their own, even if it's a shared one. I find that most children prefer privacy for their tele-sessions, and some will do whatever they must to make sure that happens, often closing a door between them and a sibling (or parent) who'd love to learn what's going on.

Parents first need to make sure the room chosen for tele-sessions is clear of sharp objects and anything someone could fall or trip over. Parents also need to be ready to make a quick exit, so their kids can move and play unfettered by observation. Still, some children, especially younger ones, will want a parent present at the first session. And I may invite a parent who's gone out of the room back into a tele-session to try bouncing on an exercise ball, for example. When parent and child do this together, each using separate balls, the parent/child duo bouncing, bumping into each other, and recovering into balance, we're engaging what Erik Erikson called "playfulness confirmed by mutuality" (1978, p. 57). It's an elegant way of saying that our parents have given the "OK" to this level of fun, a big support for me as a therapist who's interested in ways kids can stretch their bodies, minds, and concepts of self.

Pat Ogden, founder of the Sensorimotor Psychotherapy Institute based in Colorado, and Bonnie Goldstein, founder and director of the Lifespan Psychological Center in Los Angeles, which specializes in individual and group therapy for children, adolescents, and families, write eloquently about engaging the body, creating presence, and building a relationship between therapist and client in video conferencing (2020).

Focusing on somatic resources for clients, they cite John Bowlby and his work in identifying proximity-seeking actions like reaching out to secure the nearness of attachment figures. In Embodied Play Therapy (EPT) online via video, I'm looking to build a secure sense of attachment. Ogden and Goldstein (2020) portray working online with an adult client by "moving closer to the computer camera, and then apart, leaning towards the screen, and reaching" (p. 58). I use similar approaches with my own online behavior in live video sessions with children. Particularly with older children 10–11 and up, I employ the metaphor of reaching toward what they want and pushing away what they don't.

Ogden and Goldstein (2020) give specific guidance to body-centered clinicians offering live "video conferencing" tele-sessions. I've selected a few of the adjustments they recommend and comment on them below:

> Use a large enough room so that you can stand, and move away from the computer without adjusting the screen to make the entire body visible to track and model posture, stance, walking and so forth. (p. 63)

EPT Online: The size of the room I use and the one the clients choose are especially important to teach something like a breathing technique using a large exercise ball. The therapist and client each require sufficient space, and my camera needs to be angled appropriately, for the most part tilted down to capture a full view of the ball on the floor as I'm demonstrating for a child or parent how to drape their body belly down on an exercise ball. (See Figure 2.3 in the "Breathing" section of Chapter 2: The Four Pillars of Embodied Play Therapy with Children.)

> Use a rolling chair to easily adjust distance in proximity to the computer screen to more easily demonstrate posture, gesture, and other movements. (p. 63)

EPT Online: For tele-sessions, I sit on an adjustable stool mounted on a rounded base that allows me to both roll from side to side on screen and raise myself to different heights. I'm particularly focused on the power of my gestures and facial expression to deliver positive encouragement as a child is building a clay monster, engaging with me in a guessing game, or dictating a story to me about their sand world. I stand up and move my stool when needed.

> Encourage having props, (e.g., therapy balls, pillows, and ropes for boundary work) available to you and your client. (p. 63)

EPT Online: Some clients, especially those in small apartments, are reluctant to have a large exercise ball, and in that case, I have to improvise to demonstrate abdominal breathing as a child places their hands on their own belly to push the air out and allow it back in. Pillow fights between parents and kids online lighten up the atmosphere and are great for building attachment between them. Throwing a pillow down on the floor with force, picking it up, and doing that multiple times is a way to mobilize a child's assertive capacity and blow off steam about an upsetting situation or person, and it's also a lot of fun. If I ask a child to imagine something, like the teacher who's given them a ton of homework or the test at school they fear, I remind them that this is something to do here in therapy or in the safe space of their own room. The relief or levity that results from such pillow-throwing tends to lighten a child's anxiety as permission is granted to consciously choose acting on aggressive impulses in the circumscribed container of a session and in my presence. I have yet to have a parent report any misbehavior afterward.

Regarding ropes, I do use ropes during in-person sessions to delineate boundaries or stage a tug-of-war. I don't use ropes in tele-sessions specifically because I'm a little worried about not being able to monitor safety in a remote room. Dropping a rope in a tug of war match between a parent and child could mean someone ends up smashing into a piece of furniture, and I don't want that.

Especially for children reluctant to engage in narrative building, I'm constantly scanning for what's in their remote room, often asking a kid to show me what's on the walls and on their shelves. All of this can help me prompt a child to begin a story with a drawing. As they are drawing, I'll often ask whether they want me to put on a music soundtrack, which I'll select from a streaming service and share live with them via my computer audio. This often amplifies the drama that's unfolding in their minds and on the page.

Expanding Tele-session Video Beyond Its Two Dimensions

As a college student studying film production, I needed to learn the capabilities of camera lenses whose light sensitivity settings could be adjusted to yield what's called depth of field, where less or more of a two-dimensional landscape is brought out of or into focus. Now, as a therapist, I feel the longing of many children to escape from the mandates of a "fixed focus" enforced by parents and schools adhering to rule-based regimens. Today, therapy delivered via tele-session gives us particularly potent opportunities to experiment with depth of perception, emotion, and expression. Especially so because today's children are digital natives, familiar with change in viewer perspective, even as they remain vulnerable to manipulation by the pacing of those changes in the electronic games they play and videos they consume, which set them up for screen addiction and emotional dysregulation.

Effectively adapting Embodied Play Therapy into live two-way video connections with kids demands extra sensitivity to the one-to-one therapist-to-child relationship we are looking to foster. Throughout tele-sessions, the therapist's consciousness of proxemics – in this case, the distance perceived between me and my child client – can serve to deepen our therapeutic relationship. When we play with pendulations of closeness and distance, we can adapt more effectively to each other, whether in person or online. Tele-sessions can play with what a child sees as a therapist moves toward them onscreen, then away. As a child mirrors the therapist's behavior, the atmosphere of the session lightens into a game of motion, often punctuated by laughter, especially when I walk offscreen and return into view, and the child follows my lead, disappearing and reappearing. It's the electronic version of the hide-and-seek game kids know well, preceded by its earlier incarnation when a parent plays peek-a-boo, provoking delight and pleasure by alternately covering and uncovering their eyes as an infant looks on.

Many a child ups the ante on me, covering their face with their hair or, better yet, hiding something under it.

> *My 10-year-old client, Clancy, hiding behind her bangs, asks me to guess what's behind them. Lo and behold, it's a dollop of orange clay pasted in the middle of her forehead. "A third eye that can see even when my eyes are closed!" I respond by disappearing and coming back with two globs of blue clay, one above each eye. "Antennae like a Bug!"*

And So, a Trusting Relationship Grows via Play in Virtual Space

To get and keep kids engaged, especially online, I've become much more "dramatic" in the virtual therapy room with young people. I'm uncomfortably aware that my onscreen image on a child's laptop or tablet needs to be seen as much as possible in CLOSE-UP. Preferably a view that connects me, adult to child, as what I call a "co-player" in our shared virtual energy field. A teletherapeutic play space must be effective enough to convert physical distance into closeness online. Consider, for a moment, the power of a parent's face for an infant. How the perceived mood of the parent's face can elicit tears or smiling gurgles. Fast forward to a depressed or anxious child who's just started teletherapy with me. I may need to modulate my facial expressions at first, but after getting an idea of a kid's level of emotional fluency and range, what I call "response-ability," I get adventurous with my words and the non-verbal expression, which includes dramatic and humorous pantomime. Modeling emotional range for a kid who seems a bit frozen and mirroring the highs and lows of emotionally labile kids prone to acting out. Each kid is masking something similar, namely, difficulty in getting through tough emotional places, including terror, fear, sadness, and grief. Returning a kid to joy in life is my key goal, whether therapy is online or in person.

For online tele-sessions, I play with camera movement so my client's view of me ranges from close-up to full-body, when needed. An example of a situation where I need my client to see me in more of a full-body view is demonstrating belly breathing using an exercise ball or showing a child how to hit piled-up pillows on a bed or chair with a bat. (See Figure 2.1 in Chapter 2: The Four Pillars for what it looks like when a child hits a foam cube during one of my in-person sessions.) To get that fuller body view, I'm moving further away from the camera mounted on the 42-inch monitor I use to view online clients. I manually tilt that camera up or down to capture me more fully in the frame.

For sound, I employ a compact "beam-forming" tabletop conference room microphone unit that sits on the desk below my monitor, which follows my voice as I move across a room. I was taught the critical role sound plays in maintaining "audience attention," so while I'm willing to play a lot with camera movement, it's especially important that remote clients can at least hear me!

Using the camera on my phone, I pan across shelves of sandplay figures at my location, using that same phone to transmit live video, capturing what I'm doing for my remote client. Sometimes I want to minimize my shaky handheld camera as I'm showing what kids direct me to build in a sand world, or the clay monster I'm building to engage theirs in battle across virtual space. In that case, I mount my phone on a mini-tripod or prop it on a nearby shelf. But there are other times where I want to emphasize something. My handheld camera may swoop toward a remote child's choice of sandplay figure or closer to the crunch and splat of my clay monster's virtual defeat. In this way, all may be seen and felt even though a child is many miles away.

Of course, other inputs emanating from the home where the tele-session is happening, from the "annoying" voice of a sibling in the next room to the child's unconscious longing for the parent now at work, are fodder for therapeutic exploration.

> *Ouch! Seven-year-old Shari has gotten a splinter through her socks as she steps off the carpet onto a hardwood floor in her remote room. Even though her busy dad is teleworking from home and she's reluctant to reach out to him, I tell her to let him know what's just happened. The reality of the isolation Shari feels is brought powerfully into focus as her dad comes in to help and takes out the splinter. A clear message that my young client is not being abandoned when dad is working. A moment of physical healing for Shari and of relational healing for both daughter and dad.*

Speaking of injuries, actual and potential, please note the following cautions. This list is by no means exhaustive, and any questions need to be answered on a case-by-case basis through therapist-parent dialogue. (See Chapter 11: Injury Prevention.)

- Remember that the play therapist may not always have a child in view. That view will depend on both the camera angle and whether the child wants to be seen!
- Always have a parent available to step into the remote room to help a child or otherwise participate. They must be available by text and voice call for me and within ear-shot of a child. So, NO NOTIFICATIONS SILENCED by parents working at home. Online play therapy is not babysitting!
- No kicking. This includes anything in the home. I can't judge the safety of any surface a child may kick because I'm not there to assess it. That decision was made after one very active ten-year-old convinced me she needed a snack, bringing a large floor pillow into the kitchen while we were discussing having her kick against the well-padded foam chair in her basement playroom, where she'd just been. While she didn't get hurt lying on her back and kicking the pillow perched on the floor of her kitchen's center island, I decided to never risk that again.

- Punching with well-padded boxing gloves only, ideally with a hanging heavy bag supplied by the parent. If a child could benefit from using fists to hit pillows piled up on their bed, on a couch, or on a chair, talk to the parents first, have them supply appropriate pillows, and practice first with a parent in the room to monitor the situation.
- Slips, Trips, and Falls: Talk to parents about avoiding such possibilities and keep everyone aware of potential hazards in the remote room. You want to avoid anything that a moving human could bump into, knock over, or break. One excited child wanted to show me their over-sized turtle tank. Running around in a dysregulated state became a concern for me, especially when the child went outside of camera view. This prompted me to have a parent come in to see what was going on and have a follow-up discussion with both parents about where the remote sessions would be held in the future. (See more safety ideas in Chapter 11.)

Of course, I'd love it if parents would do the ideal thing and utilize a home theater-size screen as I do, mirroring from a computer with a camera perched on top of their own large screen to capture the action on their end. But few parents can set up their kids for home-based tele-sessions that way. We're used to communicating so much on small phone screens. For the most part, parents have their children participating in online video sessions using a laptop or a tablet. I discourage parents from using phones for video sessions wherever possible. This is because I want Embodied Play Therapy to pack some visual impact. For that purpose, bigger displays are better.

Remember the scene in the classic "The Wizard of Oz" film where the man masquerading as the Wizard is discovered? Like that Wizard, I have more than one identity in play. Joining with children to create fantasy worlds, we become bigger than everyday life, and yet, as when Dorothy yanks back the curtain, I'm just an ordinary human operating behind what, in this case, is an online curtain. Better that the image behind the online curtain be convincing, closer to the size of real life. A phone image is a bit too small and too commonplace as a child's receiver for the sound, visuals, and potential impact of Embodied Play Therapy Online. My goal for our live video sessions is that children will pay attention to the feeling of play both in their actual space as well as in our interaction in online space. It becomes, for all participants, a hybrid dance of transmission, reception, and perception. We are each in our own space, and we are striving to communicate within the imperfect realm of live online video.

What does online video Embodied Play Therapy look and feel like for a child and/or parent? They will usually see my head and upper body transmitted first in what filmmakers call a medium shot or mid-shot. This allows remote clients to see my facial expressions and body language. Still, as child clients get more comfortable in live video Embodied Play Therapy sessions, I like to use some unpredictability as an added element to keep them on their toes. You never know how that zany Neal will show up.

> *It's session time for seven-and-a-half-year-old Sean. Sean's mom has logged him into Neal's Online Embodied Play Therapy Video Room but where's Neal? Sean's really bummed out because he's stuck at home with a cold. The primary red, yellow, blue and purple geometric forms on Neal's carpet seem muted in the dim light. Suddenly, a high-pitched voice says, "Sean? Sean? Is that you?" Rising into Sean's view is a smiling dragon hand puppet. "How are you doing, Sean?" And so an online session begins…*

During the early days of the pandemic, my practice was pretty jammed with depressed, anxious, and often angry kids who were having a hard time adapting to forced online school, to which they were given no alternative. Part entertainment, part caring engagement, Embodied Play Therapy Online began serving as a forum for getting through tough times. While I had ideas, children were in charge from the standpoint of reduced attention spans and sheer boredom as they were bombarded with so many screens. Everything I did in person, from teaching deep breathing to clay monster building to sandplay, needed to move onto live video.

Here's what I developed that I still use today, years after the COVID-19 pandemic put us all into isolation. I present this now because I believe there are many applications for Embodied Play Therapy video sessions. Among these are kids in remote locations, or kids who see therapists sometimes in person and other times online because of parent work and family schedule conflicts, illness or inclement weather, or travel.

Embodied Play Therapy Online involves a certain amount of juggling for the therapist. As I stand up and step away from my large screen where my stationary camera sits and transfer the tele-session to my cellphone, I'm controlling the video image a child or parent sees. While I'm the cinematographer who pans or tilts to display sandplay figures on my shelves, it's the child or parent who tells me to "Stop!" and grab a particular shark or dragon to use in a sand world. Then my phone gets secured to a flexible gooseneck phone holder attached to one wall of my sandbox so I can shift a child's or participating parent's view as needed from me to the sand world they gave me marching orders to build.

We play in sessions with an underlying sense of appreciation for the variety possible in our electronically mediated Embodied Play Therapy Online sessions. We convey flexibility along with a sense of humor. Expressions change. Life changes. A child can walk in their world with alternating lightness, power, and purpose. And the therapist or client who retreats and even disappears at times from onscreen to off always comes back in the end.

Because the ubiquitous phone world populated by flashing Instagram and text exchanges feels so ephemeral, I recommend establishing a strong parental component for online therapy. If anything, I see parents more with online clients than I do with those I meet with in person. Young people are used to "ghosting out." Left to their own devices, they may not always show up for sessions. That's why it's always the parent logging in first, and if they're not participating, they move out of the online space. This is not a time for a parent to share concerns about a child. That's better left to parent-only sessions. What we're demonstrating here, using parent and therapist behavior to begin, is a commitment to the valuing of human relationships, communication, and care, whether these relationships are in-person, online, or both.

Here's my checklist on working with client families and kids online:

- Schedule one or more 50-minute to one-hour parents-only online sessions to fully cover all items below and answer any questions. If necessary and possible, the therapist visits the home in person to advice on safety. Note that online sessions, interspersed with one or more home visits or in-person sessions at the therapist's office, can be helpful to build the bond.
- Parents and the telehealth provider agree on the room at home where the young person will first attend sessions, preparing the room for the safety of the child.
- Consider soft carpeting or play or yoga mats to protect children who will be rolling on exercise balls and jumping.
- I encourage a parent to join the first online session before turning the young client over to me, introducing us, and allowing the young person to decide when they are ready to have the parent exit.
- Parents give me their cell numbers for emergencies.

My intake form for children filled out by parents includes information on what I request they have on hand for tele-sessions:

- Large exercise ball for sitting and movement
- Hand towel for wiping off sweaty hands
- One or more small flat pillows for throwing on the floor
- A lightweight hollow plastic "wiffle ball bat," tennis racket, or "bataka" (padded bat) for hitting a few piled-up pillows on a chair, or a couch

- Yoga or other mat if the teletherapy room has no carpet
- Tennis ball to "ground" energy in the feet and wake up muscles
- Drawing supplies and a large block of plasticine clay (which won't dry out between sessions)
- Well-fitting boxing gloves for punching

No later than after their first online video session, I want a child to help choose the virtual meet-up room at their location. I see this choosing process as especially important for children who are shy or feel some shame about needing to be in therapy. Just as I have the habit of asking adolescents whether the time their parents have selected for therapy is good for them, I make the process of choosing a room for Embodied Play Therapy Online for all children part of the therapeutic process.

I do this for two reasons. First, because the child's involvement in the choice of online room supports a child's agency within the therapy as well as the parent-child relationship that anchors it. A child's expression of preference in the matter of room choice sends a message that they are not being "sent off" to a space selected for them by adults. And second, because while on one level it may be fine that your therapist is "dropping in" for an online session, a child is being asked implicitly or directly to put down their activity of the moment to "play online" with an adult. Maybe not their first choice! Especially when Embodied Play Therapy Online becomes more than just an occasionally scheduled activity, that can be a big ask. It's vulnerable to be seen in your own home. At the very least, having a big say in the choice of location for Embodied Play Therapy Online is one important step in having a child buy in. My main requirements are that it be a location affording privacy for the child's play, while also allowing for expressive movement, sound that may at times get loud, and access to a parent if needed. I also prefer the space not to be a parent's bedroom or a common room where others walk in and out.

Nomi, a 10-year-old who suffered from night terrors and habitually slept in her single mother's bed, needed encouragement to move weekly sessions out of her mom's bedroom. Her desire to show me the birthday gifts she just received provided the impetus she needed to experiment with us conducting online sessions from her bedroom. The good feelings she felt sharing her space for play began making her room more of a center for her and contributed to her eventual returning to it and sleeping there on her own.

Bea, a 12-year-old client who was refusing to attend online classes as the pandemic months wore on, appeared rooted in a rocking chair over her first five or six sessions in the family's living room. Her knees were crossed, arms held tightly across her body, eyes darting to her dog, Amadeus (named after Wolfgang Amadeus Mozart) napping peacefully in a plush dog bed nearby. What might Amadeus be dreaming? Bea began drawing pictures of the dog's dreams as I shared selections from Mozart via my computer audio. Increasingly animated, Bea acquiesced to sessions in the family's home gym where her parents hung a punching bag at my urging. Donning red padded boxing gloves, she delicately moved the bag in circles to the soft opening strains of Ravel's Bolero. As the music moved towards a crescendo, the circles she created widened. The opening of her body posture to motion and breath was emblematic of her growing willingness to let go and take a step back toward life. Sure enough, Bea's parents reported in the next monthly parents-only session, that she had begun to attend classes again.

A good number of the young people in my practice come from families where there is parental conflict, separation, or divorce. There's a special opportunity for therapists working online when we interact with families from different spaces, as children move between the homes of divorced or separated parents. In such situations, I tend toward more onscreen involvement of parents with their kids to reinforce parent-child bonds that might be challenged as families split and reconfigure.

When nine-year-old Niki's mother moved out of the house previously shared by the family, I asked Niki if we could invite her mom to her next session, each of us in a separate, remote space. As I tracked my Zoom-connected cell phone camera across the shelves in my office holding sandplay figures, I offered to serve the mother-child duo as their "world construction manager." Pouring a pail of water into the deep sandbox to allow for digging and building up sand, I asked Niki if she wanted to start with a cave or a mountain, placing my cell phone into the crane-like holder mounted on the side of the sandbox. Niki wanted a mountain which I built, checking that the height and shape worked for her, then wiping my hands on a towel so I could take notes on what each of the two said about their sand worlds.

Giving Niki and Mom each a chance to pick eight figures off the shelves, I created a separate pile for each on the floor near the sandbox in my office. Mom, followed by Niki, instructed me on where to place the figures. Mom chose a tiger mom carrying a tiger baby in her mouth, searching for a treasure chest. A group of warriors supporting the tiger mom feared going to the far side of the mountain, sticking to their quest for the treasure, and the safer side. As I see it, the daughter's anxiety and tension over her mom's recent exit from home got expressed by a Queen dressed in gold and green who trips on a pebble and gets flipped upside down, head buried in the sand. Sea creatures can't escape from a moat circling the mountain. A dragon breathes fire "straight into the sky."

Thus, a multi-session dialogue between parent and child begins with the mom in one home and the child in another, miles away.

Transitioning Clients from In-person to Online and Back Again

When pandemic limitations on travel and mask mandates prevailed, I began to seek remedies to deal with my feelings of entrapment and helplessness over not seeing my clients in person. The first experiments began with my cell phone camera as I went on "virtual excursions" outdoors in sessions with clients.

I asked 10-year-old Maureen, a musician whose orchestra couldn't meet during the pandemic, to bring her flute for her tele-session. As I gingerly made my way across the meadow right outside my window, cell phone camera directed forward to the path ahead, she gave me one toot on her flute when she saw something she liked and two toots for things she didn't.

My home office in Connecticut is set in a wooded landscape of glacial moraine, rocks of all sizes strewn across the ground. This inspired me to begin heaping stones into cairns in session with children under their direction. As "construction manager," kids tell me which rocks to pick up and add to a growing tower. During cold weather, my online work needed to move inside, and the building with stones turned into building towers of blocks under the direction of my young client "architects." The kids love controlling their adult therapist, laughing with me when unstable structures fall.

Smashing clay happened equally well remotely in tele-sessions with the added advantage of my moving a handheld video shot into close-up for emphasis. I often build a clay monster along with my remote client. Instigating a battle between us, I switch the tele-session from my laptop computer to my cell phone, swooping the camera view down to capture the action on my end. My conference room microphone tracks my voice as I move around the room. "*Keowwww! Take that!*" I intensify my battle sounds, moving close to the microphone, encouraging a youngster to let loose with their vocalization, all in the service of fun and energy release, which is especially important for young people who spend many hours behind a desk or riveted to their devices.

More Tales from the Tele-session World

Nine-year-old Molly picks up a pair of binoculars to look at squirrels skittering through the trees outside her Brooklyn apartment. She wants to tell me a secret she hasn't told her parents. "My goal in life is to be alive, and I stay inside almost all the time… to be safe." Molly's mother, an information technology executive, has been reluctant to insist that her daughter reduce her screen time below the present four or more daily hours Molly demands. Still, the family plans to move soon to their beachside summer home, and Molly's resistance to outside activities means both she and her siblings will forego a lot of fun.

Molly needs to get her body into motion. But the only move happening is our return to online sessions because the family's driven hundreds of miles away to their home near the beach. She's ensconced in her room, refusing to budge. So, at Molly's next session, we take a virtual "walk on the wild side" down the suburban lane where I live. On my end, it's Neal and his handheld cellphone camera ready for an impromptu adventure. If she won't go outside, the outside will go to her!!

I tell Molly her job will be to guess what she's seeing. I turn off my camera, move it impossibly close to a clay turtle-shaped planter, and then flip the camera back on. "No clue," she says. I flip the camera to face me and say, "If you get five things I show you today, you'll win this zirconium diamond!" Molly seems pretty engaged as we move from object to object. A rock in the garden. A patch of moss. A flower. A tree. She's increasingly getting the answer right.

I know Molly's angry that her mom wants to take away hours of screen time, which helps her feel safe. She believes she has little choice in the matter. So I decided to play a game of choice for our online session outdoors, where Molly could pick her favorite tree from a number I headed us towards. I show her the texture of different ones. There are deciduous trees with broader leaves, but she prefers the evergreens and picks the one she likes best – the one with sharp clusters of dark green. She names that tree "spikey."

Reflection: I thought the "spikiness" of Molly's tree selection reflected how she felt inside, defensive and, to some extent, alone. Screen use may have given her some comfort, but it also distracted and disconnected her. Yet here we are using one of those screens to connect us in service of something more powerful -- the one-to-one relationship embodied in our play. I sense something is healing in this outside sojourn. A game outside the bounds of her parents' prioritization of family togetherness. Inspired by Molly's engagement during her one-to-one session with me, that at the next parent-only session I recommend Mom give her daughter some one-on-one time. Just the two of them, as opposed to the larger, inclusive family festivities her parents had been emphasizing. Molly took to this like a charm, helping Mom with outdoor clean-up and trips to a nearby park. An online session with Neal outside led to a stronger in-person connection with Mom at home.

Eight-year-old Max has had it with online school. He's been diagnosed with attention issues and sitting in front of another screen for an Embodied Play Therapy Online video session is the last thing he wants to do. He comes on screen, gives me a cursory smirk and runs off. What am I to do? I know Mom and Dad are working virtually from home, so I text Dad to come in for a moment. We've already cut weekly session length from the usual 45 minutes to twenty-five and while Dad looks a bit dazed having just stepped away from work, I ask him if he'll help out today and join us. Max is getting curious because I spy his body in the background, popping in behind his dad.

Max jumps onto the mini-trampoline that his parents bought to help him burn off energy and recover from all those hours listening to his teachers, who've been struggling to keep an online class of diverse students adequately occupied. Maybe Max feels a little guilty that he's blown off part of the session he knows his parents have paid for. But he's back. I ask Dad to pick up a large floor pillow that Max sometimes lounges on in our sessions when I sense he needs to take a break. Dad holds up the pillow as a shield and I ask Dad, "Are you ready for Max?" Dad nods in assent, and I say to his son, "Ok, Max...Ten, nine, eight, seven, six, five, four, three, two, one...Charge!" Max, with a running start, slams into his pillow-protected dad, doing this multiple times until he falls to the floor, grinning and spent. Dad joins him on the floor, and for a few moments, beaming at each other, they rest…until Max starts to tickle his dad!

Reflection: I sometimes feel a little bit out of control when following the lead of children in session, including figuring out how to deal with outright refusal to participate in online sessions. Parents needed to be a bigger part of the mix in Embodied Play Therapy Online. In making a film, a director will often have their cinematographer position a camera to give a character's perspective – a "Point of View" (POV) shot. Often hand-held, sometimes shaky, this POV shot brings us closer to a character. It can help us empathize more with the challenges facing them (Nashville Film Institute, n.d.) while bringing us into visceral appreciation of the instability of things, providing a shock to perspective and what we thought we knew.

That's where I found myself, a therapist who had an established way of doing sessions in person who then needed to pivot radically in what I was doing to help children and parents. Ironically, that shift in perspective, where kids got wilder, and I was more at their mercy, led me to a renewal of focus on family therapy that involved parents more. Having a child like Max receive an opportunity with his father to feel the full impact of the boy's frustration provided an experience of how emotions, expressed in an embodied way, can make way for what is next. In this case, a moment of closeness between Dad and son. I sensed that each of them, in the midst of chaos in the COVID-19 pandemic, would benefit from a little Embodied Play Therapy pandemonium. Moving father and son from isolation within separate virtual worlds into togetherness – and a shared Point of View. All accomplished online.

Max continued to hate online school. My sessions with him were sometimes brief, with Mom and Dad taking over to talk with me. But even this limitation had its silver lining. Max and I kept in contact until we could find a therapist closer to his home, with whom he could benefit from a mix of in-person and online sessions (something I couldn't provide because during the COVID-19 pandemic years, I'd given up my in-person office that I was renting part-time in NYC). And I was able to help the parents consider the additional services at school they'd need to support their son in his learning, as a neuropsychological work-up with an allied clinician helped identify the strengths that would move Max's education forward.

Limits: Online vs. In-person

It's a reality that many kids get bored with online interaction, and I've had to experiment in accommodating reduced attention spans. This is especially true with neurodiverse children and with kids who spend a lot of their time in front of screens. They often want to return to the snap, crackle, and pop of fast-paced gaming with which I can't compete. My answer has been to alter my session lengths, customizing who in the family participates and for how long to individual family needs. Since my session time is reserved in 45 or 50-minute session blocks, I prepare one or both parents to meet with me if the child is just not up to it. This helps me learn what's going on with the child and family from a parent's perspective and also for the parent to have some playtime of their own.

Many parents are understandably frustrated with their child's behavior. They may need to work some of their tension out with me using that lightweight hollow plastic bat to hit pillows piled up on a couch or chair. Or the parent may enjoy opening further into their imagining selves to direct the creation of a sand world where my hands place figures they've chosen. When I do this, we're honoring a play domain often occupied solely by children in the family. As a parent slows down to their own play process, freed from the constant inner demand to be the grown-up, child parts inside the parent often emerge.

If we do switch to a parent as the onscreen focus, I may ask the parent to change rooms and close the door to create a boundary that avoids, as much as possible, a child overhearing a parent's thoughts to me about their child. Or use their phone or laptop to play some white noise, creating a privacy barrier around what they're saying.

I've found that some parents, in both in-person and online sessions, speak to me about a child in the third person, almost as if the child were not in the room with us. I view this as a backhanded way of disciplining a child by complaining about them in front of another adult. Not only do I believe this is ineffective in achieving parent goals, but it can also threaten any trust I'm building with that child, possibly undermining the therapeutic relationship. So I encourage closed doors. Of course, hearing a parent hitting or having an interest in what a parent may be drawing may cause a child to re-enter the session. Then we have a new opportunity to return a child who's had a break from the action to fruitful interaction with the parent. *"What's that you're drawing, Daddy? I can do it better. Watch this!"*

Tools of the Online Trade: Creative Use of Audio and Video

"Digital Native" children who are more fluent in the online sphere than we adults love to show us who's boss in that world. I have had no choice but to play along and adapt what I'm doing to their expertise. Unlike some of my colleagues, I am not engaging in sessions with multi-player games like the ones my clients play. I will never be able to compete, and I'm interested most in using the online interaction for children to experiment with how that mode of interaction affects their senses and relationship with me.

My first introduction to the video gaming world happened a long time ago in the era of "Pac-Man" as I watched masterful animators Eli Noyes and Kit Laybourne create the first episode of the "Braingames" series for kids at HBO from my job as a manager in the network's original programming area. Now, 40-plus years later, I'm using that inspiration in guessing games with kids, whether it's me outside, as in this chapter's case vignette of Molly remotely identifying items in my yard, or using sound to have kids connect with what's right in front of them in their room.

Nine-year-old Claudine is stuck inside her room. Even though she's only a few miles away from me in Connecticut, she's home from school with a cold, and we have no choice but to do her session online. She doesn't feel up to bouncing on her exercise ball, smashing clay, and doesn't want me to build a sand world. Dad is working remotely in the room next door and can't be disturbed. What am I to do with the remaining 15 minutes of session time?

I move out of camera view, stepping into my shoes and off the carpet onto the echoey tile floor.

"Claudine, can you hear me? Guess what's making this sound?" She guesses it's me clunking around. Back up on screen, I hold up my shoes for her to see: "Right, Claudine!"

"Ok, Claudine, what's this?" She hears a clicking sound that I repeat. "Are you clicking a pen? Plugging in your HTML cable?" (I hold up my stapler in close-up view.)

Then something louder. Claudine: "It sounds like thunder!" I hold up my "thunder machine" for her to see, a hands-breath cylinder with a spring attached.

Now it's Claudine's turn, and she's bent on tricking me. Claudine moves off screen, and I hear the faintest crackling sound. "Is that a piece of paper? I ask. Smiling, Claudine holds up a cellophane bag of cookies she's been crinkling. But then she gets crafty, and I hear nothing as hard as I try. Claudine comes back in, fanning her face with a paper plate.

Reflections: The above relates directly to Claudine's time in Embodied Play Therapy since her issue was, in fact, around volume, her own and that of her family. While she often provoked parental attention when she got hurt and would cry, it was difficult for her to pause, gather her energy, and speak up on her own behalf in conflicts with her older sister. After this session with its contrast of loud and soft sounds, I decided to raise the volume on my request that her parents buy a heavy punching bag and boxing gloves for their basement rec room. When they hung that, Claudine got a chance to punch it with me in remote sessions and then in between sessions whenever she needed to release some of the feelings she had been submerging.

Props in Remote Rooms of Online Clients

The room or rooms being used for tele-sessions are a potential treasure trove for me. I'm constantly scanning client space: walls, toys on shelves, pillows on chairs. Whatever we might enlist as a prop beyond the tools I've asked parents to buy for remote Embodied Play Therapy. Also, if there is nothing on the walls of a child's room, I am curious why. Is that child afraid to place a stamp of their individuality in their space and with the people who surround them? Are we looking at a cry of protest spoken through the empty vacuum? I've seen multiple situations where the emptiness I observe online in a video session speaks to the richness that could be – a blank canvas ready for the precious imprinting of childhood hopes and dreams. (See more on "Props" in Chapter 9: Toolbox for Embodied Play Therapy.)

A Note on Mobilizing Aggression Online

If parents don't want their child using a bat at home outside of session, which may be the case where there's sibling conflict, and it could be misused, I show the child how to throw a pillow repeatedly down onto the floor and underscore how it's a possible way to express and rebalance themselves when not in session. In all instances, we're focused on a level of emotional expression and containment that makes sense contextually within a child's family, at school, or other public venues.

Mess-ups Online

Now that most of the world has moved the COVID-19 pandemic into its rear-view mirror, it's worth looking back at how shifting Embodied Play Therapy exclusively online led to some crazy times with kids and parents. Adapting to families who just craved a return to a sense of normalcy helped me mine some useful therapeutic nuggets, some technical, and some influencing how I would run online sessions and who I would run them for.

With children forced to attend online school, many had their fill of video-enabled interaction. Obstreperous kids would jump on screen and then off, and I had to invent ways that would engage them for at least half of the usual 45-minute in-person sessions I was used to giving. This found me playing not only with props. I played with proxemics (in-out-toward-away-and-back), prosody (vocal volume, pitch, and accent), and whatever technical wizardry kids knew about and were ready to instruct their sometimes hapless and helpless Embodied Play Therapist in.

Kids who had worked with me for a long time in person weren't afraid to blow out of session to be replaced with an apologetic parent. What drew them back were not only the games I initiated, but also the games they began. Games I continue to use today. Throwing nonsense words at me in a chat window had me set up a guessing game where I dared a kid to find a word hidden in a long string of random nonsense letters. A child used filters on Zoom to turn themselves into a bear, or a chipmunk, or a devil, and taught me how to respond in kind. The key in all this was that we were hanging on to a relationship amid the chaos of the COVID-19 pandemic lockdown. Connecting in the craziest of ways, even if that meant staying with each other for a briefer time in shorter sessions.

It was a time of irregular innovation made of necessity that taught me to surrender to compromise around the idea I would always know best how to be and what to do. As I stretched to accommodate to children on their native turf, I began to accept that I didn't always have to look good, look like the expert, and know the routes that play would take online. It became clear that while Embodied Play Therapy Online could be effective, with children's parents as more equal co-participants, my role as guide and master of ceremonies in challenging times needed to grow beyond what I foresaw as possible.

Bonus Notes for Therapists – Sandplay on Live Video in Embodied Play Therapy Online

For the sandbox, I use a metal 30-inch adjustable, folding cell phone stand that has springs and tension adjustment knobs at each joint. The stand is securely clipped to one sandbox wall, which frees my hands. I snap my iPhone into the holder at the top of the stand, mirroring the live video session (usually a Zoom meeting on my phone) via AirPlay to a 32-inch TV monitor mounted behind the top of my sandbox. The enlarged image on the monitor helps me better track responses of young people and, at the same time, see an image of the box in whole or in part, including figures I'm placing there at my client's direction. (You can probably use Chromecast to mirror the signal to your monitor if you are using an Android phone.)

Neal: Do you want your mountain in the center of the box or over here in the corner?

Child: In the center. Now dig a cave in the mountain!

Neal: Where? In the back of the mountain or the front?

Child: The side!

Neal: Which side? This side, or that side? *(Neal points)*

Child: The one you're pointing at now! *(Neal digs a cave in the chosen side)*

Neal: How's that? Deep enough?

Child: Perfect. Now put the treasure in there!
(Neal swings the long arm of the phone stand that had been angled down at the sandbox up towards his face to make eye contact with his client, and then back down to the world being created in the sand.)

Neal: OK, what goes in next? *(Wiping the sand off his hands, Neal takes the phone off its cradle and brings a group of figures into view that the client had selected for him to grab one by one off shelves in his Embodied Play Therapy office.)*

Child: The dragon. He's not letting anyone near that treasure!

When I am doing tele-sessions outdoors, at the beach, for example, I mount my phone on a mini cell phone Tripod so my phone's camera can maintain stable focus on the world I'm building with figures at a child's or parent's direction.

> *I've carted a bagful of my young client's favorite sandplay figures to the beach to change up the online environment we've been using during the COVID-19 pandemic. The wind is blowing, and it's hard for me to see my client's reactions on my little phone screen, but I'm doing my best. I've gone from hundreds of figures on my shelves to rummaging through a plastic bag of about 20. Ahhh…there's the dinosaur! And what's this… a golden goblet! I know my client is very sad today, stuck at home in NYC so I've brought along a colorful "magic wand." I've also carried in my stash of sandplay figures a "hero" that this client has been using in past sessions, whom he calls "Map Boy" because he knows the way to find "the gold."*
>
> *(Into a plastic golden goblet, Neal pours some water from the nearby ocean whose waves can be heard lapping on the shore. He waves the wand over the goblet.)*

Neal: This is the magic potion. Is Map Boy ready?

Child: Yes. Map Boy is ready…
(Neal tips the figure of "Map Boy" down towards the goblet to drink.)

Neal: Gluuuggg! Gluuuuggg!
(Map Boy falls into the goblet…)

Child: *(Cracking up in laughter)* Neaaallllllll! C'mon! That's not the end of the story!!!!!

References

Erikson, E. H. (1978). *Toys and Reasons: Stages in the Ritualization of Experience*. Marion Boyers Publishers.

Nashville Film Institute. (n.d). *Point of View Shot: Everything You Need to Know*. https://www.nfi.edu/point-of-view-shot/

Ogden, P., & Goldstein, B. (2020). Sensorimotor Psychotherapy from a Distance: Engaging the Body, Creating Presence, and Building Relationship in Videoconferencing. In H. Weinberg & A. Rolnick (Eds.), *Theory and Practice of Online Therapy: Internet Delivered Interventions for Individuals, Groups, Families and Organizations* (pp. 47–65). Routledge.

11

Injury Prevention

Some years ago, I became aware that, although rare, some children with a variety of often undiagnosed heart conditions were collapsing on athletic fields due to cardiac arrest (Liu, 2023). When I headed up a personnel department for a local public housing agency, I was given some training in what is called "risk control." Risk control is basically prevention. Looking around an environment for potential dangers and using your common sense to mitigate the potential of bad things happening.

I brought that "risk control" attitude to decreasing the chances that children could get hurt in my practice of Embodied Play Therapy. What that meant for me was taking a class in CPR, even though chances were small that a child in one of my sessions would require that level of care.

Those using embodied play methods may be working with a wide range of children having different abilities and endurance levels. Show parents what the child will be doing: jumping on a mini-trampoline, using boxing gloves to punch a padded shield or bag, and using a hollow plastic bat to hit a foam cube or piled-up pillows. Whatever you select for your menu of embodied practice, think through not only what you hope to achieve, but what could go wrong.

DOI: 10.4324/9781003328186-14

A Child Standing on Something They Could Fall Off, Jump Off, or Pull Down

Look around your office and all it contains. The chairs, desk, and file cabinet. Kids may want to climb them. Do you need to consider having these items elsewhere?

Are there any sharp edges that need to be shielded or padded?

I was once working with a child who had been brought in by panicked parents because she was walking into heavily trafficked city streets. All she wanted to do was climb up on my foam cube, stand up, and walk around on its spongy surface. Of course, I was somewhat scared she'd fall off, even though that would have been onto a carpeted floor. And yet, her knowing I was watching close by and could catch her if needed, became part of the healing. After two sessions of this, she stopped climbing and moved to floor level, jumping on my mini-trampoline, bouncing on an exercise ball, and making sand worlds. No further reports of sudden sojourns into risky streets were ever reported by parents again.

What's the Floor Covered With?

If I were building or renting another office now, I would look at having thick wall-to-wall carpeting in the area where kids will be playing with certain equipment, like exercise balls. When a child flies off, it may be onto their hand, elbow, or head. When a rope is used for a tug of war, that rope may get dropped, with a child, parent, or therapist headed to the floor.

I've opted for carpet including under my sandbox, even though it needs to be vacuumed regularly. Children often use water in their sand worlds. Better that you and your clients have the traction of carpet rather than slippery tile underfoot. Most sogginess will dry out or can be blown dry with a hair dryer.

Dry and Clean Washcloths

I keep a stack of these available on the shelf next to my sandboxes and wash them after each use. Since slightly moist sand is better for shaping mountains or caves, and a certain amount may stick to their hands, and get in their eyes, I tell children to wipe sand from their hands after they finish building a sand world. Parents using sandboxes often request a washcloth, too!

Masks Available for Kids, Parents, and Clinicians

With the experience of the COVID-19 pandemic in mind, I have a stack of fresh cellophane-wrapped masks for kids, parents, and me to wear to aid in preventing transmission of infection.

Air Purifier for Use in a Space with Multiple Active People

I have a purifier with a HEPA filter that I turn on, especially if a child comes in sniffling and the parent has forgotten to tell me they or a family member was sick or exposed to something.

Monitoring Children Who Use Water in Sandboxes

Many kids love to flood a sandbox with lots of water. Since kids can get carried away, I have taken to assisting some with bringing water to the box, or in extreme cases, being the only one who brings water to the box. In my view, it's fine to set limits. Know what your limits are.

Tie-down Cables and Electrical Cords

For offices that do double duty for online and in-person clients, there are usually more than a small number of cables and cords.

I bundle these together with zip ties wherever possible and move them against walls and away from space used for active play.

Gloves to Prevent Blisters for Kids Handling a Bat (See Chapter 9: Toolbox for Embodied Play Therapy)

I use lightweight fabric gardening gloves or batting gloves to protect hands. Some fabric gloves can be laundered after single use.

Wipe Down the Handles of Bats and Wash Off Sandplay Figures at Reasonable Intervals

Given multiple users, it's best to consider having some cleaning regimen in place. You can use an antibacterial spray or hand wipes. I periodically dunk plastic and metal sandplay figures in a solution of dish soap and water before air-drying.

Have a First Aid Kit Available

The worst I have experienced is a child getting a splinter who needed a Band-Aid. My first aid kit includes antiseptic wipe packets as well. Because I conduct some sessions outdoors, I want to know from parents whether children have allergies, including any allergies to bug bites or stings. I discuss with parents how the family handles such issues. My sessions are held either with the parent nearby in a waiting room, parked in my home office driveway, or with the parent in the room so they can be involved in any necessary care.

Important: This list is not exhaustive. Clinicians, body-centered practitioners, and parents should discuss risks on a case-by-case basis and tailor activities to specific children with safety foremost in mind.

References

Liu, X. (2023, January 25). *Youth Athletes Shouldn't Skip a Beat When It Comes to Heart Health.* Mayo Clinic Health System. https://www.mayoclinichealthsystem.org/hometown-health/speaking-of-health/young-athletes-and-heart-health

Afterword

Inner Children Surface in an Embodied Play Therapy Group for Adults

While this book focuses on Embodied Play Therapy with individual young people, my therapy practice contains a large number of adult clients and couples (including parents of children and adolescent clients). These adult folks often find themselves STUCK, repeatedly using unproductive strategies to handle dilemmas thrown at them in domains ranging from work to family. Grateful for the learning granted through play with brave and enterprising young clients, the frequency of my daring to suggest Embodied Play Therapy in my work with adult clients grows daily.

For adults, as with children, willingness to "play" into new roles and have fun releases tension and expands rather than contracts the body. Many modes of expression become possible. A combination of play with somatic psychotherapy increases the probability of lives lived with less rigidified musculature and more in flow, pleasure, and joy. (see book by Alexander Lowen (1970/2004): *Pleasure: A Creative Approach to Life*, especially pp. 43–44). A more elastic and expansive window of tolerance is developed in response to changing personal circumstances and in relationships with others (Siegel, 1999, pp. 253–258).

Live Video Online Group for "Adults and Their Inner Children"

In my online video group for adults whose chronological age stretches from their mid-twenties through their seventies, experiments in play are gaining traction. It's 7 PM on a balmy evening in Florida, where my wife and I have set up shop for some weeks of remote work free from the freeze up north. While I'm ready to rock and roll tonight in what I expect to be multiplying profusion of play, only one of my five group members is in the virtual waiting room. Low energy tonight? Sure enough. As the group trickles in, no smile crosses a single face as each entering member adjusts their camera and notes the sparse attendance so far.

I begin, as always, with movement to music. Picking up on a paucity of breathing and sluggish motions of arms and legs, I notice the atmosphere of resistance and refusal that began with late arrival. Usually, I prompt group members to begin with embodying and energizing feelings they tend to hold back in daily life. This may include an exercise of protest to let out their frustration – sharp arm and elbow movements up and over their shoulder blades as they yell, "Get off my back!" or bringing their arms up to push away others, grunting, "Get away!" or "No!" Tonight, there's none of this. Just a somnolent rocking in place on one screen, arms circling in front of the chest and languidly behind on another. Remembering the waves earlier that day from my walk on the beach, I encourage everyone to swim through the evident emotional muck pervading tonight's group space. Each member responds to my prompt, one doing the breaststroke, another doing the crawl through what they might perceive as dense, viscous, and icky. Welcome to the "goop-y group!"

During the 10 minutes of "group check-in" which follows, the source for each group member of this evening's contagious lethargy is spoken. Included in the mix are packed work schedules, family illness, and challenges with money, children, love, and keeping a complicated adult life in balance when all you want to do is crawl under a rock and hide.

"Enough, I say! We're going on a mission!" I tell the group that I often take kids in my Embodied Play Therapy practice on a "Hero's Journey." I also say that the first stage of any such journey is often "Refusal of the Call." Refusal to take that first courageous step out of our comfort zone and embark on the uncharted waters of a Hero's Journey–a reticence as old as Odysseus (See Campbell (2008), *The Hero with a Thousand Faces* and Rylee Blake (2024), *The Hero's Journey Through Therapy*.)

"Find your No!" "Refuse this call!" I say, moving my head close to the camera for impact. I raise my voice for the conference room-style table microphone that tracks me wherever I move in my space and, for greater emphasis, move my face right up to it. "Tell us your truth!" "Let's get real," I blast out at the group. "What part of you wants to protect yourself and stay stuck right where you are on the hamster wheel?!" One group member blurts out, "I won't move!" Another yells, "You can't make me!" A third: "I'll stay a victim forever and make you suffer!"

I encourage group members to feel the muck they're in tonight, squishing it through their fingers, imagining now they've grown webbed hands like a salamander's. We're all underwater. All helpless. Drowning in it. Sensing this could go on and on, I take a risk to provoke the group, and shift the dreary energy.

"Is anyone willing to take a bite outta this mudcake?!"

What's it taste like, this yuck?! One says it's like jiggling jello. "What color is it?" "It's yellow!"

Ok, I say, "We're on the Yellow Jello Mission…!"

"Who's the captain? Who's the first mate? Who'll lead the mutiny? The heck with what Neal wants!" I fume. Everyone for themselves! Take no prisoners!"

A group member raises a hand in defiance. This group member, who said their life was like moving through mud, picks up a yellow plastic bat and begins activating energy, holding the bat over their head and slamming it down on pillows piled up on a chair in their room. Other group members cheer the mutinous one on. "Go for it! You're in charge! No one's going to boss you around! No more swimming upstream! Go with the current! It's the only way!"

"Spit out what you're swallowing!" I yell. "All this muck!" One member purses their lips and makes a sputtering sound. Another follows. Still, I discern a decrease in energy level as group members collectively reach the edge of how far their comfort zones will allow them to go tonight. I sense the reassertion of adult personas who learned to repress emotion, modulate facial expressions, and speak words well-fitted to families of origin. But, still we've had a dose of outlandish role-playing tonight. And fun. We've begun to play with the possibility of breaking through habitual ways of being through play together.

I know our group's experiments in play will need to live on in future sessions. We've reached our limit for now in letting out the vociferous and vocal inner children inside us, and adult personas will need to be heard, too. This role expansion, to allow our "inner kids" to surface, especially where aggression gets involved, demands a level of patience for a therapist, not needed with children whose "masks" of looking good have not had so many years of use.

We will need to play more, trying on new roles to see how they feel. To get in touch with the young ones inside that once held abundant levels of invention. Together, we will risk being seen in these vulnerable places where our inner children live. Slowing down where necessary. Checking in with each other along the way to make sure we're all OK. While some of my "adult group" members have parented children, others hope to undertake this noble task in the future. I, for one, feel grateful they can work on themselves and contact, if only briefly, unprocessed parts of themselves that emerged in childhood. Hidden "inner children" who reside beneath the mask of adult veneer. Often, silenced. Often in pain.

Reflection: I believe it's never too late to allow young parts of ourselves, potential fonts of great creativity and problem-solving prowess, to surface. While it's hard to do this work, to play, to stretch, and to grow in adulthood, the alternative is getting stuck. This is what Erik Erikson (1950/1993) defines as a key task key task of adulthood: "Generativity vs. Stagnation" (p. 266).

I received this gift later in life – the opportunity to play together with children, with parents of these young people, with adults, and couples questing for a greater sense of vitality as they pursue what's vital in their lives. Taught by my clients, I am learning that we can play with our partners and friends, with our co-workers, and even with our own surviving parents who may have longed for levels of lightness they never got a chance to experience as kids.

As Dennis McCarthy (2012) says, and has written about so eloquently, things often need to fall apart to grow back together in ways we may not have dreamed. It's a journey worth the risk, as presence with our own breathing, pulsating, always changing state of being, puts our hearts into play. Seeing my clients' willingness to connect with parts inside they may have previously rejected, I feel such gratitude. Their courage inspires me to search for new arenas where Embodied Play Therapy may grow further as a kind of "Petri Dish for Play," mixing components of attention and care into living loam so clients can move forward, less fettered, and more free.

Digging down with clients amid the roots of their stories, I feel their hurt, their hope, and the potential for joy we all share. Each of us is a steward of a unique and precious constellation of personalities. Collectively embodied on this small blue orb to circle each other and resolve what generations past could not. May each of us, vulnerable and indispensable humans, not waste the precious life given in the mysterious darkness of our mother's womb. May you, my readers, birth a multitude of productive play spaces that help folks, young and older, open into lives filled with curiosity for what may yet unfold.

References

Blake, R. (2024). *The Hero's Journey Through Therapy: A Literature Review.* Expressive Therapies Capstone Theses. 768. https://digitalcommons.lesley.edu/expressive_theses/768

Campbell, J. (2008). *The Hero with a Thousand Faces* (3rd ed.). New World Library.

Erikson, E. H. (1993). *Childhood and Society*. W. W. Norton. (Original work published 1950)

Lowen, A. (2004). *Pleasure: A Creative Approach to Life*. Bioenergetics Press. (Original work published 1970)
McCarthy, D. (2012). *A Manual of Dynamic Play Therapy: Helping Things Fall Apart, the Paradox of Play*. Jessica Kingsley Publishers.
Siegel, D. J. (1999). *The Developing Mind: How Relationships and the Brain Interact to Shape Who We Are*. The Guilford Press.

Addendum

"Core for Kids Playshop"

A Group Experience

In early 2015, I wanted to see how a group workshop could "road test" some of the techniques I had collectively called "Core for Kids," because I'd adapted adult techniques from Core Energetics to my work with children. I also saw this as an opportunity to introduce parents and children to the activities they would encounter in individual sessions with me. So, I invited a small number of families with kids ages 7–11 to join me and my colleague, art therapist Elaine Oswald LCAT, a Core Energetics practitioner like me, in a one-time group experience. Four individual parents showed up with one child each in tow for a total of eight participants.

Soft strains of music from East Africa seeped through into the hallway leading to my Manhattan office, where parents and children took off their shoes, piling them next to the heavy wooden office door. After brief introductions, we invited everyone to walk slowly around the large room, circling it and making the space they'd be occupying for the next 90 minutes their own.

Emotional parts within a child and the inner children of adults struggle between obeying authority and not. The specter of disapproval from family, schools, and society is so strong that playing with the possibility of non-compliance is something I wanted to have parents and kids experience today. To have kids see their parents allow for the place inside themselves that embodies and says "No!"

Couch pillows were scattered around the room, and we encouraged individual parents and children to pick them up and throw them down on the floor, repeatedly saying the word "No!" for the pure joy of giving voice to the refusal that's often under wraps. To get the energy moving further, I then led a group jump with everyone beginning at the four corners of the room, moving toward each other and back, experimenting with activating the body in space. As I jumped in, it felt like being part of a human accordion made up of moving bodies pumping in and out.

Next, we showed the group how to discharge the energy they each had built up in their bodies by softening their knees, supporting the lower back with their hands, and tilting the body backward into a grounding "bow" position. Asking the parents and kids to connect with their breath, we encouraged them to make eye contact with their family member. And then playing with making a face at that person, perhaps daring to stick their tongues out at each other. Elaine and I noticed the energy change in the room as initial awkwardness shifted into lightness and laughter.

Since embodied play with young people involves a good deal of movement, I told the group about my basic rules of safety, respect, and reasonable boundaries. First and foremost: "Don't hurt yourself, don't hurt us, and don't hurt the room." To demonstrate, I put on boxing gloves and gave one parent a padded shield. As I punched the shield held by the parent, I said, "You could hurt your hand if you punched without these gloves." You could hurt your parent by punching above or below the shield! No one gets hurt as we play." I asked everyone to look around the room. "How could you hurt the room?" One kid piped up, pointing to a plant on a windowsill: "Don't punch the plant!' Everyone laughed and nodded. "Yes," I said. "And don't punch or kick the wall or break anything, even if part of you would like to!" Looking at the parent holding the shield, I said, "You need to set up a contract with your kid around safety. No one gets hurt."

I tell the group that another pattern I notice is the degree to which the voices and movements of people in families get silenced. Sometimes kids or parents get explosive from sheer frustration. How many kids have been asked to close their mouths as they eat? To stay quiet. To sit still. I want to play with the opposite.

I pointed to shelves that held a myriad of sandplay figures and asked everyone to pick an animal they most wanted to be right now. "An animal from the forest, the desert, or the ocean!"

As the parents and kids headed over to the shelves to make their selection, I turned on a recording of sounds you might hear deep in the forest at night. Crickets, bird calls, and hoots from other animals. I said, "As you walk around with your animal figure, imagine you're waking up in the forest! You're hungry! The time has come to stalk your prey! You may need to hide from danger, but you need to eat!" I demonstrated by taking large, stealthy, low-to-the-ground steps around the room and signaled for the parents and kids to follow my example. Elaine and I made exaggerated movements with our arms, opening our jaws wide to make chomping sounds as we consumed our imaginary capture. Parents and kids answered us, their growls and yelps resonating off the walls in the room. Again, the energy of the room was loosening up. People playing freely in animal guise.

After a break, we gave each parent-child dyad a large piece of paper from a roll. Each person got an orange plastic cup. "Imagine that each of these cups has a magic potion that will turn you into a monster! Take a make-believe sip and draw that monster." As the drawings were completed, I asked the parents and children what they had drawn. "What's your monster's name?" "What does your monster do that's so monstrous?" Now let's get up and be our monsters! Move around the room like your monster! Make a sound like your monster! You may meet other monsters!" Elaine and I demonstrated moving in and out of the monsters as they gyrated, hissing with open jaws, and their hands turned into claws. We had a real "Monster Mash."

After we settled down, I described what a "Core for Kids" session with an individual child might look like. How a child participating in-person or online uses similar equipment. A tennis ball that a young person steps on with varying pressure, one foot at a time, while the other foot remains firmly on the floor. Deep breathing is encouraged while this is happening. All this is to ground energy. Tennis balls were passed around, one to each parent and child, and after I demonstrated, they tried this out.

I told the parents how I look for ways a child moves. Are they active or passive? Risk-averse or adventurous? A large exercise ball is a great way to check that out. I brought out two exercise balls and asked two kids what they would like to do. One sat and bounced. Another flopped onto a ball, belly down, and rolled. This, I told the parents, could be used to open up energy at the beginning of an individual session with careful spotting by me or a parent in concert with self-awareness by their child.

Next, I brought out a large foam cube covered in corduroy fabric and demonstrated how a child could hit it with a padded bataka or slam their body into it or kick it. All active motions that move a child in session out of the quiet zones that parents or schools demand. Better to get some of that obstreperous energy out here than at the dinner table! Demonstrating how to hit the cube with a bataka, I asked a few parents and kids to try it, noticing their energy, and asking how they felt: "Self-conscious? Relaxed? Energized?" Could they imagine that this mobilizing and movement of their energy would open them to more possibilities in their lives? Could it lead them to reach more for what they want in relationships with family, friends, and at work or school? I talked with the parents and kids about having a life where they feel centered and grounded, returning to what Core Energetics calls your "Center of Right Energy," or "Core," recovering from places where you feel out of balance and out of sorts into that Center, which just feels right to you.

The final part of the workshop was quieting down and grounding. Parents and kids chose a place in the room where they felt comfortable sitting or lying down on the carpet, eyes closed or looking at something that they liked in the room.

I turned on calming music and led a minute of slow breathing. Then, I invited each person to pick two figures from the sandplay shelves, representing how they felt now after our 90 minutes of being together, placing what they'd selected into a single shared sandbox. I noticed a parent selecting a female lion with a baby cub carried gently in its mouth and a child picking a roaring tiger. Another, a dragon. Another, a roaring bear.

Together, we gazed at our group masterpiece in the sand. Ending our playshop, each child received a "Core for Kids" stress ball as a parting gift and each parent got a handout. We bumped hands with a smile as energized kids and parents exited back into the bustling streets of Manhattan.

Handout – Two Techniques Used at "Core for Kids Playshop" for Quieting Down and "Being Present" on a Body Level

The "Heartbeat Exercise"

Jump up and down in place for one minute and then sit back down, placing your hands on your heart. Close your eyes. Sense your heartbeat. Feel your breath moving in and out. In the silence, imagine you are scanning every part of your body from head to toes. See where there's tension and let it go.

The "Squeeze, Squish, and Relax Movement Meditation"

Lie down with your eyes closed. Now, squeeze every muscle in your body as tightly as you can. "Squish" your toes and feet in. Tighten the muscles in your legs up to your hips. Suck in your belly. Squeeze your hands into fists. Raise your shoulders toward your head. Hold this squeezed/squished-up position for a few seconds … and then fully release and relax with a loud "Ahhhh" sound!

Acknowledgments

Deep gratitude goes out to:

- Judy Gotlieb, my "first and last editor," who does all she can to make my life and words sing.
- Those who read drafts with such careful and caring eyes – Sue Erikson Bloland, Elizabeth S. Carl, William J. Doherty, Stuart Friedman, Brian Gleason, Dennis McCarthy, Deborah Vilas, and Karyne B. Wilner.
- For their patience and diligence: At Routledge - Amanda Savage, Sophie Dracott, and Alison Mcfarlane, plus Prabhu Chinnasamy and the KnowledgeWorks Global Ltd. team.
- My assistant in all things editorial, informational, and organizational, Kathryn Keaton
- Illustrator Evan Neidich of Fox & Crow Art for her keen vision and sensitivity to kids in motion (Find Evan at https://www.foxandcrowpaper.com)
- My Mom and Dad of blessed memory, Norma and Seymour Brodsky, who first showed me the importance of caring for kids, and my brother Paul, for embodying that care.
- All the children and parents who jump into Embodied Play Therapy with power, heart, and soul, now and in days yet to come.

Index